To Olivia

Happy 40t

Love

Mum & Dad

BATTLES FOR THE THREE KINGDOMS

BATTLES
FOR THE
THREE
KINGDOMS

THE CAMPAIGNS FOR ENGLAND, SCOTLAND AND IRELAND 1689—92

JOHN BARRATT

SUTTON PUBLISHING

First published in the United Kingdom in 2007 by
Sutton Publishing Limited · Phoenix Mill
Thrupp · Stroud · Gloucestershire · GL5 2BU

British Library Cataloguing in Publication Data
A catalogue record for this book is available from the British Library.

Hardback ISBN 978-0-7509-4358-1
Paperback ISBN 978-0-7509-4359-8

Typeset in Photina MT.
Typesetting and origination by
Sutton Publishing Limited.
Printed and bound in England by
J.H. Haynes & Co. Ltd, Sparkford.

Contents

List of Illustrations

List of Maps

Preface

The literature on the Jacobite movement and the later attempts of the exiled House of Stuart to regain its British thrones is extensive. The '45 Rebellion is one of the most popular, and frequently over-romanticised, episodes in British history, and the earlier '15 and '19 Rebellions have attracted their share of interest.

Much less well known as a whole is the first serious Jacobite attempt to reverse the verdict of the Revolution of 1688. For the next three years both Scotland and Ireland were the scene of bitter and prolonged fighting, while England was the target of invasion attempts and Jacobite conspiracy. Some incidents of the war, notably the siege of Derry and the Battle of the Boyne in Ireland, and the encounter at Killiecrankie in Scotland, have secure places in British history, and, in the cases of the first two, still arouse strongly partisan feelings.

The war as a whole, however, is much less well known, particularly in England. So much so, in fact, that no universally accepted name for it has emerged, and it is variously known – among other titles – as the War of the British Succession; in Ireland as the War of the Two Kings, or the Williamite War; and, in its wider European context, as the War of the League of Augsburg and the Eight Years' War. After some thought, I have opted for none of these, and as this book is primarily a military study of the conflict as it affected the British Isles, I have called it the War of the Three Kingdoms.

As always, thanks are due to a number of institutions and individuals. The Sydney Jones Library of the University of Liverpool provided much of the basic material used in researching this book, while the unrivalled resources of the British Library contain much contemporary material. The staff at Sutton provided much useful advice, not least in settling on the title of the book!

As this is primarily a military study, I have, with some relief, minimised discussion of the political and religious events leading up to the 1688 Revolution and the Settlement that followed. The debate over such questions as the exact motivations of James II and William of Orange in their actions that precipitated the Revolution remains heated, even after more than three hundred years. Published as I was completing this book was the magisterial study *Revolution*, by Tim Harris, which I would warmly recommend to anyone wishing to delve further into the murky but fascinating politics of 1688 and its aftermath.

John Barratt
Henllan
2006

Chronology

1685
6 February   Death of Charles II, succeeded by his brother as James II
16 July   Battle of Sedgemoor

1688
10 June   Birth of Prince of Wales
5 November   William of Orange lands at Torbay
10 December   Failure of James II's first attempt to flee to France
23 December   James II's second attempt to escape to France successful

1689
January–
  February   English convention declares James to have abdicated. William
      and Mary accept the English throne
12 March   James II lands in Ireland
14 March   Hamilton routs Ulster Protestants at 'Break of Dromore'
24 March   James enters Dublin
27 March   Hamilton fails to take Coleraine
Mid-April   Dundee begins Scottish Jacobite rising
15 April   Ulster Protestants defeated at Clady and Lifford
17 April   James II fired on from walls of Derry; siege begins
1 May   Battle of Bantry Bay
11 May   William and Mary accept Scottish throne
13 June   Duke of Gordon surrenders Edinburgh Castle to Williamites
27 July   Jacobite victory at Killiecrankie; Dundee killed
31 July   Siege of Derry raised; Hamilton defeated at Newtownbutler
13 August   Schomberg and Williamite forces land at Bangor Bay
21 August   Highland army defeated at Dunkeld
7 September   Schomberg's advance halts at Dundalk
Early October   Schomberg withdraws to Lisburn; James pulls back to Dublin

1690

1 May	Scottish Jacobites routed at Cromdale
14 June	William III lands at Carrickfergus
30 June	French naval victory at Battle of Beachy Head
1 July	Battle of the Boyne
4 July	James II quits Ireland for France
7 August	William commences operations against Limerick
12 August	Sarsfield captures William's siege train at Ballyneety
27 August	Williamite assault on Limerick repulsed
29 August	Siege of Limerick raised
29 September	Marlborough takes Cork
15 October	Marlborough takes Kinsale

1691

9 May	St Ruhe takes command of Irish army
8 June	Ginkel takes Ballymore
19 June	Ginkel begins siege of Athlone
30 June	Fall of Athlone
12 July	Jacobites defeated at Battle of Aughrim
21 July	Galway surrenders
25 August	Second siege of Limerick begins
14 September	Surrender of Sligo
3 October	Limerick surrenders; Treaty of Limerick ends war in Ireland

1692

13 February	Massacre of Glencoe
19 May	Battle of Barfleur
23–24 May	French fleet destroyed at La Hogue; end of James II's invasion plans

1701

16 September	Death of James II

ONE

········

Introduction

When James II succeeded to the British thrones in February 1685 following the death of his brother, Charles II, he seemed as secure in his inheritance as any monarch in Europe. Yet, in less than four years he would be a dethroned exile, overthrown by the 'Glorious Revolution' of 1688 and poised to engulf the British Isles in bloody civil war in an effort to regain his crown.

There were always those who doubted James's ability. In his earlier career, fighting in exile in the service of France and Spain, James had been an energetic and apparently courageous soldier, although always in a relatively junior capacity, and had displayed similar bravery of a passive kind as a fleet commander against the Dutch.

James's instincts were always authoritarian, with compulsion the first resort, as demonstrated when he was given responsibility for suppressing the Protestant Covenanters in Scotland. Indeed, religion was the key motive in most of James's actions and in his eventual fall. Converted to Catholicism during his exile, James fervently embraced his religion, and this was a major cause for the widespread opposition that the prospect of his succeeding to the throne created.

In the end, the strong grip that Charles II had established in his later years, and the support of the dominant Anglican–Tory interests, were enough to secure James's accession with little opposition, and indeed with some enthusiasm, although conditional on his working within the existing political and religious framework. Yet within less than a year, encouraged by the easy defeat of the rebellions of Monmouth and the Duke of Argyll, James would be embarking on a collision course with increasing numbers of his subjects.

Nobody ever credited James with great intelligence. A cold and generally humourless man, he lacked the cleverness and wit of his elder brother. The Duke of Buckingham said of the brothers: 'the king could see things if he would; the duke [of York] would see things if he could.' Catherine Sedley, one of the numerous, usually remarkably ugly, mistresses kept by James in contradiction to his strong devoutness, commented: 'we are none of us handsome, and if we had wit, he has not enough to discover it', while Charles himself feared that 'my brother will lose his kingdom by his bigotry and his soul for a lot of ugly trollops'.[1]

With haste sharpened by his advancing years, James attempted to push through policies favouring his Catholic co-religionists. As they comprised only 2 per cent of the English population, otherwise predominantly anti-papist Protestants, a collision was virtually inevitable, and James's readiness to ignore or override existing legislation and Parliament in order to gain his ends led to growing alarm.

James's long-term plans remain the subject of debate. Was he aiming at a British version of the absolute monarchies that were a feature of contemporary Europe, or was he following the narrower plan of emancipating his Catholic co-religionists, with the hope that their greater prominence would be followed by increasing numbers of conversions among the rest of the population?

There were grounds for concern because of his known authoritarian tendencies, and still more due to his steady expansion of his regular army, where commissions were now granted to Catholics, although even by 1688 only about 10 per cent of the officers were of that faith.

Alarm grew when James's activities in his kingdoms of Scotland and Ireland were observed. In Scotland, where the proportion of Catholics was similar to that in England, James tested out his pro-Catholic policies before applying them in England, but encountered so much opposition, especially from the Presbyterian section of the community, that by 1688, even before the Revolution in England, royal government had almost broken down.

In Ireland James began with the advantage of 97 per cent of the population being Catholic. But the social and political situation was complex. There was a complicated divide between the 'new' settlers (those who had arrived in the post-Reformation period, and particularly during the Cromwellian Settlement of the 1650s), the 'Old English' (descendants of the pre-Reformation settlers, who had remained Catholic), and the 'native' Irish or 'Gaels'. The remaining 3 per cent of the population were Protestant, of whom the most hostile to James and his plans were the mainly Scottish Presbyterians of Ulster.

Prominent in Catholic Ireland was Richard Talbot. Born in 1630, Talbot was an 'Old English' Catholic who fought against Cromwell, narrowly escaping from the massacre at Drogheda in 1649. A close friend of James in exile and procurer of his mistresses, Talbot was described by Bishop Burnet as 'a man who had much cunning, and had the secrets both of his master's pleasures and of his religion'.[2] Talbot opposed the Restoration Land Settlement which left the 'New English' settlers in possession of most of their recent territorial gains, and became regarded as the principal spokesman of the 'Old English'.

Talbot prospered both financially and in influence under James, who, in 1685, created him Earl of Tyrconnel, and two years later appointed him Lord Deputy, with the task of expediting his Catholicisation programme, particularly in the Irish army. In 1685 nearly all the troops were Protestant; a year later 67 per cent of the privates were Catholic, along with 40 per cent of the officers. As a result, increasing numbers of alarmed Protestants fled to England.

Matters came to a head from the spring of 1688. James, like his brother before him, had accepted financial subsidies from King Louis XIV of France. He had been unhappy with Louis's insatiable ambition to expand French influence in Europe, and attempted to remain neutral in the contest between Louis and his principal adversary, the Protestant William, Prince of Orange, Stadtholder of the Netherlands and James's son-in-law by marriage to his daughter Mary. However, popular opinion in England regarded James as a virtual French puppet.

In 1686 Emperor Leopold of Austria and a number of other European states, including the Netherlands, had formed the League of Augsburg, pledged to resist further French expansion. Two years later, Louis invaded the Palatinate, ostensibly in support of the claims to the territory of his sister-in-law, the Duchess of Orleans. By 1688 French troops were launching devastating raids deep into Imperial territory. The League of Augsburg was activated, and Europe was once more at war.

William of Orange, the moving force behind the League, and Louis's inveterate foe, was an unattractive man. Cold, cynical and suspicious by nature, William reserved any warmth for his female mistresses and male lovers; and for his troops, who regarded him with enthusiasm despite William's uninspiring military record.

From the opening of hostilities, William's overriding aim was to bring England into the war on the side of the League. This was clearly unlikely while James was on the throne, and, as early as April 1688, William was considering a landing in England if he could be assured of sufficient support there to overthrow or neutralise James. Matters in England were brought to a head by two events. First, the strength of popular opposition to James's policies was demonstrated by the acquittal of the seven bishops, tried for their refusal to endorse the King's latest Declaration of Indulgence suspending all anti-Catholic legislation. Secondly, on 10 June James's queen, Mary of Modena, gave birth to a son. Attempts were made to suggest that the new Prince of Wales had been 'planted', but in reality there could be no doubt that James now had a male heir, who would be brought up a Roman Catholic and supplant as heir to the throne his two Protestant half-sisters, Mary and Anne. Instead of a temporary religious aberration under James, the king's opponents were now faced with the prospect of a Roman Catholic dynasty stretching into the future.

The outcome was the invitation three weeks later, by seven leading figures in the Church, aristocracy, army and navy, to William of Orange to land in England to settle affairs there – and, if as yet only tacitly, to overthrow James.

William landed at Torbay on 5 November with an army of 15,000 men. Although James could theoretically muster almost three times that number, after he had called in reinforcements from Ireland and Scotland, his regime literally fell apart. Shaken by the desertion of trusted officers such as John Churchill and the Duke of Grafton, James suffered something approaching mental collapse, and fell back on London virtually without striking a blow, disbanded his army, and attempted to follow his wife and son in flight to France. His first attempt ended in failure. Brought back to London, James briefly met his chief Scottish supporters, the Earl of Balcarres and John Graham, Earl of Claverhouse, recently created Viscount Dundee. A kinsman of the great Montrose, though with less of his military talent, Claverhouse had gained some notoriety for his ruthless suppression of Scottish Covenanters and was the natural choice to lead any Stuart counter-revolution in Scotland. He and Balcarres were sent back north to await instructions.

On 23 December, an embarrassment to his Dutch son-in-law, James was permitted to make a second, this time successful, escape attempt. In France he was warmly welcomed by Louis, and installed in the palace of Saint-Germain. In England and Scotland, James's flight was presented as de facto abdication, and Conventions in both countries proclaimed William and Mary as joint monarchs in his stead.

William had achieved his immediate aim of bringing Britain into the League of Augsburg, and a declaration of war on France followed in May. In Scotland there was no immediate opposition to the change of regime, but in Ireland, after some apparent initial hesitancy and abortive negotiations with William via Richard Hamilton, an Irish officer taken in England who had been paroled to talk with Tyrconnel, the latter declared for James and began raising troops, and Hamilton joined him.

In England, once James's stranded Irish troops had been rounded up, the new regime seemed shakily established, and there were hopes that James might accept the status quo and comfortable exile in France.

This at first seemed not unlikely; James still wanted to be king, but lacked the determination to attempt this, while the French courtiers were unimpressed with the prematurely aged and indecisive monarch. But, although his War Minister, Louvois, wanted to concentrate all efforts on the war in Europe, Louis had some personal regard for James, and both he and his Naval Minister, the Marquis de Seignelay, saw support for James in Ireland as a useful diversion of enemy resources, and as a way of perhaps eventually restoring him as a client monarch.

James proved reluctant to oblige. Tyrconnel in the end had to demand of the king whether 'you can with honour continue where you are when you possess a kingdom of your own',[3] and assured him that he need remain in Ireland only for a short time to organise matters there, and could then return to France. The great French military engineer Vauban commented caustically to Louvois: 'I have an idea that when a man plays his last stake he ought to play it himself or be on the spot. The king of England seems to be in this condition. His last stake is Ireland; it appears to me that he ought to go there.'[4]

In the end, pressure from Louis and a certain recovery of confidence on James's part, tipped the scales. On 25 February 1689, seen off by Louis with the enigmatic comment 'the best I can wish you is that we shall never see each other again', James left Saint-Germain bound for the port of Brest and thence to Ireland. In his Irish kingdom, Tyrconnel's troops were preparing to march on Ulster, where Protestant-held Derry and Enniskillen defied him. The War of the Three Kingdoms was about to begin.

TWO

· · · · · · · ·

Warfare in the Late Seventeenth Century

Late-seventeenth-century Europe was overshadowed by the legacy of the Thirty Years War. Its terrible impact had led to a widespread desire to limit the effects of conflict.

This did not mean that no atrocities took place, whether carried out by unauthorised individuals, or as deliberate acts of policy – such as the notorious 1670s *dragonnades* by the troops of Louis XIV against the French Huguenots. But, overall, most governments and commanders made conscious efforts to moderate the effects of their military operations.

Warfare remained largely seasonal. Communications were, generally, fairly basic and bad weather quickly turned most roads into muddy quagmires, unusable for up to seven months of the year, while it was customary to lay up the largest warships for the winter.

The rise of professional armies, which had been a feature of much of the century, also played a fundamental role in the nature of late-seventeenth-century warfare. Such armies were expensive to raise, equip and train, and casualties were difficult to replace quickly with recruits of the same calibre. Consequently, siege warfare was generally preferred to pitched battles, as the latter were both expensive in terms of casualties and risky in their outcome.

LOGISTICS

Objectives were often limited by supply considerations. Logistics were a nightmare for most commanders, worsened by the steady growth in the size of armies, which by the end of the century had, on average, doubled to around 100,000 men. This increase was not the result of population growth, or indeed desired by most generals, who preferred smaller and more manageable forces, but was seen by monarchs as a visible sign of their power and prestige. The development of relatively efficient centralised governments also made it easier to recruit and equip such large forces.

The growth in the size of armies was not matched by a corresponding increase in ability to maintain them. The horse remained the predominant means of bringing supplies to an army in the field. The unauthorised foraging which had been a feature of the Thirty Years War was now usually discouraged.

As a result, it was necessary to maintain huge depots, from which supplies were carried to the army by means of horse- or ox-drawn supply convoys along the frequently appalling roads, or, when possible, by water. Only fairly densely populated and heavily farmed areas produced the quantities of food necessary to feed these large armies. It was not only the requirements of the combat troops themselves that had to be met, but also those of the large numbers of civilian camp followers of various kinds, who often added as much as half again to the numbers of an army.

Supply demands were huge. Even a relatively small force of 60,000 men needed 95 million pounds of bread in a six-month period,[1] and this in turn would require the services of 60 ovens and 240 bakers. Nearly 60 tons of bricks would be needed to construct the ovens, and 1,400 wagon-loads of fuel would be required each month to fire them.

On campaign, 40,000 horses, drawing 10,000 wagons, required 10,000 quintals[2] of fodder a day, while the team of horses drawing a supply wagon would consume much of what it carried for its own subsistence before it reached the army.

It is not surprising that even the best logistical arrangements frequently proved inadequate. In such circumstances an army was forced to revert to more traditional and unwelcome methods of foraging. The 'Grand Forage', as it was known, frequently saw the bulk of troops in an army being employed in systematic ransacking of the surrounding countryside, which might yield sufficient supplies to last for four or five days.[3]

Even in good weather, it was usually impossible for a depot adequately to feed an army more than five days' march (about 70 miles) away. Strategy was increasingly dictated by the need to keep an army supplied, and this led to sluggish and formalised campaigning, in which a general could not risk out-marching his supplies.

As a result, commanders became increasingly obsessed with real or imagined threats to their lines of communication. Enemy garrisons to their rear had to be either reduced or neutralised, a process that consumed both time and manpower, which meant that even a major victory, unless gained very early in the campaigning season, could not be fully exploited. Such a situation faced William III after his victory at the Boyne in July 1690, which proved too late in the season to allow him to reduce Limerick before the weather broke.

Given an average daily march of about 10 to 12 miles, these factors meant that, after a victory gained in the middle of the campaigning season, an army might have left to it an effective range of no more than 300 to 350 miles, and this in practice was frequently considerably less, because of the need to spend time neutralising enemy garrisons or detachments threatening lines of communication. By the time this had been achieved, the onset of winter would provide opportunity for the enemy to recover.[4]

The major supply worry for any commander lay in obtaining sufficient fodder for his huge numbers of horses. Each horse on a daily basis ate about 18–30 kilos of green fodder in summer, and half its own weight in corn in winter. As a result, a large effort had to be concentrated on providing sustenance for the horses.

The monetary costs of war were always high. Sometimes they could be partly met by wintering in enemy territory, as the Williamite forces in Ireland did, particularly in the winter of 1690–1, or by foraging. It was rare for a war to be fought to a decisive conclusion, and a negotiated compromise, hastened by the economic exhaustion of both sides, was more common. When both sides wanted to retain the overall status quo, although with adjustments to their own advantage, wars were usually ended by compromise.

It was not surprising, therefore, that major battles were rare and were frequently indecisive, and that siege warfare played such a major part in campaigning.

SIEGE WARFARE

The late seventeenth century saw the development of complex systems of fortifications. These reached their apogee in the extensive chain of fortresses, often the work of the great French engineer and siege expert Sebastian Prestre de Vauban, which dotted the Low Countries and guarded the frontiers of Eastern France.

In all, Vauban was responsible for the design of some 160 fortifications, mainly on the frontiers of France. The systems devised by Vauban, and his nearest rivals, the Dutchman Coehorn and the Swede Erik Dahlberg, dominated campaigning of the late seventeenth and much of the eighteenth centuries. In the Nine Years War, of which the War of the Three Kingdoms formed a part, there were seventeen battles, as compared to twenty-one major sieges.

A siege in the late seventeenth century was a complex affair that usually followed several clearly defined stages. As he himself was liable to attack by a relieving force, a besieger normally surrounded his own siege lines (lines of circumvallation) with protective defences (lines of contravallation). If a fortress was to be reduced by means other than starvation, a breach had to be made in its defences wide enough to be stormed by infantry. At this point the commander of a garrison was held to have fulfilled his main duty of delaying the enemy, and was free to seek terms of surrender, which, in recognition of his willingness to avoid unnecessary casualties on both sides, were usually generous.

Creating a breach in the main defences of a fortress was often a lengthy business, requiring the use of heavy siege pieces, which, laborious to transport and emplace, also used up huge quantities of frequently scarce gunpowder. They were normally effective only at ranges of 100yd or less, meaning that prolonged operations were often necessary to breach a fortress's outer defences before the main bombardment could begin. Complicated siege works and approach trenches had to be constructed by the besieger, who was subject to disruption by enemy fire and frequent sallies by the garrison, before work on the final emplacements for the siege guns could begin.

As a result, sieges were liable to be prolonged unless the defenders' morale collapsed or they were betrayed. It was quite unusual for a fortress actually to be stormed, as this involved an attacking force having to cross open ground under heavy enemy fire, and usually incurring severe casualties despite covering fire from its own artillery. Once it was possible for troops to approach a breach, ideally by means of a 'covered way' along the top of the 'glacis' or open ground in front of the defences, the final stages of the siege began. If a breach had been blasted in the curtain wall of a fortress, the defenders could only hope to plug it by a hastily improvised barricade. If, even then, they chose to defy their attackers, they were no longer regarded as being entitled to any quarter, while the captured town was liable to be plundered by the victors for up to three days. Unsurprisingly, it was rare for any garrison to continue resistance to this point.

There were few, if any, fortifications in the British Isles that rivalled those of the Continent, although this was counter-balanced in some cases, such as Derry and Athlone, by the inadequate resources of the besieger. The major exception was Limerick, whose defences, although disparaged by many professional soldiers, proved strong enough to withstand two lengthy sieges.

TROOP TYPES

The horse

Cavalry, often known as 'horse', included several different categories. The cuirassiers, or heavy horse, were shock troops, intended to break opponents by the force of their attack. Employed in a number of European armies, but not in the British until 1691, were carabineers, who were armed with both sword and pistols, as were other horse, and also 'musketoons' – a type of blunderbuss.

The bulk of the horse of any army consisted of regiments of line cavalry. By the late seventeenth century the use of armour, even by heavy cavalry, was in decline. The English Royal Horse Guards abandoned breastplates in 1688, although other units, both in Britain and on the Continent, continued to wear at least breastplates for another decade, and buff coats were also often to be found. Breast- and sometimes backplates continued to be worn by many cavalry officers, and senior officers sometimes wore three-quarter armour, although helmets were generally going out of use. Some cavalry troopers wore a metal skull cap, or 'secret', under their broad-brimmed hats. A trooper had heavy thigh boots, and was armed with a straight sword, a pair of pistols and a carbine.

The other principal variety of mounted soldier was the dragoon. These were still theoretically regarded as mounted infantry, and were normally armed with carbine, bayonet and hatchet, sword and pistols. They never wore armour.

Dragoons had always been seen as military 'jacks of all trades', and were expected to perform a wide variety of duties, including reconnaissance and escort missions, raids into enemy territory, and building fortifications. In 1691 the English army included nine regiments of dragoons, as compared with thirty-one of horse. As the establishment of a dragoon regiment was larger than that of its cavalry equivalent, there were a total of 3,440 dragoons in 52 troops, compared to 8,702 cavalry in 144 troops.

In the English army at least, dragoons were always seen as 'poor relations', expected to live on less pay and a lower subsistence rate than the horse. Particularly unfortunate were the men of those regiments designated as 'Dragoon Guards', who, although equipped and serving as regular cavalry, were paid at the dragoon rate. Among them were the Queen's Dragoons, the third most senior British mounted regiment.

The largest cavalry formation on campaign was the brigade, formed from between eight and fifteen squadrons. It was a fairly ad hoc formation that normally existed only for the duration of a particular campaign. A brigade would be led by a brigadier-general (normally colonel of a cavalry regiment), assisted by a brigade-major. The strength of an individual cavalry regiment, and the number of troops comprising it, fluctuated sharply. A squadron was formed from two or three troops. A regiment's field officers were its colonel, lieutenant-colonel and major, and usually a surgeon and chaplain.

In a line cavalry regiment a troop was led by a captain, with a lieutenant, cornet and quartermaster. There were usually two or three corporals and one or two trumpeters. A reasonably well-recruited troop might total around fifty officers and troopers, and a regiment between 300 and 450 officers and men.

Dragoon troops or, more correctly, 'companies', were larger, with sixty or seventy officers and men.

In action, cavalry were normally deployed in three ranks, with intervals of 3ft between each rider.

On the march, especially in hostile territory, the role of the cavalry was to reconnoitre ahead and to guard the flanks and rear of the foot and baggage. When the army was in camp, cavalry patrols were sent out to guard against surprise attack, and they would also forage and attack any small enemy convoys encountered.

In battle, cavalry were intended to counter enemy horse, but their main role was pursuit if the enemy infantry were disordered. They were intended to cut down fugitives and to prevent the enemy from regaining its balance. If the battle were lost by their own side, the cavalry were to cover the army's retreat.

The importance of the cavalry was declining by the late seventeenth century. Even before the arrival of the bayonet, improved infantry firearms and tactics were making the foot less vulnerable to cavalry attack and, unless their formation was broken, infantry units could often repel attacks by horse, who usually 'charged' at a brisk trot.

The foot

There were several categories of infantry soldier. In rapid decline were the pikemen, with pikes of up to 14ft in length, who, in the earlier part of the century had comprised up to a third of an army's infantry strength. The arrival of the socket bayonet around 1700 sounded the death knell of the pikeman.

A relative newcomer, appearing in the French army in 1667 and in England around 1680, was the grenadier. A battalion might have one grenadier company, comprised of hand-picked troops, which formed on the right of the battalion in battle. They were described as 'soldiers armed with a good Sword, a hatchet, a firelock slung and a Pouch full of hand-Granadoes'.[5]

As elite troops, grenadiers were intended to stiffen the remainder of the foot. They would also take the lead in storming attempts, using their hatchets both in combat and to clear a way through enemy defences and palisades. Their grenades, normally three per man, most commonly consisted of earthenware pots filled with incendiary or explosive materials, which were ignited by means of a fuse and thrown at the enemy.

Grenades were seldom used in ordinary battle situations because they were too indiscriminate in their effect. Grenadiers quickly lost much of their original role, and became instead an elite company which otherwise employed the same weapons and tactics as the ordinary infantry.

Another specialist type of infantryman was the fusilier, who was armed with a 'fusil' – a flintlock musket that was lighter than the standard infantry matchlock, and which was provided with a sling so that it could be shouldered while the fusilier was carrying out his primary role of assisting and guarding the artillery train.

The bulk of the infantry, however, were still the musketeers of the line infantry regiments. The older, heavier matchlock was being replaced with the new, lighter flintlock. This had a number of advantages. As well as being easier to handle, it had a faster rate of fire than the matchlock, and was more accurate. However, in 1689 the changeover was still a long way from completion. Although many of the established regiments of the British army by now were armed with flintlocks, the French army did not complete the changeover until 1693, and the majority of Jacobite troops in both Ireland and Scotland carried matchlocks. Infantry normally also carried cheap swords, more often used for cutting wood than in hand-to-hand combat, when the butt end of the musket was usually preferred, and bayonets. Most of these were still of the 'plug' pattern, which had to be screwed into the muzzle of the musket, transforming it into a miniature pike, but having the disadvantage of making it impossible to fire.

It was noted of the raw recruits who made up many of the Williamite foot in Ireland in 1689–90 that: 'A great many of the new men who had matchlocks had so little skill in placing of their matchlocks true and that scarce one in four could fire their pieces off, and those that did thought they had done a great feat if the gun fired, not minding what they shot at.'[6] The same faults were evident in their Irish opponents.

The matchlock had an effective range of about 250yd, although it was rarely accurate at more than 60yd. Loading and firing the matchlock was not, in practice, as complicated as is suggested by most contemporary military manuals, and a rate of fire of two or three shots per minute was not uncommon. The matchlock was sturdier than the flintlock, but it was also less reliable – particularly in wet or windy weather, when the 'match' used to fire it could often be extinguished.

Each musketeer carried a length of match, which was lit at one end at the onset of battle. On average, match burnt at a rate of 1in every 15 minutes, although the rate could be slowed by diluting the combustible nitrate solution in which it was soaked. A major disadvantage of match was the huge quantity that had to be carried with the army on campaign.

The flint, or firelock, was, in some respects, more reliable and accurate, with 'only' about one in three of its shots misfiring, but in other ways it was little better than the matchlock, and more susceptible to damage. In consequence, its introduction was slow and met resistance, notably from military conservatives such as Louis XIV and the French War Minister, Louvois, who delayed its introduction in any numbers in the French army until 1693.

In the English forces grenadiers had carried firelocks from 1678 onwards, but in 1690 only about half the foot in Ireland had them. In the rush to expand the English forces on the outbreak of war, many flintlocks were bought abroad, but all too often proved to be faulty. At this time no fewer than about fourteen varieties of firearm were in use in the English forces, including three types of matchlocks and four of flintlocks.[7] It would be 1691 before a reasonable degree of standardisation followed the expansion of home manufacture in London and Birmingham. As late as 1697 there was still a matchlock/flintlock ratio of 2:3. The Dutch forces, by contrast, had completed their changeover to flintlocks by 1692.

Few English regiments had more than one battalion, although regiments of several battalions were common in Europe, especially among 'guard' units. In England only the 1st Foot Guards normally had a wartime establishment of two battalions. The number of battalions in French regiments varied, although by 1690 they generally closely resembled the English pattern of one battalion of 745 officers and men, formed into thirteen companies.[8] A regiment was normally raised by its colonel, who financed its recruitment and whose property and investment it effectively remained. The colonel was often absent from his unit, perhaps occupying a more senior command, and the regiment was frequently led in battle by its lieutenant-colonel or major – often an experienced professional soldier. Most battalions were formed from thirteen companies – one of grenadiers and the remainder 'line' infantry, although in the Irish Jacobite army some regiments initially had many more. The normal established wartime strength of a company was sixty officers and men, each having a captain, lieutenant and ensign (grenadiers had a second lieutenant instead of an ensign, as they did not usually carry a company colour into action). A company would normally also have two sergeants and two corporals or 'senior men'.

A colonelcy, particularly of a guards regiment, where competition for officer vacancies was keen, could be a very lucrative investment. Vacant posts were generally sold to the highest bidder, with candidates for guards units attracted both by their prestige and by the higher rates of pay often offered. In an English guards regiment a lieutenant would receive 11s a day, together with 8d to pay for a servant, while his line counterpart could expect only 4s 8d. A guards private was paid a daily rate of 10d, twopence more than his counterpart in a line infantry regiment.

TACTICS

The amount of training a new recruit received varied according to circumstances. In time of war a recruit might have to pick up the necessary knowledge as he went along, assuming that he survived long enough.

If possible, however, he would at least be trained in the basics of drill and weapon-handling. When more time was available, he would be given long hours of more elaborate drill, which was intended to result in a military automaton with little individual initiative. Apart from some of the Dutch and other foreign units, there were probably few soldiers in the Scottish and Irish campaigns who attained this level of training.

So far as basic drill was concerned, no detailed procedures were laid down, much being left to the judgement of individual colonels. In essence, however, a recruit had to be taught to load and fire his musket, and how to advance in order to close contact with the enemy and engage in a firefight. He had to know how to follow up with an advance, or, if worsted, how to retreat in good order and hold off attacking cavalry. He would also need to know how to defend a fortification or other fixed defences.

On the march, most units formed what was known as a 'column of route', on a frontage of between eight and twenty files. This inevitably forced many troops to make their way through the fields on either side of the road, with the result that progress was slow.

This formation supposedly made it easier for an army to take up position when it deployed for battle. It remained, however, a vastly time-consuming process. Once deployed, a battalion formed three blocks, with pikes in the centre and musketeers on either flank. It was not unusual for several weak battalions to be 'brigaded' together to form one body. Grenadier companies were either deployed on the right, or split to take up position on either flank.

Musketeers were normally formed into five ranks, with an interval of four paces between each rank in order to allow space for reloading, when the rank that had just fired fell back to the rear and was replaced by the rank immediately behind it. A properly deployed battalion occupied a block of ground of roughly 190yd by 14yd. The overall aim was a situation in which a battalion produced the highest possible volume of fire. In theory at least, half of the musketeers were always loaded. There were various procedures laid down for firing. Fire was by ranks, files or divisions, each retiring to the rear of the formation after it had fired. In the case of firing by files, two files totalling ten men would move six paces out from the front of the battalion, fan out to deliver their fire, and then retire, to be replaced by the next ones. In firing by 'division', either four or six files would carry out the same manoeuvre. The main problem was the almost inevitable confusion following from the successive movements involved in reloading. This resulted in a marked reduction in volume and accuracy, especially when raw troops were involved, or in prolonged actions.

Actual hand-to-hand fighting was rare; it was more usual for one side or the other to retire, or even rout, after getting the worst of the firefight.

The Dutch infantry were generally acknowledged to be the best foot on the allied side, arguably the best in Europe. French infantry were thought by many to be of inferior quality. Indeed, it was said by an English commentator that when the French encountered the Dutch at the battle of Fleurus in 1690, 'The French infantry could not so much as dare look them in the face; could the Dutch be left alone to them, they would esteem them as nothing.'[9] Despite the initial inexperience of many, the English foot quickly gained a reputation almost as good as that of the Dutch.

It was common for infantry battalions to be accompanied into action by two or three light guns, which could be manhandled by their crews. When faced by cavalry attack, two or three battalions often united to form a square, which, provided it kept its order, could generally repel horsemen by means of a mixture of musketry, pikes and a hedge of bayonets. Some authorities reckoned that a battalion could remain in line to repel cavalry, but this was a highly risky option if formation was lost.

Pikemen, with their pikes varying from 13ft to 18ft in length, although frequently cut shorter to make them easier to handle, were deployed five deep in a body at the centre of each battalion. Protected by buff coats and leather gauntlets, but by now rarely wearing armour, they had the primary role of repelling enemy cavalry by forming a 'hedgehog' of pikes, beneath and in the midst of which the musketeers could shelter.

Although officers and sergeants retained halberds and spontoons, both as 'badges' of rank and as a means of ordering the ranks of their troops, other pole weapons went into rapid decline after the introduction of the 'socket' bayonet – which had the advantage of allowing the musket still to be fired when fitted with it – invented around 1678 and variously credited to either Vauban or the Scottish General Hugh Mackay. It was gradually introduced into most European armies over the next decade.

In battle, infantry were normally formed into double or triple lines about 200yd apart and arranged chequerboard fashion, so that the reserves could move up to fill the gaps left for that purpose in the first line. A battalion of 700 men occupied a frontage of 200yd, and was drawn up in five or six ranks, of which usually only one fired at a time, so that around half of the musketeers were always loaded.

Battles fought in the open, in which neither side had the advantage of prepared defences, were generally of fairly short duration, although confusion quickly reigned, mainly because of the dense clouds of smoke produced by the large quantities of black powder that were expended.

ARTILLERY

The most noticeable feature of any seventeenth-century army on the march was the vast number of wagons that accompanied it and its artillery train. In England these were administered by the Board of Ordnance, a steadily expanding and influential department controlled by the Master General of the Ordnance. As well as supplying the guns required by the army, the Board of Ordnance – and its equivalents in other European countries – also supplied munitions for the whole of the army, and, in the case of England, for the navy. It also was responsible for such services as bridging trains and their transport, and the engineer and pioneer services. In 1689 the Master of the Ordnance was Frederick, Duke of Schomberg, with five principal officers, the Lieutenant-General, Surveyor General, Clerk of the Ordnance, the Keeper of Stores and the Clerk of Deliveries, who in practice were responsible for the running of the department. Under them were about 160 subordinates divided into about fourteen categories, of whom the bulk were the Gentlemen of the Ordnance, some of whom were attached to each field artillery train. Other specialists were responsible for arranging the manufacture and testing of guns, dealing with supplies of munitions to fortresses and barracks, and there was a group of sixty trained gunners responsible for handling artillery in action, although these always had to be supplemented by detachments of other troops.

In the English forces the regular gunners and their assistants, termed 'matrosses', wore red coats faced with blue. Artillery trains were not permanent units, but were organised as required for specific missions and campaigns. When such a train was required the normal procedure in England was for the appropriate Secretary of State to issue a warrant to the Master Gunner or his Deputy, calling for a train whose composition would be specified in the warrant.

The 38-gun train in Flanders in 1692 included some 250 officers and men and around 400 wagoners and boys. It carried 11,200 cannon shot, 200 barrels of powder, 209 barrels of match, and 200 7in grenades. It also transported a good deal of material intended for the army in general. In this case, that included 600 barrels of powder, 10 tons of match, 4 tons of musket and carbine shot, 4,000 grenades and 6,000 fuses.

There were three main classes of artillery: (1) siege guns and field pieces; (2) mortars, designed to fire explosive or incendiary shells at a high trajectory into the interior of besieged garrisons; (3) howitzers, which combined some of the characteristics of both of the other types.

The main types of cannon used in England were the 24-pounder whole cannon, the 16-pounder culverin, the 12- and 8-pounder culverins, the 6-pounder saker and the 3-pounder minions, falcons and falconets, the latter ranging from 2½lb to ½lb, and used mainly as light pieces and battalion guns in support of the infantry. The French tended to use a higher proportion than the English of the heavier 36- and 24-pounder cannon.

Guns fired solid balls of stone or iron, mainly against enemy fortifications or formed bodies of troops. In the latter case sufficiently skilled gunners would attempt to make use of ricochet fire to cause the maximum number of casualties. Employed in an anti-personnel role were various forms of case or canister shot, known to the English as 'partridge' shot, which burst in a spray effect, rather like shotgun fire.

With, at best, rough and, at worst, impassable roads, moving the artillery was one of the major problems that confronted a general. Horse teams to draw guns and wagons were supplied by civilian contractors and were usually administered by civilians, who had a tendency to make off in the heat of battle. Artillery was, however, essential in any major campaign, both for its supporting role in battle and for the part it played in siege operations. Indeed, by the late seventeenth century its increasingly significant role was widely recognised. Louis XIV's appreciation of this was demonstrated when he had his guns engraved with the motto 'Ultima Ratio Regis' ('the last argument of the king').

The main disadvantage remained the huge size of artillery trains, and their snail-like rate of progress, which slowed the march of the rest of the army. Guns averaged 3 tons in weight, and needed teams of six to eight horses to draw them. Hundreds of wagons were needed to carry the ammunition and the vast paraphernalia of equipment required by the gunners and engineers. The guns and their attendant wagons of necessity occupied the roads on the march, in wet weather rapidly turning them into quagmires of mud and forcing the rest of the army to make its way, with difficulty, through the fields and enclosures on either side.

The artillery train and other wagons of an army could occupy many miles of road. In Flanders in 1692 William of Orange had a small artillery train of thirty-eight guns, which required 240 four-horse munition wagons, and several others for baggage and provisions. Fodder was as great a problem for the artillery train as for baggage trains, and it could be almost impossible to move in bad weather. Civilians were either hired or conscripted to drive the wagons, and, not unnaturally, were frequently unenthusiastic about involvement in battle. Theorists saw the ideal train for an army of 50,000 men as comprising fifty guns, which would need around 1,220 horses and 183 wagons.[10]

In battle the main role of the artillery was to provide defensive fire or to be concentrated in batteries to support attacks at key points. In sieges its role was to breach the enemy defences and provide supporting fire in general. Many armies built up huge numbers of guns. In the Nine Years' War the French at one stage had around 14,000 cannon, although many of these were static fortress guns.

THE SOLDIER'S LIFE

Between 1640 and 1680 most armies adopted fairly uniform dress. In England red had become the favoured colour by the time of the formation of the New Model Army in 1645, with individual regiments identified by their differently coloured coat-linings. In the Dutch forces blue was the predominant colour, while most French line regiments wore off-white or grey. The Jacobite armies never entirely resolved their shortage of uniforms; the Irish troops, seeing themselves as the legitimate 'British' army, strongly preferred red, although they were more often issued the grey coats of their French allies.

A soldier's life was inevitably hard. With only fairly basic medical services available, more men died from the effects of disease than were killed in battle. But contemporary civilian life was so subject to disease and the effects of violence that many men felt that the risks of military life were compensated for by the promise, though by no means always the reality, of regular issues of clothing, food and pay. The latter might be fairly low, and reduced further by various stoppages, but it could be supplemented by extra payments for such things as construction work on fortifications, or sometimes for dangerous duty in the trenches during siege operations. In times of peace, at least, there were also unofficially accepted opportunities for 'moonlighting' – as, for example, in helping to bring in the harvest.

It was never possible to fill the ranks by voluntary methods, and all armies included a large number of conscripts and pressed men. In England and Scotland, even many 'volunteers' who had enlisted for the bounty money of the 'king's shilling' had to be kept in prison until they were able to be taken to their units, otherwise they were very liable to desert – and possibly re-enlist under another name in order to obtain the bounty again. Desertion was rife and, in theory, liable to harsh punishment, although in practice the need for men was usually so great that suspected deserters were rerecruited with few questions being asked.

All nations in the late seventeenth century made increasing use of foreign mercenaries. Unlike earlier times, these were not generally recruited from private contractors, but were obtained from foreign governments, as individuals, as specially raised units, or as detachments from their own regular forces. The Swiss, for example, provided both the French and the Dutch with complete units already formed as battalions. For many years the Dutch also maintained an Anglo-Scottish Brigade, whose officers provided an invaluable core of experience for the rapidly expanded English forces after 1689. The German states of the Empire were another valuable source of troops for both sides. At times, Louis XIV's armies included up to 50,000 Germans.

As well as selling commissions in their regiments, colonels were also responsible for providing their men with uniforms, which they naturally tried to obtain as cheaply as possible, with the result that both clothing and shoes quickly fell apart in campaign conditions, and were generally entirely inadequate for bad weather. A commanding officer's expenses were reimbursed by the state at an official rate, from deductions made in the soldiers' pay.

Corruption was inevitable and rife. A common practice in all armies was to hold 'false musters', in which civilians would be hired, or troops 'borrowed' from other units, for the duration of official musters, while the regiments were deliberately kept under strength for the remainder of the time, with the officers pocketing the difference in allocated pay.

The majority of officers in all armies came from aristocratic, or at least gentry, backgrounds, although it was not unusual for technical posts, such as engineers, to be occupied by men of middle class origin.

WAR AT SEA

The predominant feature of the seventeenth century had been the three wars at sea between England and the United Provinces of the Netherlands. On balance, the Dutch had had the better of the conflicts, but it also had become apparent that the rigid naval tactics that had followed the English Fighting Instructions of 1653, which made the 'line ahead' the standard fighting formation, had made truly decisive victories very difficult to achieve. The difficulties encountered by all admirals in the areas of command and control discouraged initiative among their officers, and led to slowness in exploiting advantages. Nonetheless, the 'Fighting Instructions' had helped the English navy gain the advantage in the first of the Dutch Wars, when they had been a distinct improvement over the unregulated free-for-all that had hitherto often passed for naval tactics, and this led to their being followed by every European nation.

The Dutch Wars had also led to the further refinement of naval gunnery, of which the English fleet in the time of Queen Elizabeth had been the principal proponent, especially in its campaign against the Spanish Armada. The English preference for building ships that were primarily floating gun platforms, designed to win their battles by means of firepower rather than by boarding, had been copied by all the other nations of Europe.

Ships were rated according to the number of guns they carried, ranging from first rates of 100 guns or more, through the particularly versatile third rate of about 50 to 60 guns, down to the smaller, fourth- and fifth-rate vessels, used for scouting and convoy escorts, but not deemed sufficiently heavily gunned to stand in the line of battle.

In the earlier part of the century, war at sea had still been a very seasonal business, with most of the warships, especially the larger first and second rates, laid up for the winter, and only a skeleton force maintained. Most naval campaigns had been relatively brief, and usually fought not far from home waters.

The wars of Cromwell's navy in particular, during the 1650s, had brought changes. The English Admiral Robert Blake had been first to introduce prolonged blockading of an enemy port, during the war with Spain in 1656–7. The same period, with the trend intensifying during the later Dutch Wars, had seen many more examples than previously, of squadrons clashing in various relatively far-flung corners of the globe, whether in colonial rivalry or over trading issues. All conflicting nations, but especially the Spanish, compensated for or assisted regular naval forces by widespread use of privateers or small warships in attacks on enemy trade. Navies were also increasingly being employed in support of land operations, whether in supplying troops operating overseas or in providing artillery support.

THREE

•••••••••••

The Rival Armies

THE BRITISH ARMY

Following the Restoration in 1660, the Cromwellian New Model Army was largely disbanded. A distrustful government had no wish to risk another military takeover and was reluctant to authorise more than the smallest force required for internal security.

Nevertheless, British troops saw action over the next two decades in a wide variety of situations. The unwelcome dowry of Tangier that Charles II's bride, Catherine of Braganza, brought with her, with constant clashes with hostile Moors, proved an excellent if harsh training ground for many British officers. And if British troops were distrusted at home, they were eagerly sought by several European powers. They were loaned to Portugal, fighting to maintain its independence from Spain, and distinguished themselves on several occasions, as did the British brigade that served with the French under the great Turenne from 1672 to 1678. British troops served at different times with Louis XIV of France and with the Dutch Republic. Many of their officers were young gentlemen in search of adventure, and the semi-mercenary nature of the units in which they served tended to turn them into professional soldiers and adventurers whose loyalties were more changeable and easily bought and sold than was desirable in a national army.

The army at home was maintained from the king's own revenues, had a somewhat unclear legal status, and was seen primarily as an instrument for internal security. Unlike Charles II, his brother and successor, James II, had a keen interest in military matters, stemming from his service while in exile with Marshal Turenne. His regard for his regular troops seemed justified in 1685, when they smashed the Duke of Monmouth's Rebellion on Sedgemoor. James took the opportunity presented by the Rebellion to raise further units for the three regular armies in the British Isles – for separate armies (under the Crown) were maintained in Ireland and Scotland. Dismay mounted when it became apparent that he intended the new regiments to be a permanent part of the military establishment.

Parliament had been particularly concerned when the King commissioned a number of Roman Catholic officers, in clear breach of the Test Acts, which debarred 'papists' from holding any office under the Crown. Even by 1688 no more than 11 per cent of the English officer corps were Catholic. Considerably more were career soldiers, mercenary professional adventurers who had fought for years in Europe. As a result of their previous frequently chequered careers, most of these professional soldiers had strong instincts for self-preservation, and they viewed the purge of Protestant officers in Ireland with considerable foreboding. When William of Orange landed in England in November, something like two-thirds of the officer corps in the country were in a state of discontent.

By December, James's previously excellent army, ravaged by dispute and desertion, was in a state of disintegration. William's decision initially to rely on a considerable number of Dutch and other foreign troops was dictated by necessity as much as by policy. Caught up in the maelstrom was the small but highly efficient Scottish army of 2,964 men, which had been brought south of the Border to face William's threatened invasion, together with 2,820 men of the Irish army.

William had not expected this total collapse of the British army, which proved a serious hindrance to his major short-term aim of employing it in his war on the Continent. His preferred solution might have been to disband the existing army and completely reconstruct it. But the threats in Scotland and Ireland, the demands of the war in Flanders, and the possibility of Jacobite insurrections in England meant that there was no time available. The result was a hasty attempt to put the old army back together again.

William opted to keep in post James's Secretary at War, William Blathwayt, who, early in 1689, began reconstructing the English army. He had three main tasks. First, he had to deal with the religious divisions in the army. This was tackled ruthlessly by dismissing all Catholics. The Irish troops that had been brought over by James, numbering about 1,500, were interned on the Isle of Wight prior to disbandment. From here at least 300 had escaped to France by the end of April 1689. The remainder were sold to Emperor Leopold of Austria to fight the Turks. There were still a number of Irish soldiers roaming around the English countryside, mostly trying to reach ports on the Irish Sea coast to seek passage home. The majority were too hungry and frightened to be a serious threat, and they were gradually rounded up.

Problems remained with some of James's Protestant soldiers. The bulk of the rank and file displayed little enthusiasm to serve King William. The reaction of the officers was equally mixed. A third of them were willing to serve the new regime; another third retired or resigned; the remainder either joined James's forces in Scotland and Ireland or went to France.

William distrusted even those who professed loyalty, but he had no option but to make use of them. For able and hardbitten commanders like John Churchill, Percy Kirke and Sir John Lanier, the change of regime primarily meant a change of paymaster.[1] This core of veteran mercenary officers was essential in keeping together the remaining English troops of James's army, who had been moved out of London.

The officer corps was supposedly thoroughly purged of dissident elements. But grave doubts remained regarding the reliability of the army in the event of a Jacobite uprising or invasion. Mass desertions were continuing, albeit from a reluctance to serve in the war in Flanders rather than from sympathy for King James. The Royal Scots, indeed, mutinied. Mutiny by one of James's favourite regiments was perhaps not unexpected. But even here the discontent had been occasioned at least as much by being sent to Flanders as by loyalty to the fallen monarch. Despite the government's fears, the example of the Royal Scots was not followed by others; some regiments even sent 'loyal addresses' to the new monarchs.

John Churchill and William's Dutch favourite, William Bentinck, Earl of Portland, played a key role in the reorganisation of the army, by recommending suitable officer candidates to the king. So far as the rank and file were concerned, the assurance of regular pay was a major factor in securing their support. In January 1689 Parliament had promised that all arrears of pay would be settled forthwith, and at the same time that efforts would be made to ascertain the actual effective strengths of the individual regiments.

However, major problems remained. On 1 April Sir John Reresby said of the troops being sent to Scotland that they were 'unarmed, unclothed, and without sufficient pay to clear their arrears'.[2] It was recognised that, although the bulk of the rank and file might be unenthusiastically loyal, grievances over pay and conditions might easily change this, and a special commission 'for reforming the abuses in the army' was set up on 10 May, headed by leading Whig politicians and Lanier, Kirke and Brigadier General Charles Trelawney, but it achieved very little. However, by the end of 1689 a viable British army existed, even though it would require bolstering with Dutch and other foreign units for at least the next two years.

Army officers tended to be quarrelsome, arrogant and lawless. They spent no more time at their duties than was absolutely necessary, and generally led a life of card-playing, drinking, dancing, horse racing and cockfighting, with the occasional session of basic drill for their men. The main friction in the officer corps remained the long-standing antagonism of gentry versus professionals, especially as large numbers of the latter, such as Hugh Mackay, Kirke, Churchill and Thomas Tollemache, were rising rapidly in the more fluid conditions in the aftermath of 1688. Junior vacancies were increasingly being filled from the ranks of the lesser gentry and the mercantile classes, who saw the army as a career and whose attitudes clashed with those of the traditional officers of more aristocratic origin.

William was not, on the whole, impressed with the officers of his British army, compared with those of continental armies and, indeed, the Anglo-Dutch Brigade. He was used to the Dutch system, whereby officers were promoted strictly on merit, but his problem was that he required to field a British army as quickly as possible, and therefore had neither time nor opportunity to carry out the large-scale reform and reorganisation he would have preferred. Instead, only absolutely essential changes were made, usually on an ad hoc basis. As a result, a host of abuses were perforce allowed to continue. Most junior officers were men in their late teens or early twenties. As might be expected when so many hot-blooded young men were gathered together, disputes ending in duels were frequent, despite official bans of the latter. The practice of false musters continued, with the hiring of 'faggots', and pay being claimed for dead soldiers and for officers' servants.

As for the genuine soldiers, there was no guarantee that they would receive the payments due to them. There were numerous complaints of officers holding back payments intended for quarters and subsistence to line their own pockets. The consequence was that men either lived at 'free quarter' in civilian houses or extracted money from local communities. None of these problems was solved during William's reign, and the King was fairly indifferent to them, provided that the fighting ability of the troops was not seriously affected.

There was no formal professional training for officers, and it was probably only the influx of experienced Huguenot officers into England, driven out of France by the *dragonnades* and in search of employment, that made the expanded British army of 1689–90 possible. This situation inevitably resulted in a mass of totally raw recruits, whose training and learning – if they survived long enough – had to take place on active service.

Innate conservatism and a desire to preserve the status quo meant that the overwhelming majority of army officers had no desire to take the radical step of declaring for the exiled James. Although a number of them, like Marlborough, kept in touch with the Stuart court, James would have had to have a more realistic prospect of success to have persuaded them to turn coat.

William, however, retained doubts about his British senior commanders, in particular. None of them, with the exception of the self-seeking Marlborough, demonstrated any great enthusiasm for the new regime. Consequently, the new king preferred to put his trust mainly in his continental commanders, such as Schomberg, Ginkel and the Duke of Württemberg, and, so far as British officers were concerned, he really placed reliance only on veterans of the Anglo-Dutch Brigade, such as Hugh Mackay and Thomas Tollemache.

In theory, soldiers were recruited from the county militias, which themselves, just as theoretically, included the entire male population aged between 16 and 60. In practice, the numbers this provided were insufficient. At the height of the War of the British Succession there was an average annual demand for 50,000 British troops, both to meet the continuing commitments of the war and to replace the wastage from all causes. Most regiments were constantly under strength, averaging around 70 per cent of their formal establishment.

All recruits were supposed to be volunteers, but most were raised by roaming recruiting parties, 'at beat of drum', often by dubious methods. Officers attempted to take advantage of local and family connections, such as recruiting men from family estates, when the extent of their being true 'volunteers' was often questionable. In Ireland, 'native' Irish, including men who had previously fought for James, were used to fill out the ranks. In Scotland, where the 'press' was not illegal in raising land forces, compulsion was practised openly. It usually concentrated first on 'all idle and loose and vagabond persons' and then was extended more widely to the unmarried. As the demand for men grew, 'pressing' was also carried on illegally in England. Such dubious methods were connived at, if not encouraged, by senior officers, while the civilian authorities saw this enforced recruiting as a way of ridding their towns and villages of undesirables and riff-raff of all kinds. From 1691 onwards, convicted criminals were regularly 'pressed'.

The typical British private was a man in his twenties, usually a former artisan, with unemployed tailors, weavers and shoemakers the most common trades. Many others had been casual or occasional labourers, with no fixed abode. Indeed, even after enlistment, many soldiers continued to do casual work in their long periods of military inactivity. However, they were not welcome in civilian communities, and there were frequent complaints of soldiers stealing and committing acts of violence.

Married men were supposedly exempt from enlistment, and soldiers were not encouraged to marry. A number did so, however, only to find that they lacked the means to support their wives and families. A limited number of wives were often allowed to accompany the troops on campaign, to act in such capacities as cooks and nurses.

Soldiering, for the other ranks, was for life; only severe wounds, illness or infirmity might result in discharge, to rely on the charity of the 'parish'. Ex-soldiers found it hard to fit back into civilian life. The large-scale discharges of early 1689 were followed by an upsurge in crime. However, desertion was both easy and common, especially if troops were stationed in large towns. Most deserters were from the foot; few cavalry troopers or dragoons fled the colours, mainly because most of them were volunteers. Many infantrymen claimed that they had been forced to desert as a result of poverty. Of their pay of 8d a day, 2d went to their officers as 'officers' reckonings', which, after various other deductions had been made, generally left the soldiers with only 4d or 5d, and even that was frequently much in arrears.

A soldier was thus left with virtually nothing with which to support a family, or, if quartered on a civilian, for himself, once he had paid his dues to his landlord. In such circumstances, some kind of 'casual work' was often essential for survival. Another way of making some money was to be a 'bounty-jumper', switching from one regiment to another to obtain the bounty – often as much as 20s – that was paid to 'volunteers'. Some attempts were made to apprehend ordinary deserters, especially if they were newly issued with their uniform, as this would represent a financial loss to the officer concerned. In practice, however, few 'runners' seem to have been caught.

Very little is known for certain about what the ordinary soldier actually wore on campaign – as opposed to what official regulations said he should wear. In 1677 newly raised troops were supposed to be issued with 'a cloth coat lined with bayes . . . one pair of kersey breeches lined with pockets . . . one pair of shoes, one pair of yarn hose, one hat edged, one hat band, one sash and also one sword and belt'.[3] Coats, following the tradition established by the New Model Army, were normally red, with cuffs in the regimental facing colour, although blue and sometimes grey coats were issued. 'Royal' regiments tended to have blue facings, while white, yellow, green, tawny and, rather surprisingly, red, were commonly selected by colonels of other regiments. Hats were usually made from black felt, with a trim of coloured tape around the brim, often white.

Cavalry now rarely wore the buff coat that had been common during the Civil War of the mid-seventeenth century. As with the foot, red seems to have been the most common coat colour, for both cavalry troopers and dragoons, although on campaign undyed cloth was often used instead.

Discipline became somewhat harsher under William, although flogging of troops seems to have been common only in Flanders, possibly because the soldiers could desert less easily there. Discipline in England was ultimately the responsibility of general courts martial, which could impose the death penalty for mutiny, sedition and desertion, with other crimes subject to the penalties of English common law. There were also regimental courts martial to deal with non-capital offences. The regimental provost marshal was responsible for the administration of punishments such as running the gauntlet, or flogging, the latter initially limited to thirty-nine strokes. Most disciplinary problems resulted from boredom or drink.

For troops seriously wounded in action, the first port of call was the Royal Hospital, Chelsea, founded by Charles II and paid for by the soldiers themselves by means of a levy of 1d a day. The Hospital proved inadequate for the demands of a full-scale war, and all its 472 places were taken by March 1690. To ease the situation, some of those in need were classed as 'out pensioners'. These more lightly wounded who lodged outside the Hospital were formed into companies to carry out light garrison duties. A few, fortunate disabled veterans received pensions from the Crown or became almsmen supported by local charities. But the majority had to rely upon parish relief as 'maimed soldiers' whose applications had to be proved before the appropriate county Quarter Sessions. The pension granted might be around £2 a year, but was dependent upon continued 'good behaviour', and initially relied on the petitioner's being able to produce a certificate from his old commanding officer. In many cases, ex-soldiers had to subsist as best they could.

Abroad, medical provision was even more abysmal, although slightly better in Ireland than in Flanders after the summer of 1690, with the establishment of a base hospital in Dublin, and a 'marching hospital' accompanying the army. Some regiments also employed additional surgeon's mates.

FOREIGN TROOPS

The Dutch

The army of the United Provinces, although referred to as 'Dutch', in fact included German, French, English and Scottish units. Every year the States General, made up of representatives from the seven provinces and the largest cities, had unanimously to approve the petition of the Council of State for funds to maintain the army. Each province had a Stadtholder, who commanded the troops paid for by that province, with the Stadtholder of the largest province, Holland, commanding the field army as a whole, although he was ultimately responsible to the States General.

The army was normally considerably reduced in peacetime, running the risk of being overwhelmed by a sudden invasion such as that mounted by Louis XIV in 1672. It was thanks to the indefatigable leadership of the young William of Orange that the United Provinces weathered that storm and gradually forged the Dutch army into a highly respected fighting force.

By 1685, despite William's warnings, the Dutch army had been reduced to about 30,000 men, with the result that the force with which he launched his invasion of England in November 1688 included troops from several parts of Europe. The elite were twenty-four companies of the Dutch Guards, and some of the cavalry. With the outbreak of war in the southern Netherlands, the Dutch army was steadily expanded, reaching over 85,000 men by 1694.

Most uniforms were of a similar basic design, of undyed brownish-greyish cloth, sometimes distinguished by cuffs in regimental colours. The result was that, on campaign, the uniforms of all the armies involved tended to assume the same hue, because natural, undyed cloth was the material most easily obtained for replacements.

Although Dutch troops were, at least in the case of the foot, regarded as the best troops in Europe, as with many veteran forces there was little uniformity of arms and equipment. Weapons were manufactured in Holland, Germany and the Spanish Netherlands, or assembled from components 'cannibalised' from various sources. Many made use of captured French arms and equipment.

The Huguenots

There had been French Huguenots (most notably the Earl of Feversham) serving with the English forces before the 1688 Revolution, but the accession of William, and the security that this afforded to English Protestantism, resulted in an influx of French Huguenots into English military service, eventually reaching a total of five regiments. Three foot regiments were raised between March and June 1689. So many former officers arrived, perhaps around a thousand in all, that the Huguenot regiments had a large number of 'reformadoes' attached, although most of these were gradually transferred to fill vacancies in British regiments. Most of the rank and file were not Huguenots; indeed they included a fair number of French Roman Catholic deserters and, all in all, were a fairly cosmopolitan mix.

William had a high regard for his Huguenot troops, whose strong, personal hatred for Louis XIV was a highly motivating factor. They were, however, unpopular with the British officers and men, which was one reason why they were eventually settled in Ireland on lands confiscated from James's supporters.

THE WILLIAMITE FORCES IN IRELAND

The army at the Boyne in 1690 numbered 37,000 men, and included English, Dutch, Danes and Germans in the Danish regiments, and Huguenots. The foreign troops were seen as being the best in the army. There were also large numbers of newly raised English troops and Ulster Protestants, who made up about one-sixth of the total. In April 1689 William had been intending to employ 30,000 men of the British army in equal numbers in England, Holland and Ireland. Of these, six regiments of horse, three of dragoons and eight existing foot battalions were earmarked for Ireland, with seventeen more foot battalions to be raised for service there.

There were also plans to raise a large force in Ulster, and the irregulars raised in Londonderry and Enniskillen were placed on a regular footing by the time of the siege of Derry. The Derry forces were eventually consolidated into three regiments from the eight that had existed during the siege, while the Enniskilleners ultimately formed a large regiment of horse, two regiments of dragoons and three battalions of foot. The commander of the Ulster horse, William Wolseley, was an English career soldier, as were most of the other

Ulster colonels. Marshal Schomberg had a poor opinion of the Ulster troops because of their plundering tendencies, likening them to 'so many Croats'. But in 1690, despite Schomberg's opposition, the Ulster troops were placed on the same rates of pay as the rest of the English forces.

New recruits suffered particularly heavy losses through disease during Schomberg's abortive autumn campaign of 1689, although Captain Robert Parker of the Earl of Meath's Regiment would recall how the veteran Dutch and Huguenot regiments built themselves 'good warm barracks which preserved them the wet weather that came on immediately, but the English being raw soldiers neglected the duke's orders till it was too late to provide either timber or straw'.[4] By February 1690 some 5,674 out of Schomberg's army of 16,728 men were dead, mostly as a result of contracting pneumonia in the cold wet conditions.

There was also a major breakdown in supply, mainly because insufficient horses and wagons had been sent over to Ireland to transport supplies disembarked at the ports. William Harbottle, the paymaster, believed that if the army had been properly supplied Schomberg could have been in Dublin before the end of the 1689 campaigning season.

By the spring of 1690 most of the worst deficiencies had been rectified, with 850 wagons and 2,500 horses earmarked to carry supplies. Field bakeries were set up and the experienced Amsterdam military provisioner William Perira was made commissary of the bread. A 'marching hospital', consisting of 30 six- and 12 four-horsed wagons, each with driver and boy, was set up under the direction of the Physician-General, Sir Patrick Dunn, who was paid 10s a day.

As well as large quantities of provisions, 15,000 new muskets and 5,000 pikes were shipped from England, together with the 'new-invented wheel engines, which discharge 150 musket barrels at once, and turning the wheel, as many more'.[5] Disappointingly, there is no record of these predecessors of the Gatling gun seeing action.

Throughout the summer of 1690 a major operation continued to keep the Williamite army adequately supplied. Almost 10,000 horses were shipped over from England by the commissioners of transportation, who hired ships to carry them at a rate of 12s per ton per month, although payments were long in arrears. During the summer 341 merchant ships, mostly of around 200 tons, were retained for transport duties at a cost of £32,000. Their major cargo was fodder for the horses, to compensate for the shortage in Ireland that resulted partly from the Jacobite scorched-earth strategy. A cavalry trooper was expected to buy his own fodder for his horse at a cost of around 1s 3d a day.

More recruits arrived in the first half of 1691. In all there were between 4,000 and 5,000, although the veteran Dutch and Danish complained of their quality, the Danes complaining that most of the English were 'boys and beggars'.[6] The fall of Limerick in October 1691 reduced the need for such large numbers of troops in Ireland. Between November 1691 and the following February most of the regulars under orders for the Continent were embarked. To bring them up to strength a number of Jacobite prisoners and former soldiers were enlisted in their ranks – 2,000 in December alone. However, Catholic recruits were barred from those units that were to remain in Ireland.

In March 1692, when the Irish war was officially declared to be at an end, government forces there, under the new commander-in-chief, Lieutenant-General Ruvigny, Earl of Galway, consisted of one regiment of horse, two of dragoons and fifteen battalions of foot.

THE IRISH JACOBITE ARMY

The basis of the Irish Jacobite forces was the Irish army, which had formed part of the pre-Revolution British forces, although classed as a separate establishment. In 1685 this force had consisted of seven regiments of foot, three of cavalry and one of dragoons. On paper this army totalled 8,500 men, but at least 40 per cent of its personnel were stranded in England by the 1688 Revolution. What remained formed a totally inadequate core for Tyrconnel's greatly expanded army, which would reach a total of 40,000 men in sixty regiments. This rapid expansion, while deterring William from launching an immediate invasion, resulted in military chaos. The establishment of the Irish army, as eventually fixed in 1689, was to be forty-five regiments of foot, eight of dragoons, and seven of cavalry, plus the Lifeguard. This nominal establishment did not change greatly for most of the war. Total strength of the Irish forces varied considerably. In 1689 it was around 36,000 men, reaching 45,000 in 1690 before slipping back in the following spring to 30,500 and to 28,400 by the end of the war.

The latter part of the war saw two auxiliary forces added to the regular army. The first, varying almost daily in strength, but potentially fielding several thousand men, were the guerrillas known as 'rapparees'. The second was the semi-autonomous 'Gaelic' army of Hugh Balldearg O'Donnell, which proved virtually worthless.

In time, Irish foot regiments mainly settled down to the standard British army organisation of thirteen companies, including one of grenadiers. Only the Foot Guards retained two or three battalions. The regulation company mustered sixty-two privates, although fifty was more usual, together with one captain, lieutenant and ensign, two sergeants, three corporals and a drummer. This gave a battalion a theoretical strength of 771 men. Not surprisingly, this was rarely achieved, and in action two or more battalions had often to be combined to reach the required strength.

The squadron, of approximately 100 men, formed the cavalry tactical unit. Regiments might have between six and nine troops, with the latter the regulation strength. At full strength, a regiment would have 527 men, although in practice 300 to 400 was more common. The Lifeguard was formed after James arrived in Ireland, and initially consisted of two troops, each of 100 men, all ranked as officers. A single troop of horse grenadiers was later attached to the Lifeguard. The effective combat strength of the Jacobite cavalry during the war varied from 2,500 to 4,000. There were a similar number of dragoons, formed into companies of ten to twelve per regiment.

The exclusion of Roman Catholics from the British standing armies until shortly before the 1688 Revolution meant that the Irish Jacobites faced a chronic shortage of trained officers, although there were a number who had served with the British forces in Holland and France. Among them was William Dorrington, colonel of the Foot Guards, and Justin MacCarthy. Cavalry colonels with similar regular army experience included Patrick Sarsfield, Henry Lutterell and John Parker. At least two Scottish professional soldiers, the dragoon colonel Thomas Maxwell and the infantry commander John Wauchope, also served in Ireland, along with a number of Englishmen, including Dominic Sheldon, a senior cavalry commander. One cavalry colonel, Lord Sarsfield of Kilmallock, a brother-in-law of Patrick, was an impoverished Irish peer who had served in the ranks in the French army.

Most colonels were appointed because of their wealth and local influence. John Lord Bellew of Duleek, for example, owned more than 6,000 acres, and Lord Louth 4,000. More than one-third of the colonels were peers or sons of peers. Whenever possible, these amateur colonels were given an experienced officer as their lieutenant-colonel or major; however, no more than about one in twenty of the Jacobite officer corps had any previous military service, so that, even spread equally, they would have amounted to no more than two per regiment. The situation was somewhat eased after the opening days of the war by a number of French officers being attached to Irish regiments. Many of the amateur soldiers became highly competent during the course of the war; one, Michael Rothe of Kilkenny, a captain in the Foot Guards, eventually became a lieutenant-general in the French service.

Most colonels tended to recruit their officers from among their relatives, dependants and neighbours. Other ranks were nominally volunteers, except in the emergency following Aughrim, when all males between 16 and 60 were liable to conscription. Although there was generally at least some moral compulsion on men to join units raised by their landlords, there was initially a good deal of enthusiasm to enlist. In 1686, of forty men recruited for a company under Lord Enniskillen, leader of the dispossessed Maguire clan, half bore the name Maguire, and all the remainder had Gaelic surnames from the same locality.

Maintaining the army placed a tremendous burden on the Irish economy. Until the territory under their control began to shrink, the Jacobites were generally able to supply sufficient horses, fodder and provisions, but they could never provide enough arms, clothing or military experience. Initially, Tyrconnel was able to provide only 1,000 muskets, taken from the Protestant militia, and there were reports of whole regiments armed only with sticks and clubs. The Jacobites always relied heavily on the French for military equipment. In all, eight major convoys sailed for Ireland. Two in 1689 consisted of over 60 ships, three in 1690 had over 100 ships, with similar numbers in 1691, the last reaching Limerick after the Jacobite surrender. Besides these, there were the products of individual trading ventures with the Continent. Merchants of Lisbon supplied cannon and flintlocks.[7] Mary of Modena purchased 2,000 muskets by pawning her jewellery. As well as munitions and other supplies, the French convoys also brought officers, engineers and technicians. D'Avaux reckoned that by August 1689, 17,000 muskets had been dispatched.[8] Convoys arriving in the same year also brought 3,000 swords, 16,000 sabres, 1,000 pairs of pistols and 100,000lb of black powder. In 1690, 8,000 muskets and flintlocks, with powder and match, and 16,000 grenades arrived, with further consignments the following year.

Although the French naval ministry was sympathetic towards the Jacobites, the War Minister, Louvois, did not favour sending them massive support. Many of the muskets sent proved to be old and in poor condition. Tyrconnel commented bitterly: 'Could M. Louvois be gained, or at least softened, I would have no doubt of our soon being masters of this kingdom.' In March 1690 it was estimated that the army was short of 20,000 muskets, and of those men lucky enough to have them, two-thirds had never fired a shot because of lack of powder.[9]

Irish soldiers were sometimes quick to throw away their weapons when in flight, and after the Boyne half of those who eventually rallied at Limerick did so unarmed. There were few facilities to repair unserviceable weapons, and it was alleged that most of the available gunsmiths were Protestants, who sabotaged more than they repaired.[10] In the spring of 1691 the convoy that brought the French General St Ruhe to Ireland included five armourers among the additional personnel it carried.

Clothing the Irish army also proved to be difficult. Red was the desired coat colour, though French grey and occasionally blue were also issued. It proved difficult to follow the customary practice of issuing new uniforms every eighteen months. And although the army seems to have been reasonably well fitted out at the start of the 1690 campaign, by the autumn most of the troops were in rags. St Ruhe's convoy in the spring of 1691 brought with it 20,000 grey-white French uniform coats, in which the bulk of the Irish army fought its last campaign.

Between one-third and one-fifth of the Irish foot were pikemen, their weapons often tipped with scythe blades instead of pike heads. The matchlock remained the standard infantry firearm, with flintlocks issued only to dragoons, to a few infantry units such as the Foot Guards, and possibly to grenadier companies. Infantry swords were always in short supply. The cavalry were justifiably regarded as the elite of the Irish army, with the best officers, finest horses, and usually a better class of recruits, although the quality of the cavalry declined during its final campaign.

In theory, the Irish army adopted the same articles of war that were in force in the British army from 1686, although discipline was generally poor. This was partly because many officers initially lacked the authority to discipline or train their men, and even after the French had established formal training camps the Irish army never achieved the standards of its European contemporaries.

Artillery always remained the greatest weakness of the Irish army. Before the Revolution, although the Irish military establishment had included its own ordnance board, the Irish forces had effectively relied upon their English counterpart for guns and gunners. In April 1689 James appointed Justin MacCarthy as his Master Gunner. Although an experienced soldier, MacCarthy took little interest in gunnery. Following his departure to France in early 1690 it does not seem that a successor was appointed. From then on, French officers took overall command of the Jacobite guns. Their personnel were rarely satisfactory. All the pre-war gunners on the Irish establishment had been Protestants, who had fled to England following the Revolution. Their replacements were untrained and never reached the standard of their European counterparts.

There was an ongoing shortage of guns. In March 1689, during his attack on Crom Castle, Lord Galmoy had only two light 'leather' guns. Although it was estimated that there were over 250 artillery pieces in various Jacobite garrisons, no attempt was made either to make them mobile or to form a proper artillery train. During MacCarthy's tenure of office the effective commander of the artillery in the field was Garade Pointis, a French naval gunnery officer who commanded the Jacobite ordnance at the siege of Derry, his principal pieces being two 18-pounders.

By the time that Pointis left Ireland in November 1689 the Jacobite artillery consisted of eleven field guns pulled by old saddle horses, with 4 artillery officers, 100 pioneers and the survivors of 34 gunners who had come from France. At the Boyne, where the French Lieutenant-General Laisne commanded the artillery, the Jacobites had at least sixteen guns. Laisne left for France in the autumn, but in the spring of 1691 St Ruhe brought with him to Limerick four artillery officers, six guns and eight limbers. All but one of the guns were lost at Aughrim.[11]

THE SCOTTISH JACOBITE ARMY

The Jacobite forces in Scotland, lacking a secure base area from which to recruit and to obtain provisions, and consisting largely of clan forces, never achieved anything approaching the cohesion and organisation of their Irish counterparts. None of the successive Jacobite commanders in Scotland – Dundee, Cannon or Buchan – was able to expand his breadth of support much beyond the Celtic fringe of western clans, apart from a handful of cavalry recruited in eastern Scotland. They therefore had no option but to work as best they could with the existing clan military system.

The Highland clans figure in popular imagination as fierce warriors sweeping down from their mountain strongholds in savage raids on their lowland neighbours. But the idea of a clan as being entirely composed of hardened fighting men is an over-simplification. The clan was headed by its chief, who, theoretically, led it in war. Next in importance to the chief were the heads of the different branches of the clan. They and other leading members normally held their lands from the chief by leases or 'tacks', which gave these tenants their name of 'tacksmen'. It was not unusual for tacksmen to be from families not originally part of the clan, and hence to have different surnames.

Inter-clan fighting often took the form of cattle-raiding, in which armed clashes might occur, although usually with little bloodshed. Most were carried out by men known as *cearnachs* or *caterans* to the Scottish Lowlanders. The word meant 'soldier', and they were noted for their violence and disorder, not necessarily being members of the clan whom they currently served. Below the *cearnachs* in the hierarchy of clan warfare came the *ghillies*, who in peacetime were normally outdoor servants of various kinds, and below them came the ordinary clansmen, who were not necessarily trained in warfare and were generally called out only in emergencies. All ages, from young boys to old men, would be called upon, and they were often little more than a poorly armed mob. When a clan went to war, its gentry and leading tacksmen became its officers, and occupied the front rank along with the *cearnachs*, with the *ghillies* and ordinary clansmen massed behind. In practice there was considerable confusion, with companies and clans varying greatly in size, and usually with too many officers.

The dress of the clansman varied. A chief might present an air of barbaric splendour, with feathered bonnet and bristling with weaponry, but most clansmen were much less well turned out. Most wore either breeches, trews or the garment known as the belted plaid, a piece of cloth about 54in wide and 6yd in length, and gathered in at the waist. Other clansmen are described as going into action in their shirt tails, probably because they had cast their plaids aside for ease of movement. The kilt does not appear to have come into use before the early eighteenth century. Nor were there distinctive clan tartans in the modern sense, although a particular pattern might sometimes be associated with a specific area.

Most clansmen travelled light, carrying their basic utensils and the oatmeal that formed their principal campaign diet in the folds of their plaids or in a small bag. Armour was rarely worn, although some of the better-equipped warriors carried the small shield known as the 'targe'. The description given by General Wade in 1724 applied fairly well to the Highlanders of forty years earlier:

> The Arms they make use of in War, are a Musket, a Broad Sword and Target, a Pistol and a Dirk or Dagger, hanging by their side, with a Powder Horn and a Pouch for their Ammunition. They form themselves into Bodies of unequal Numbers according to the strength of their Clan or Tribe, which is commanded by their Respective Superior or Chieftain. When in sight of the Enemy they endeavour to possess themselves of the highest Ground, believing they descend on them with greater force.
>
> They generally give their fire at a distance. They lay down their Arms on the Ground and make a Vigorous attack with their Broad Swords, but if repulsed, seldom or never rally again. They dread engaging with the Cavalry, and seldom venture to descend from the Mountains when apprehensive of being charged by them.[12]

The mass of clansmen forming the rear ranks were often very poorly armed indeed, with long dirks rather than swords, axes, both short-handled and the long-handled Lochaber variety, and occasionally even agricultural implements. On the whole, Highlanders were unused to firearms, and they were certainly less commonly used in 1689 than in the later rebellions, although a considerable number were captured at Killiecrankie. The tactic described by Wade was the famous 'Highland Charge', in which the leading ranks of well-armed men did most of the serious fighting, the mob behind providing moral encouragement and crowd pressure, and only really coming into their own in the pursuit of routed fugitives.

Ireland, 1689–91

FOUR

•••••••••

Jacobite High Tide

On 12 March, after an uneventful voyage, King James II and his convoy of twenty-two ships arrived at the south-west Irish port of Kinsale. As he travelled to Dublin, the King received a tumultuous welcome from the population of the towns and villages on his route.

It was a very different reception from any that James had ever received in either of his other two kingdoms, but did little to alter his views about Ireland's role in his plans. Among the King's first actions on arrival was to set up an inner cabinet consisting of himself, the French envoy d'Avaux, Tyrconnel and Secretary of State John Drummond, Earl of Melfort. The royal advisers were at cross-purposes regarding future Jacobite strategy.

Tyrconnel, as might be expected, wished priority to be given to completing the Jacobite conquest of Ireland, and to training the newly raised Irish troops before considering a landing in England or Scotland. Melfort, on the other hand, pressed for an early landing in Scotland, leaving behind only enough men to contain the Protestant garrisons in Ulster. There was, however, no immediate prospect of the French providing the necessary shipping, as Louvois believed that an over-hasty attempt might lose James all three of his kingdoms. D'Avaux took a similar line, opposing any invasion until Derry had been taken, and even then feeling that James should remain behind in Ireland.

James himself had never seen Ireland as more than a stepping-stone on his journey back to Whitehall, which he now saw as being via Scotland. He envisaged an army of 10,000 Irish troops being landed at Troon by the end of July, going on to take Glasgow, to rendezvous with Dundee and his Highlanders at Stirling and to be in Edinburgh in three days. At the same time, French troops would land on Anglesey and cut William's communications if he advanced to meet James, either trapping William's forces or compelling him to fall back on London. Here James, optimistically assuming that the English population would rally to his banner as he marched south, would fight the decisive battle. The French, however, had no intention of supporting such a plan, at least until Derry had been taken.

REORGANISING THE ARMY

The Jacobites' first task must be to end Protestant resistance in Ulster, but the forces available were clearly inadequate. Throughout the winter Tyrconnel had given individual colonels a free hand in recruiting, so that their units varied widely in both size and quality. A horrified d'Avaux reported to Paris that there were regiments with thirty-five, forty or even forty-four companies, and that the officers appointed to command these units were often totally unsuitable. Many had been appointed by means of patronage, or elected by the men of their companies, reportedly including tailors, butchers and shoemakers. D'Avaux's accusations were slightly exaggerated, but the Irish army was poorly prepared for the start of the campaigning season.

However, the 200 Jacobite and French officers who had accompanied James to Ireland, and tough-minded individuals such as the young Colonel Patrick Sarsfield, strove to bring some order. Only a smaller, better-regulated army was viable in the longer term. The establishment of the Irish army was fixed at seven regiments of horse and seven of dragoons, with thirty-five regiments of foot, each of the latter (apart from the Guards, who had two battalions) consisting of thirteen companies. The reorganised army would have an estimated strength of 35,000 men.

The disbanded troops, although claiming that their attacks were aimed at Williamite supporters, caused considerable disruption by what amounted to banditry. Jealousy resulted from the deployment of French officers into the Jacobite units. Each officer received a step-up in rank on appointment, and General the Marquis de Boisseleau raised a regiment of his own in the Cork area.

The army remained short of everything but manpower. The muskets brought from France were of poor quality, many of them damaged, while only one in twenty of the firearms confiscated from the Protestant population, many sabotaged by their former owners, proved to be serviceable. As most of the armourers in Ireland were Protestant, and hence of suspect loyalty, repairs would take a long time, and d'Avaux requested that more armourers be sent over from France. One regiment sent to take part in the siege of Derry had only seven muskets. The Jacobite artillery train was woefully inadequate for siege operations, with no more than twelve guns and two mortars fit for action.

Experienced, well-equipped French troops were urgently needed, but Louvois would consider sending them only at a price. On 26 February he wrote to James's most competent general, Justin MacCarthy, telling him that he would send some troops the following winter, but only in exchange for 5,000 Irish troops commanded by MacCarthy himself. Although he must have known that they could ill be spared, MacCarthy replied promising personally to select the best officers and men. James disliked the proposal, especially when Louvois announced that no French troops could be spared until the end of the campaigning season, and even then only 4,000 to 5,000 in return for 6,000 to 7,000 Irish. Argument rumbled on for much of the summer. D'Avaux eventually appealed to Mary of Modena to talk James around.[1]

THE INVASION OF ULSTER

Operations had begun in Ulster before James's arrival, with the dispatch northwards by Tyrconnel of 2,500 men under the turncoat Lieutenant General Richard Hamilton. The Ulster Protestants had been alarmed by rumours of the size of the army that Tyrconnel was raising, which they rather obviously concluded was 'not intended for their safety or advantage'. The result was a general call to arms, and the setting up of a Council of the North, headed by Lord Mount-Alexander, and including many of the leading Protestant gentry of Ulster. The Council's first act was to appeal to William to send it 10,000 infantry, 1,500 cavalry and 20,000 muskets. There was no prospect of such assistance materialising for a long time to come but, as the weeks passed, hopes rose that Tyrconnel would submit and conflict would be avoided.

By now Tyrconnel's hesitancy regarding his commitment to the Jacobite cause was at an end, and he was able to inform the newly arrived James that Richard Hamilton and his army were on the march to crush resistance in Ulster. Also sent north by Tyrconnel was a Presbyterian emissary, Alexander Osbourne, with the mission of trying to persuade the Council of the North to agree to terms. However, Osbourne lost no time in informing the Council that Hamilton's men were poorly equipped, and that his cavalry were 'but contemptible fellows, many of them having lately been cowherds etc.'. He advised the Council to resist, rather than trust in Tyrconnel's promises of moderation, and the Protestant leadership, further encouraged by promises of assistance by William, returned a defiant response.

The Council had become so caught up in its own debate that Hamilton was upon its troops almost before it realised it. Hastily, a small force of yeomen cavalry under the 'Cock of the North', Arthur Rawdon, one of the more celebrated Ulster leaders, was sent to meet the Jacobites near the County Down village of Dromore. The short skirmish that followed, known as the 'Break of Dromore', proved that Hamilton's cavalry were rather more than 'contemptible . . . cowherds', as they easily routed Rawdon's men, and Protestant resistance in eastern Ulster collapsed. Many of the leading Ulster Protestants, including Lord Mount-Alexander, fled to England.

However, the resolute Rawdon collected several thousand men and on 15 March occupied the town of Coleraine. Hamilton failed to capitalise on his success, wasting an invaluable fortnight while his men indulged in an orgy of looting. This gave the defenders of Coleraine, confusingly commanded by Major Gustavus Hamilton, a kinsman of the Jacobite commander, time to strengthen the scanty defences of the town, already protected on one side by the River Bann.

It was 27 March before Hamilton reached Coleraine. At ten o'clock the next morning the five Jacobite guns began a bombardment of the town, whose defenders replied energetically. Hamilton sent his infantry forward using available cover, and an ineffective firefight continued until dusk, when snowfall brought an end to the skirmishing.

His repulse at Coleraine came as a shock to Hamilton. He had been unprepared for a siege, having with him only two days' provisions. Knowing that Jacobite reinforcements were moving up from Charlemont, he decided to leave the reduction of Coleraine to them, while he led his own troops against Derry. For the next ten days, in cold, wet and windy weather that had serious effects on the health of both sides, Hamilton's troops skirmished with detachments from the Coleraine garrison, along the River Bann, until the Jacobites found some boats and crossed the river at Portglenone.

Hamilton was now in County Londonderry, and both Derry and Coleraine were under serious threat, with communications between them cut. In these circumstances, Gustavus Hamilton decided to abandon Coleraine and fall back on Derry before he became completely isolated. As his ragged levies, accompanied by crowds of terrified refugees, made their way through the gates of Derry, it seemed certain that the small town would shortly come under sustained attack.

THE SIEGE OF DERRY

The governor of Derry was a professional soldier, Robert Lundy (nominally of Lord Mountjoy's Regiment, which was now serving with the Jacobites). Lundy, as a veteran of the Tangiers garrison, was experienced in the defence of a town under threat. He worked energetically in preparing Derry to meet attack, and was described by one Ulsterman as 'very much esteemed not only for his forwardness in their Majesties' service but for his military knowledge and courage and his extraordinary care and vigilance'.[2] He strengthened the walls and gates, originally constructed to protect the settlement from attacks by the Irish population, repaired the carriages of the guns mounted on them, and cleared some of the approaches. For much of their length the walls were further protected by the River Foyle or by steeply falling ground in front. A ravelin was constructed to strengthen the approaches to Bishop's Gate, on the weaker defences on the southern edge of the city.

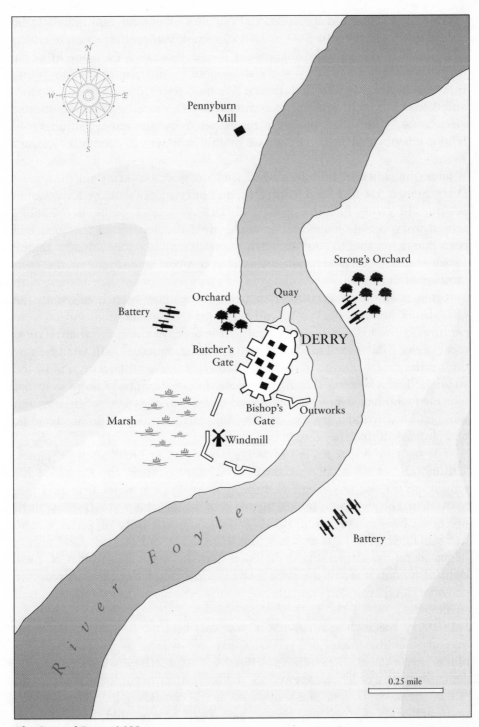

The Siege of Derry, 1689

Lundy also arranged for additional supplies of powder and match to be purchased, together with 500 matchlocks from Stirling Castle, while efforts were made to recruit more soldiers for the garrison. Not everyone in Derry was convinced of the wisdom of resistance, but for the moment the prevailing view was expressed in the declaration: 'We have resolved to stand our ground, and defend our walls and not to admit of any Papists whatsoever to quarter among us.'[3] Confidence was strengthened by the large numbers of reinforcements that began to arrive, mainly followers of nearby Protestant gentry.

James, meanwhile, had decided to lead his principal army north against Derry himself. He had been assured by his commanders that the town would fall quickly, giving him the prestige of an easy victory, while, if resistance proved unexpectedly stubborn, he could avoid the accusation that this had been due to his absence. An underlying motive may have been that by taking personal charge at Derry, James was able to avoid attendance at the Irish Parliament in Dublin.

While as many as 20,000 Irish troops may have been involved in the operations against Derry, not all were present at once, as units were continually rotated. James may initially have brought north less than 10,000 men, of decidedly mixed quality. D'Avaux was unimpressed with what he saw during the march north: 'There was scarcely a soldier that they saw in the way who had a weapon that he could use; in every company there were not four men who had swords, the old muskets and bad guns were of no use; and they marched without powder, match and balls . . . they come like bandits, and plunder all that they find in their path.'[4]

D'Avaux feared that a siege of Derry would end in humiliation for James. The march got off to a poor start when, after a week, the King and his entourage arrived at Omagh to hear that an English relief fleet had just arrived in Lough Foyle. James turned and headed back for Dublin, until overtaken by a message from his illegitimate son, the Duke of Berwick, who had remained with the army, reporting that the rumour was false and urging James to return, expressing confidence that the mere appearance of their rightful monarch would be sufficient to bring about the surrender of the defenders of Derry. James, with no great enthusiasm, did as his son had suggested.

In Derry, meanwhile, a council of war was held on 10 April to agree on measures for the town's defence. The first step was to fix regulations for a place under siege. Remaining suburbs outside the walls were to be demolished, and orders were given for the building of a 'pair of gallows . . . in one of the bastions upon the south-west of the city, whereupon all mutinous or treacherous persons of this garrison shall be executed, who shall be condemned thereunto by a court martial'.[5] In recognition of the possibility of a prolonged siege, rations for the troops were also laid down:

That every soldier of the garrison, and non-commissioned officer, shall be weekly allowed out of the magazines eight quarts of meal, four pounds of fish, and three pounds of flesh for his weekly subsistence.

That every soldier and non-commissioned officer, shall be allowed a quart of Small beer per day, as soon as the same can be provided, until some money shall come to allow them pay.[6]

On 13 April the first Jacobite patrols were sighted from the city walls, and, although they quickly pulled back, it was clear that the crisis was at hand. By now Lundy probably had elements of some thirty, mostly understrength, Ulster regiments in Derry, all raw recruits, totalling about 7,000 men. Lundy had ordered various outlying garrisons to be abandoned in the face of James's advance. Some of these garrisons still contained significant quantities of supplies when their defenders pulled out and, when the key town of Sligo was evacuated, this opened a new route into Ulster for the enemy from the west.

The orders made sound military sense, for the small outposts could not have resisted determined attack, but to some of the anxious citizens and refugees crowded within the walls of Derry such a precipitate withdrawal smacked of treachery. Disquiet focused on Robert Lundy, who had, as his opponents were quick to point out, originally received his army commission from James. Perhaps, they hinted, he was suffering from a crisis of conscience at the prospect of drawing his sword against King James, and was concentrating nearly all the Protestant forces of Ulster at Derry in order to surrender them. For the moment, however, most of the local leadership retained confidence in Lundy, and on 13 April a hastily convened council of war appointed him commander-in-chief of a force that was to march out and block the Jacobite advance on Derry. It was ordered:

That, on Monday next, by ten o'clock, all officers and soldiers, horse and foot, and all other armed men whatsoever, of our forces and friends, enlisted or not enlisted, that can or will fight for their country and religion against a common enemy, shall appear on the fittest ground, near Claudy-ford, Lifford, and Long-Causeway, as shall be nearest to their several and respective quarters; there to draw up, in battalions, to be ready to fight the enemy, and to preserve our lives and all that is dear to us, from the enemy.[7]

Lundy is sometimes credited with this strategy, which in effect pitted one untrained mob against another. This, however, seems questionable; as an experienced officer, Lundy can have had few illusions about the quality of his troops, and might have been expected to have preferred to fight behind fixed defences. It seems more likely that he was forced to accept the proposals of some of the civilian activists within Derry. Early on Sunday, 14 April, Lundy ordered the crossings of the River Finn, south of Derry, to be secured by detachments of troops, one of which, at Lifford, reportedly repulsed several enemy attempts to cross during the night. Next day the outposts were reinforced by Lundy's main force from Derry, which probably totalled in the region of 7,000 men, roughly equal in numbers to their opponents.

As the two sides prepared for action, the relief fleet from Liverpool, whose arrival had earlier been rumoured, finally anchored in Lough Foyle. Aboard were reinforcements, one of whose officers, Colonel Andrew Cunningham, sent a message to Lundy offering the support of two regular battalions. However, the offer arrived too late. The first clash between Lundy's men and the advancing Jacobites occurred near Lifford, with the Derry forces deployed to defend the various crossing places. Lundy accurately estimated the poor quality of the Jacobite infantry, but he seems to have discounted the ability of their cavalry. Although his raw levies could probably have held their own against the Irish foot, they lacked the training and steadiness to withstand horse.

The debacle was complete. The Jacobite cavalry who came charging across the river were led by the ferocious General von Rosen, a Livonian soldier of fortune who, after entering French service, had married his colonel's daughter and adopted her family name. Von Rosen was described as 'always in fear of accidents and subject to passion even to a degree of madness and at these times he was incapable of listening to any representation'.[8] He was, nevertheless, an excellent combat commander, and the Protestant foot, despite a stand by a body of troops under the young Colonel Adam Murray, who fought until they ran out of ammunition, were quickly routed. Von Rosen pursued Lundy's fleeing men about 5 miles towards Derry, killing or taking some 400 of them, until Richard Hamilton came up and halted the pursuit.

The defeat was a major blow to Lundy's confidence. He began to entertain serious doubts of being able to hold Derry. It may have been because of this that he persuaded Colonels Cunningham and Richards, commanding the troops aboard the relief fleet, that if they landed them in Derry they would be caught up in inevitable defeat. One immediate consequence of the debacle at the fords was a decision by the leadership within Derry to open negotiations with the enemy. While some have seen this as a delaying tactic, Lundy may have hoped to reach a settlement that would have allowed him to withdraw his own troops intact, to fight another day.

James arrived before Derry early on 18 April, ignorant of the fact that Richard Hamilton had already begun negotiations with the defenders. He had offered generous terms, including a 'general Pardon, and [to] order Restitution of all that had been Plunder'd from them'.[9] Hamilton had also agreed that, while negotiations continued, no Jacobite troops would approach nearer than 4 miles. James and von Rosen, however, seem to have felt that a show of strength, with their forces drawn up in sight of the town, would suffice to bring about its speedy surrender. In fact, the sight of James, von

Rosen and their entourage approaching the walls was considered by those in Derry as a deliberate disregard of the agreement.

> Orders were given that none should dare to fire till the King's demands were first known, by another Messenger to be sent to His Majesty for that purpose; but our men on the Walls, wondering to see Lieutenant-General Hamilton (contrary to his engagement) approaching our walls in such order, they imagining they were by some means or other betrayed, thought it reasonable to consider their own safety, and to keep the Enemy at distance, by firing their Guns upon them, which they accordingly did . . . In an instant a discharge of musketry and cannon from the troops stationed in the church bastion, was directed against the enemy, proclaiming defiance and hostilities, with the triumphant shout of 'No Surrender!'[10]

An officer close by James was killed, along with a number of others, and the King and his entourage withdrew to a safe distance. By now, heavy rain had started to fall, and the King spent the rest of the day sitting hunched on his horse, still vainly hoping for a surrender.

The decision not to accept reinforcements from the relief convoy was made at a small council of war in Derry, the majority of whose members were supporters of Lundy, and an attempt was made to keep its conclusions from the rest of the townspeople. However, the latter were told by the clerk, who recorded the proceedings, and uproar followed. The growing opposition to Lundy found a leader in Adam Murray, whose yeomanry cavalry were among the few troops to have emerged from the humiliating defeat at the fords with any credit. Murray urged the defenders of Derry to stand firm, and accused Lundy of being 'either a fool or a knave'.

The Governor's position had become untenable, and eventually he was assisted in escaping from the city, disguised as a common soldier, by two of his principal opponents, a Presbyterian clergyman, George Walker, and another professional soldier, Colonel Henry Baker. Other supporters of negotiations also left Derry and, after Murray had refused the post, Walker and Baker were appointed joint Governors of Derry. Baker was aged 42, of English settler stock, while the 43-year-old Walker was of Yorkshire descent, with considerable influence among the townsfolk, although his widely circulated account of the siege probably exaggerated his role.

In popular legend Lundy is still portrayed as a traitor whose scheme to surrender Derry to the enemy had been narrowly frustrated. However, this seems to have been an oversimplification. While he may have felt that the defence of Derry was untenable in the long term, his decision to open talks with the enemy had the additional result of buying time.

But for the blunder by James and von Rosen, it is probable that the town would have surrendered without resistance. As it was, James was faced with the prospect of a prolonged siege. His preference would have been to blockade Derry with a small force and cross to Scotland with the bulk of his army. But, with the French unwilling to provide naval assistance, this was never an option, and besieging Derry was the only course left open to the King if he were to retain any sort of initiative. James himself never seems to have expressed a decided view on the matter, and left the decision to his generals before Derry. D'Avaux, who remained sceptical of success, commented: 'Our chief difficulty will be the irresolution of King James, who often changes his mind, and then decides not always for the best.'[11]

The problem that was fatally to dog Jacobite efforts before Derry should have been obvious to both James and his commanders. The Jacobite army lacked the means to bring a siege to a successful conclusion. Most importantly, its siege train, with only about eight guns capable of doing even minimum damage to Derry's walls, was totally inadequate. Unless the defences could be breached, there was no way the Jacobites could utilise their one undisputed advantage – greater manpower – and storm Derry. Although the Jacobite commanders were unwilling to acknowledge the fact until almost the end of the siege, their only hope of taking Derry, short of treachery within, was by starvation.

The main strength of Derry's garrison was formed by eight regiments of foot, varying in size from eight to twenty-five companies, the largest being Baker's regiment and the smallest Colonel Crofton's. The widely differing size of each regiment was mainly accounted for by the elected captains of each company being free to decide which colonel they would serve under. Two regiments would be on duty each night, with a curfew at eight o'clock, after which no drinking was allowed.

There were, on paper, a total of 7,020 other ranks and 341 officers in the garrison. George Walker would claim later that no less than 30,000 civilians had taken refuge within Derry's walls. As the total area encompassed by them was only 500yd by 300yd, this seems an impossibly high total, and Walker's figures may be as much as a tenfold exaggeration. In any case, Richard Hamilton would ease the overcrowding and supply problems of Derry by allowing an estimated 10,000 civilians to leave. This 'hearts and minds' policy was opposed by the brutally realistic von Rosen, but his protests were overruled by James. The defence was also aided in a grim fashion by the high mortality rate, mainly affecting the old and very young, that developed in the later stages of the siege, and which reduced the number of – in military terms –'useless mouths' that required feeding.

Of the defenders, only around 300 men who had formerly served in Mountjoy's regiment could be classed as experienced soldiers. The rest were raw recruits whose only previous experience of battle had been in the debacle of the fords. The majority of the officers were also amateurs. The garrison possessed about twenty guns of various calibres, which would eventually be reduced to firing back the roundshot with which the Jacobites bombarded the city. Most of the horses in Derry died through lack of fodder, or were eaten.

James had not abandoned hopes of taking possession of Derry peacefully, and negotiations continued spasmodically, with the Derry council of war going so far as to apologise to the King for the shots fired at him. But, although some of the leaders within the city still hoped for compromise, they were powerless to act against the more radical elements, including most of the ordinary citizens. Negotiations, therefore, ended with a reiterated message of defiance from Derry. Realising that there was no prospect of an easy reduction of the town, James handed over command to the French Lieutenant-General Maumont, assisted by another French officer, Lieutenant-General Pusignan, Richard Hamilton and the Duke of Berwick. With Rosen and Secretary of State Melfort, James then returned to Dublin, having issued no clear instructions on how operations before Derry should be conducted.

According to Berwick, the plan devised by the commanders on the spot recognised the reality of the situation by establishing a blockade of the town while they built up the resources necessary for a full-scale siege. Jacobite infantry were deployed on the west bank of the River Foyle, in an arc that touched the river to the north and south of Derry, with a detachment of horse and foot at Pennyburn, cutting off communications between Derry and the outlying fort at Culmore, where supplies from England might be landed. Another Jacobite strongpoint on the opposite bank of the river, on high ground at a location known as Strong's Orchard, was manned by men of Lords Bellew and Louth's regiments of foot.

Active operations began on 21 April, when the Jacobites opened fire on the defences with a demi-culverin emplaced at Strong's Orchard, and the defenders replied with a sortie by 300 cavalry and about four companies of foot, all under the command of Adam Murray. Their objective was the Jacobite outpost at Pennyburn. Leaving his infantry to act as a reserve, posted on high ground to cover his eventual retreat, Murray divided his cavalry into two squadrons, led by himself and Major Bell. A brisk encounter took place with Jacobite cavalry, and Maumont led up a reinforcing troop of horse to join the action, but was killed – according to tradition in a hand-to-hand encounter with Murray.

As more Jacobite reinforcements came up, Murray ordered his horse to pull back into Derry. His infantry reserve had been placed in ambush in ditches along the line of retreat, and opened fire on the pursuing Jacobite cavalry. According to Berwick, who led the pursuit, his men suffered heavy casualties, with scarcely a man or horse returning unscathed.

The skirmish provided a useful boost to Williamite morale. The Jacobite response was to intensify their bombardment, with four additional guns stationed at Strong's Orchard, whose fire killed several civilians and damaged a number of buildings. On 24 April the Jacobites brought up two mortars to add to the weight of their attack.

Mortars, firing a variety of projectiles, including explosive or incendiary shells and even large stones, were notoriously inaccurate weapons. However, their high trajectory enabled them to fire over the defences into the heart of Derry and, especially at night, cause confusion and dismay out of all proportion to the physical damage that they inflicted. One of the larger shells 'fell into a house while several officers were at dinner; it fell upon the bed of the room they were in, but did not touch any of them; forced into a lower room and killed the landlord'.[12] Major Baker ordered blinds to be erected on the walls to conceal the troops posted there, and had paving stones in the streets taken up to prevent casualties caused by splinters from exploding enemy shells.

On the same day that the mortars were first employed, there was another skirmish near Pennyburn, when Murray made another sortie. In a sharp cavalry skirmish, the new French commander of the besieging forces, Lieutenant-General Puisignan, was fatally wounded. Berwick was also wounded in the action, and as a result command rested solely with Richard Hamilton. He had few illusions regarding the task that he faced, complaining to James that he lacked both artillery and men. With his six infantry battalions all badly below strength, he probably had no more than 3,000 foot actually present, of whom only about one in ten had a musket fit to fire.

However, the Jacobites gained an important success when they persuaded the commander of Culmore fort, William Adair of Ballymena, to surrender. Adair and his men were allowed to march out with the 'honours of war', with their swords, horses and pistols, although not with their muskets; but on reaching Coleraine they were allegedly stripped to their shirts by the Jacobite troops stationed there.

Jacobite efforts against Derry were hampered by lack of gunpowder, which siege batteries always consumed in enormous quantities. Between 24 April and 4 May they fired only about thirty rounds. However, by early May Hamilton's men were making their first serious attempts to extend their trenches and parallels close enough to Derry's walls for their guns to be able to create a breach, and the result was the first major clash of the siege. On the night of 5 May the Jacobite infantry brigade commanded by Colonel Ramsey launched a surprise attack which took an outwork of the defences between Windmill Hill and the Foyle. A parallel was constructed from which Jacobite guns began to fire at close enough range to damage Derry's walls. Although the Jacobite artillery would have had to be still closer to make a breach, Walker and Baker decided that the outwork must be retaken.

Ten picked men were selected from each of the foot companies of the garrison, and reinforced by volunteers. According to Walker, both he and Major Baker led the attack, although it is more likely that Baker was in sole command. A sharp engagement followed, with hand-to-hand fighting with clubbed muskets, before the Jacobites broke and fled. They suffered a number of casualties, not least Colonel Ramsey, reckoned by many to be one of the most capable officers in the army, who was shot dead in the fighting. The Williamites also claimed to have taken five enemy company colours, at least two of which were triumphantly hung in Derry cathedral.

Numerous minor skirmishes followed over the next few days, with the Williamites optimistically claiming that by the end of May the enemy had lost 3,000 men in action or through disease. However, the defenders were not without their own problems. One regimental commander, Colonel Parker, deserted to the enemy, while a furious quarrel between Major Baker and another professional soldier, Colonel John Mitchelburne, resulted in a brawl during which Mitchelburne was wounded. Throughout the siege there were fears of some act of treachery by those within Derry who still secretly either favoured James or wished to surrender. There were indeed some illicit contacts between disaffected citizens and the besiegers, and the governors decided that, because of the danger of betrayal, it was unsafe to have complete regiments on duty at night. Instead, detachments from all the units in the garrison would be on duty, so that each could keep an eye on the others. Even so, there was a steady trickle of desertions as men slipped over the defences, a process which the Derry commanders did little to prevent, as such faint hearts poised less of a threat outside the walls, and their departure also helped to conserve supplies.

At the end of May, at least two heavy Jacobite siege guns arrived. They had taken so long because, lacking control of the Irish Sea, the Jacobites had been forced to move them by land. Early in June a French engineer, the Marquis de Pointis, tightened the Jacobite grip on Derry by constructing a boom across the Foyle, between Derry and the mouth of the river. His first attempt, using a boom made from oak, failed when it proved to be so heavy that it sank. A second attempt, employing a boom constructed from sections of fir joined by movable metal clamps so that it could rise and fall with the tides, appears to have been more successful.

On 4 June, the day that the second boom was put in place, another serious action took place at Windmill Hill. This time Hamilton launched a major attack with twelve infantry battalions and fifteen or sixteen squadrons of cavalry. The aim seems not to have been to break into Derry itself, but to take ground so that the artillery could be brought up nearer to the town. On seeing the enemy preparations, the garrison made a sortie in strength to meet them. The Jacobites reportedly began their advance with a loud 'huzza' and 'dreadful shouts and howlings' from their camp-followers, who were watching events unfold. The defenders quickly realised that the attacking cavalry, who were equipped with back- and breastplates, were not much affected by their fire, so switched their aim to the unfortunate horses, breaking up the cavalry attack in confusion. Of those horsemen who managed to reach the 7ft-high defences, only three escaped, the remainder being killed, or captured by the expedient of hauling them over the defences by the hair.

Meanwhile, the Jacobite infantry had launched its own assault, the front rank carrying bundles of basketwork or faggots as a flimsy defence against heavy and continuous enemy fire. Once again, some of the attackers managed to reach the defences, but found them too high to scale without ladders, which were not available. On the left, the attacking grenadiers 'came over the bog, near the Double Bastion, and beat our men thence, all but a little boy, who when they were climbing the trenches stood stoutly upon the trench and threw stones at them. Our men being reinforced from the city came down with spirit and beat them quite over the meadows.'[13] The abortive attack cost the Jacobites fairly heavily, especially as they retreated, although some reportedly saved themselves by carrying the dead bodies of comrades as shields. The Protestants admitted to only six dead, while the Irish reported that they had lost 400 killed, a high proportion of whom were officers, especially among the King's Guards.

The defeat was a major blow to Jacobite morale, and the French General Pointis felt that it spelt the end of any hopes of taking Derry by force. Only starvation, he believed, might do the business. Certainly this was almost the last serious attempt by the Jacobites to storm Derry, whose defenders' morale was shortly raised by hopes of relief.

A relief force was on its way from Liverpool, commanded by Major-General Percy Kirke, a hardbitten professional soldier with a lurid reputation. For a time he had been Governor of Tangier, where Samuel Pepys observed him to be 'a coarse drunken brute who commanded a drunken regiment'.[14] Kirke's 'Lambs', as his regiment of dragoons were known – in reference to their cap badge of a paschal lamb – added to their notoriety by their acts of brutality in the suppression of the Monmouth Rebellion of 1685. However, three years later, having refused James II's suggestion that he convert to Roman Catholicism on the grounds that he had already 'promised' the Emperor of Morocco that if he ever changed his religion it would be to become a Muslim, Kirke defected to William.

Kirke seems to have sailed from Liverpool with no clear plan of action. On entering Lough Foyle, the relief force appeared to have two possibilities open to it. The first was to use shallow-draught boats to capture the boom. The Jacobite General von Rosen believed that this could be done at the cost of a few boats. Kirke, however, felt that any such attempt would be smashed by the guns of Culmore Fort in the 100yd-wide narrows beneath it, and that the mouth of the river had been further blocked by sunken ships. As a result, Kirke decided for the second option, which was to establish a base at the head of Lough Swilly on Inch Island, and there consider the situation at leisure before, perhaps, attempting to relieve Derry by land, although he believed himself to be heavily outnumbered.

The defenders of Derry had greeted Kirke's arrival by flying flags from the walls – intended to represent to the relief force the desperate situation they were in – but Kirke's men claimed not to have understood them. The swift departure of the relief force caused a slump in morale in Derry, although any thoughts of reopening negotiations with the enemy were speedily quashed by the arrival on 24 June of the feared von Rosen, to take command of the besiegers. Von Rosen had little patience with the measured approach of Hamilton and, according to Walker, 'swore by the belly of God he would demolish our town and bury us in its ashes, putting all to the sword without considerations of age or sex'.[15]

Von Rosen's assumption of command saw a quickening of Jacobite activity. According to George Walker's rather suspect account, he

> orders 3 mortar pieces and several pieces of Ordnance against the Windmill side of the Town, as also two Culverins opposite to Butchers-Gate; He runs a Line out of Bog-street up within ten Perches of the half-Bastion of that Gate, in order to prepare Matters for laying and springing a Mine; He made approaches to our Line, designing to hinder the relief of our Outguards, and to give us Trouble in fetching Water from Colum-Kills Well . . . We countermine the Enemy before the Butchers-Gate, the Governor contrives a Blind to preserve our Work from the Enimes' Battery. The Enemy fired continually from their Trenches, and we make them due returns with sufficient damage to them; for few days passed, but some of the choice and most forward of their men fell by our Arms and Firing.[16]

It was during this period of renewed activity that, on 28 June, an attack was launched on Butcher's Gate, headed by the regiment of Donough McCarthy, Earl of Clancarty. Walker dismissed its significance, suggesting that Clancarty was motivated by 'the credulity and superstition of his Country, with the vanity of so brave an attempt, and some good Liqour'.[17] In fact, the assault was well planned, and executed with some determination. The Jacobite guns had been attempting to breach the walls near Butcher's Gate, in conjunction with attempts to bring them down by mining. And it seems that a small breach was actually made, which Clancarty was earmarked to storm. The assault was led by grenadiers, whose bombs forced the defenders back from the outworks to the main defences. Clancarty's men probably reached the breach before they were thrown back in fierce hand-to-hand fighting by Williamite reinforcements that were rushed to the scene.

At the end of June, Derry's highly competent military governor, Henry Baker, died of the prevalent 'camp fever'. The dying Baker recommended his old foe, Colonel John Mitchelbourne, as his successor, and the latter, in an expression of defiance, hoisted a red flag on the tower of the cathedral.

Aware that supplies in Derry were running low, von Rosen attempted to force the issue by driving local Protestant civilians below the walls of Derry, in the hope that the defenders would feel obliged to let them in. Mitchelbourne's response was to threaten to hang Jacobite prisoners in retaliation, and a horrified Richard Hamilton protested to King James, who rescinded von Rosen's orders, describing the Livonian as a 'bloody Muscovite'. Hamilton made his own attempt to persuade Derry to surrender, firing over the walls a hollow shell containing an offer of terms, backed by leaflets offering generous conditions to any who declared allegiance to King James.

It was claimed that those within the town were now subsisting on horsemeat, dogs, cats, rats and mice, tallow, salted hides, seaweed and whatever fish could be caught in the river. According to Walker:

> we were under so great Necessity, that we had nothing left unless we could prey upon one another. A certain fat Gentleman conceived himself in the greatest danger, and fancying several of the Garrison lookt on him with a greedy Eye, thought fit to hide himself for three days. Our drink was nothing but Water, which we paid very dear for, and could not get without great danger. We mixt in it Ginger and Anniseeds, of which we had great plenty, our necessity of Eating the Composition of Tallow and Starch, did not only Nourish and Support us, but was an Infallible Cure of the Looseness, and recovered a great many that were strangely reduced by that Distemper, and preserved others from it.[18]

In fact, the main problem within Derry was probably the spread of disease, especially dysentery, as a result of chronic overcrowding.

The condition of the besiegers was little better. Food was almost as scarce as it was in Derry, and the only shelter for the Irish soldiers from the endless rain of that summer was rough dugouts and makeshift huts. The trenches were constantly full of water, the soldiers' picks and shovels were forever breaking, and there were serious language problems and friction between the Irish troops and the French engineers. Far more Jacobite soldiers died from sickness than as a result of combat.

Von Rosen, meanwhile, disgruntled by James's condemnation of his recent actions, pleaded ill health and left the conduct of operations to Richard Hamilton. The latter succeeded in restarting negotiations, offering in return for the surrender of the city full pardons for its inhabitants and guarantees for the safety of their property and respect for their religious beliefs. Although contemporaries such as Walker play down the effects of these terms, there were undoubtedly many in Derry who found them attractive, and the council of war asked for a delay of ten or twelve days to consider. They were, however, aware that Kirke was preparing for action, having landed his troops on Inch Island, and it is likely that the talks had given them greater insight into the problems of the besiegers, among whom increasing numbers of officers were being described as being absent without leave, while their men were plain deserters. A French officer wrote that 'the troops are tired and many of them are ill, they have been out in the open for several months without tents in a country where it rains almost every day and the nights are extremely cold'.[19]

King James tacitly agreed that the siege should be abandoned if the situation deteriorated further when, on 20 July, he wrote to Hamilton telling him to continue to blockade Derry for as long as he could, but to send off his sick and wounded in case he had to make a speedy retreat. The Jacobite council of war outside Derry had already concluded that it was impossible to storm the town, von Rosen declaring that Vauban and the best of the French engineers would be unable to capture the place with the equipment available.[20] On 22 July James accepted the inevitable when he instructed Hamilton to raise the siege unless he saw some prospect of the defenders surrendering. On the same day, Melfort admitted: 'I confess it is hard to leave a town so near starved and of so much consequence for the king to have; but if it be so, that mortification must be swallowed.'[21]

By now, both William and the Duke of Schomberg, his senior army commander, were becoming concerned by Kirke's lack of progress, and he was told rather firmly to consult with naval officers about the possibility of breaking through the boom. Described by King James as a 'capricious fellow', Kirke was convinced that an attempt was possible, and returned to Lough Foyle with part of his fleet and three merchant ships loaded with supplies.

On 28 July the attempt to break the boom began. The English force was led by the frigate *Mountjoy*, moving up on the incoming tide. At a critical moment the wind dropped, and the *Mountjoy* fell away towards the shore, under heavy fire from Jacobite guns. Her captain was killed, although his ship got clear on the rising tide. HMS *Swallow* now dispatched a longboat to cut through the fastenings of the boom, setting it adrift, and the merchant ship *Phoenix of Coleraine*, accompanied by the *Mountjoy*, broke through and headed upriver, the latter towed by the *Swallow*'s longboat. The vessels came under heavy but ineffective fire from Jacobite gunners, who were subsequently accused of being drunk, although it is equally probable that their failure was the result of inexperience and lack of trained French gunners.

That night, as the supply ship unloaded at Derry quayside, the Jacobites recognised the inevitable. By 31 July the siege was over, as columns of men, guns and equipment withdrew southwards.

It has been claimed that the attack on Derry was better termed a 'blockade' rather than a full-blown siege. In fact, the seventeenth-century term 'leaguer', describing a combination of both methods, is more accurate. The Jacobites on several occasions came close to taking Derry, more often by offers of generous terms aimed at dividing the defenders than by strictly military means. Overall, they lacked the equipment and trained manpower to have any serious chance of breaking through Derry's defences so long as the morale of those within held firm. Though the Protestants of the town were by no means as united in their defiance of James as is sometimes portrayed, their fear (however ill-founded) of their possible fate at the hands of James's Catholic army was enough, in the end, to persuade them to hold out against blandishments, bombardment and starvation.

For the Protestant cause, then, and for centuries to come, the successful defence of Derry would be a potent symbol. For the Jacobites, it was to prove the turning point of the war.

FIVE

· · · · · · · · ·

The Braes of Killiecrankie

CLAVERHOUSE'S CAMPAIGN

For Dundee, the coming of spring made it possible for him to call a rendezvous of the Highland chiefs in James's name. He needed to move quickly. General Hugh Mackay was threatening to isolate Dundee from the Highlands, and on 30 March the Convention in Edinburgh declared him to be in rebellion. He had few illusions about the difficulties lying ahead. Only the Roman Catholics seemed sympathetic, and even many of them stayed quiet. In the Gordon country of north-east Scotland, a major source of support for the Stuarts during the Civil Wars, only a few gentry and the Earl of Dunfermline joined Dundee, and even here there were more active government supporters than open adherents of the Jacobites.

Dundee knew that, initially at least, he would have to rely on some of the clans of Lochaber and the Western Isles, even the largest of which was capable of raising no more than 1,000 fighting men. Only the support of major magnates could significantly increase Jacobite strength. Without them, Dundee could hope for at most 5,000 men. Most of the clans who rose had motives other than mere loyalty to James. A major factor was fear of the great Clan Campbell, disgraced under James but likely to be restored to power by the new regime. Even so, the majority of the clan chiefs who would eventually join Dundee were younger men with less to lose.

Speedy success, Dundee knew, might transform his prospects. But Lochaber, the only major mainland area where he could count on support, was a very poor base from which to mount a rebellion. A region of mountains and moors, it had scanty resources, and could not maintain any sizeable force for long. Dundee would have to take the offensive, not only to win support, but also to feed those followers he already had. This inevitably resulted in looting and foraging, alienating potential sympathisers. It was a dilemma that, as the Marquis of Montrose had found half a century earlier, could damage as much as assist the Stuart cause.

Scotland, 1689–90

Dundee's first objective would have to be to gain control of additional territory. Seemingly most promising were the north-east Lowlands. If the Gordons joined him, Dundee would have his army at a stroke. Further north, the clans were known to be 'not a stirring people at any time' and unlikely to be receptive. The third area of potential support was Perthshire and Argyll. Here, Lord Breadalbane's sept of the Campbells appeared to be hesitating which side to back. Dundee knew how vital it was to form an alliance between loyalist Campbells and the other clans. If he failed, and Clan Campbell sided with William, the Duke of Argyll might be able to bring overwhelming forces to bear against the Lochaber clans.

Other parts of Scotland offered still fewer prospects. The Jacobites of the Lowlands might make promises, but they could do nothing without the presence of either a respectable force under Dundee or an army out of Ireland. By the end of April there were also some 8,000 to 9,000 Anglo-Dutch troops quartered in the Lowlands and northern England, which not only subdued the Jacobites there, but were a source of reinforcements for Mackay.

Dundee had two main hopes. If he could hold out long enough he might be able to exploit growing dissatisfaction with the Williamite regime in Scotland over such matters as increased taxation. Ultimately, however, he pinned his main hopes on assistance from Ireland. By April it was obvious to James that his only hope of regaining his Scottish throne was through a military solution. When, in mid-April, he dispatched his commission as Lieutenant-General in Scotland to Dundee, the King also promised him a force of 5,000 troops from Ireland, including 100 horse and 150 dragoons, as vanguard of the 10,000 men James intended to bring over in person. The King had been told that the loyal clans would quickly raise 5,000 men if they received French and Irish support. He thought this an overestimate, but urged d'Avaux to provide enough transport to carry three Irish regiments over to Scotland immediately. This plan was, for the moment, foiled by French lack of enthusiasm and the decision to concentrate on the capture of Derry but, if all went well, Dundee could hope for reinforcements from Ireland in the fairly near future.

So, as spring broke across the Highlands, Dundee could consider the Jacobite cause in Scotland as by no means hopeless. With a number of magnates secretly giving assurances of support, it seemed that 5,000 troops from Ireland might be sufficient to carry the counter-revolution to success.

The Convention, hitherto somewhat complacent about affairs in the Highlands, called on 18 April for a levy of 500 horsemen from the shire militias in order to form ten troops of cavalry, with volunteers to raise two more, along with Lord Cardross's dragoon regiment of six troops. The Williamite peers offered to recruit nine infantry regiments, each of 600 men (apart from the Earl of Angus's, from the strongly Covenanter south-west, which was to be double that size). In mid-April Dundee, with fifty to sixty horsemen, mainly from his old troop of the Royal Scots Dragoons, raised his standard and headed for the north-east to begin recruiting efforts there.

General Hugh Mackay went in pursuit with 450 men, including 200 foot, part of Livingston's Regiment of Dragoons and Colchester's English cavalry regiment (which was soon immobilised by the bleak Scottish terrain). Mackay's plan was to trap Dundee with the aid of the north-eastern magnates.

Hugh Mackay was a more able general than is often credited. A Gaelic-speaking Highlander who, paradoxically, had a low opinion of Highland fighting ability, he was a highly experienced soldier who had served with the Anglo-Scottish Brigade in the Netherlands. He was described by the not entirely reliable Bishop Burnet as 'the piousest man I ever knew in a military way . . . one of the best officers of the age, when he had nothing to do but to obey and execute orders, for he was both diligent obliging and brave; But he was not so fitted for command. His piety made him too apt to mistrust his own sense, and to be too tender or rather fearful.'[1] However, Mackay would have the advantage over Dundee, himself an often overrated soldier, for much of the campaign.

Dundee reached the Gordon lands by 21 April and halted for two days at Gordon Castle, where the Earl of Dunfermline and a few other supporters joined him. Hearing that Mackay was moving north, and that Sir Thomas Livingston's Dragoons had occupied the town of Dundee, Lord Dundee himself headed north, on 24 April crossing the River Spey at Elgin.

Dundee's wife, who had been entertaining Livingston's officers, had sent a message to her husband that a number of them were ready to defect, but the Earl was dissuaded from riding to join them by news that Mackay hoped to be in Dundee by 26 April with 1,000 men. So Dundee pulled back about 33 miles northwards to Cairn Mount, and then to Huntley Castle. Mackay, his English cavalry by now decidedly the worse for wear, retreated to Feltercairn.

On 1 May Dundee returned to Gordon Castle to rejoin Dunfermline, who was to become his most trusted subordinate. Aged 47, James Seaton, 4th Earl of Dunfermline, was a 'middle-sized, well-favoured, high-nosed' soldier of fortune, who had fought in the Low Countries. He had succeeded in recruiting forty to fifty Gordon gentry to strengthen Dundee's cavalry. The combined force headed north towards Inverness, with Mackay once more in pursuit.

Throughout May and June, Mackay generally got the better of Dundee, consistently thwarting his recruiting efforts in the north-east. Mackay's main weakness was growing overconfidence, sharing as he did the Edinburgh government's view of the Highlanders as 'barbarous'. He evidently assumed that those who joined Dundee did so only because they had been forcibly conscripted. He regarded the north-east as a potentially hostile area, and his attitude was such that the recruits he managed to raise were almost as few as those who joined Dundee, and rather less enthusiastic.

Dundee had arrived at Inverness to find the town under rather lethargic siege by clansmen under MacDonald of Keppoch. The latter had imprisoned members of the Town Council and demanded a ransom for them. Dundee promised the burgesses that the ransom would be repaid, and sharply rebuked Keppoch. The latter apparently made no attempt to prevent his clansmen from following their usual practice of heading home with their booty, and Dundee was forced to abandon Inverness.

Mackay reported that he was confident of holding the north when reinforced by the newly arrived 600 men of the Anglo-Dutch Brigade under Colonel Ramsey, whom Mackay ordered to join him, marching by way of Atholl and Badenoch. Dundee, meanwhile, was heading across Badenoch into Atholl, after confirming plans for a mustering of the clans on 18 May in Lochaber. The first month of campaigning had seen no action of note, although Dundee had achieved his immediate objective of keeping the uprising alive until help could arrive from Ireland.

To occupy the interval before the clan muster, Dundee made a successful raid on the city of Perth. He also hoped to link up with Livingston's Dragoons in Dundee, reportedly ready to defect. However, riding on to Dundee on 13 May, he found his hopes of gaining Livingston's men dashed, with the town gates closed against him and troops manning the walls. The rebels lacked the strength to attack the town, while there were too many other troops there for the defectors to make their move. The rebels were forced to make an arduous retreat in foul weather, across some of the wildest parts of the Highlands, to Lochaber. Dundee marched on foot, encouraging his troopers, many of whose horses perished on the march, and, probably as a result, Dundee fell ill.

The Convention was sufficiently alarmed by Dundee's raid to summon from Berwick an extremely reluctant Sir John Lanier and his cavalry regiment, together with Berkeley's Dragoons and Hastings's and Leslie's Regiments of Foot. The latter three units were stationed in Perthshire and Angus to prevent a repeat of Dundee's recent raid. Meanwhile, the Convention's other planned regiments were taking shape. The largest of them was the Earl of Angus's Foot, popularly known as the 'Cameronians' because of the unit's close links with that Covenanting sect. Its lieutenant-colonel was a professional soldier, William Cleland, whose father had been the Earl of Angus's gamekeeper. In fact, only two of the regiment's companies were actually Cameronians, the remainder being recruited more widely.

On 6 April Highland Jacobite supporters had sent Alexander MacLean to Ireland with a direct appeal for assistance. By then King James had reached Dublin, and MacLean reported that, if 2,000 'regular' troops and supplies of arms were sent to Scotland, they would be joined by 6,000 Highlanders. James promised three Irish foot regiments under the command of another

Scottish professional soldier, Major-General Thomas Buchan. But the King made clear that these units could not be spared until Derry had been taken.

After the French refused support for the major expedition that James had planned to lead to Scotland, the King decided to dispatch a smaller force of 1,200 men in two waves. With the English navy active in the Irish Sea, it was decided that the reinforcements should take the shortest route and land in the Mull of Kintyre. Dundee was in favour of the plan, although he was in no position to assist.

On 2 May Sir Donald MacDonald, followed soon afterwards by the now knighted Alexander MacLean, landed in Kintyre. They brought no troops with them, but the local MacLeans came out in support. Sir Alexander crossed over to Mull to recruit, and in his absence the Convention dispatched by sea to Kintyre eight companies from the regiments being raised in the west under Captain William Young. On 15 May Young's men landed, evidently taking the local Jacobites by surprise, and routed them in an almost bloodless skirmish, taking a number of prisoners. However, Sir Alexander MacLean secured some small ships, and managed to outwit the local English naval commander, George Rooke, and to embark about 200 of the Kintyre MacLeans and take them to join Dundee. But the Jacobites had lost control of Kintyre, making the dispatch of any troops from Ireland considerably more difficult, and opening the way for the Duke of Argyll to advance in the west.

On 18 May Dundee held his rendezvous in Lochaber. Amid scenes of barbaric splendour, he was joined by Alistair Dubh MacDonnell of Glengarry with 300 men. The white-haired, 70-year-old giant of a man, Alistair MacDonald, 'MacIain' of Glencoe, came, and 150 Appin men, with their fur bonnets, marched under their banner of 'blue chequered with yellow figures'. Some 200 of the Camerons, with their chief Lochiel, one of the most influential figures in the Western Highlands, best known perhaps for his exploit of ripping out an English officer's throat with his teeth, arrived, accompanied by numerous relatives. Ranald MacDonald of Keppoch brought 200 of his men; and smaller contingents from other clans, as well as a handful of Lowlanders, also arrived at the muster. But all the colour and dash, skirling pipes and fluttering banners could not disguise the fact that considerably fewer men had arrived than Dundee had hoped for. In all, he had only about 2,000 men.

On 25 May the Jacobites marched to intercept Ramsey and his detachment, who were marching through Atholl on their way to rendezvous with Mackay at Ruthven Castle. But, finding the Atholl men in arms against him, Ramsey abandoned his march and fell back to Perth.

Dundee, meanwhile, was plundering in Badnoch in an attempt to feed his hungry troops. Mackay, unaware of Ramsey's retreat, left Inverness on 26 May with 450 regulars and 200 clansmen of the Mackays and Rosses to rendezvous with Ramsey. He planned then to block any further attempt by

Dundee to penetrate the north-east. On 28 May he had almost reached Ruthven Castle, which was under attack by some of Dundee's troops, when he learnt of Ramsey's retreat. At about the same time the opposing armies sighted each other.

Both commanders bungled the opportunity to fight a battle, and Ruthven Castle surrendered. Mackay now beat a retreat in an easterly direction, with Dundee in pursuit, but, despite some sharp rearguard skirmishes, the Jacobites narrowly failed to intercept Mackay. By now the government force was close to collapse through exhaustion and lack of provisions, but it was saved by the arrival of reinforcements consisting of Leslie's Regiment of Foot and Berkeley's Dragoons. Once Mackay reached lower ground around Huntley, his superiority in cavalry prevented pursuit.

The Jacobites were almost equally disorganised and exhausted, and Dundee fell ill with dysentery. With their leader incapacitated, the Highlanders began plundering and straggling. From Cromdale in Badenoch, Dundee fell back up the valley of the Spey. By now his army was melting away, and was so short of provisions that he had no alternative but to disperse most of his men on twenty-four hours' notice to rejoin. With only 200 men under Sir Alexander MacLean to act as a bodyguard, Dundee withdrew to Shone on the banks of Loch Lochy.

News of the dispersal reached Mackay, who had advanced cautiously again to Ruthven. The government commander, his already heartfelt contempt for the Highlanders reinforced, was convinced that the rebellion had collapsed and, sending part of his force under Ramsey to Elgin, withdrew with the remainder to Inverness. However, Mackay felt that only a system of garrisons would serve to keep the Highlanders permanently in check. He had had enough of the frustrations of campaigning against illusive irregulars, writing later in his *Memoirs* that 'it is certainly more fit for a man of fewer years, and more accustomed with the manner of the country', and, with the benefit of hindsight would revise his opinion of the Highlanders, admitting them to be 'absolutely the best untrained men in Scotland, and can be equal'd to our new levies though they were better armed than they are'.[2]

Some, including King William, felt that Mackay was wearing out his men in ponderous pursuits of his swift-moving opponent, and that he should concentrate on defending the Lowlands. On 13 June government complacency received a further boost when the Duke of Gordon surrendered Edinburgh Castle at the end of a desultory siege.

Dundee, meanwhile, was convalescing from his illness at Lochiel's house. Here he had leisure to ponder future operations. As a Lowlander, he hankered after training the Highlanders to fight using conventional military tactics, but was persuaded by Lochiel of the value of allowing the clans to fight in their traditional way. Reform would require both time and greater supplies of military equipment than were available, but Dundee demonstrated his willingness to adapt his tactics to those of the men who made up the vast majority of his command.

Jacobite inactivity strengthened the feeling both in the Lowlands and in London that the rising was effectively at an end. The English regiments that had been sent north as reinforcements were recalled. But the Highlanders had not been crushed. Large numbers were still willing to fight, and Dundee yet hoped for a massive rising. By the end of June, Mackay was also admitting that the danger was not over.

Writing to Secretary of State Melfort, Dundee put forward proposals for a new strategy. He opined that, as the Williamites were aware of James's plan to land troops from Ireland in Kintyre, nobody would now expect them to do so: 'So I am extremely of opinion this would be an extreme proper place, unless you be so strong that you need not care where to land. The truth is, I do not admire their mettle. The landing of troops will confound them terribly.'[3] Although Dundee believed that Mackay was deeply concerned by the threat of a landing from Ireland, in reality the government commander was more anxious about a rumour that Dundee was about to march north again. So, when he himself moved south, Mackay left behind at Inverness a strong garrison under Sir Thomas Livingston.

Mackay did not reach Edinburgh until 12 July. By now, with supplies in Badenoch virtually exhausted, the clansmen had no choice but to raid indiscriminately over a wide area. Dundee attempted to boost the faltering morale of his followers by telling them that Derry had already fallen, and that help was on its way, but he admitted at the end of June that most of them no longer believed him. Some of the clan chieftains were putting out peace feelers to the authorities in Edinburgh, and the government reacted by putting a price on Dundee's head, hoping that the clans would turn him in. Dundee himself was appealing, with scant success, to uncommitted clans, especially the Macleods, and to some of the smaller septs who were long-standing victims of the Campbells.

By mid-July Mackay was back in Perthshire. His plan now was to march through Atholl and establish a garrison at Inverlochy in order to hold down the clans. It was a risky scheme; the previous garrison placed there during the Commonwealth by General Monck had been landed from the sea. But preparations continued, even though Mackay now learnt that Dundee had at last been reinforced from Ireland.

The assistance was much less than had been hoped for. The worsening situation for the Jacobites in Ireland meant that the promised army was reduced to a raw regiment of 400 dragoons – 'three hundred new-raised, naked, undisciplined Irishmen' was how their enemies described them – under Colonel Purcell and Brigadier-General Thomas Cannon, a Lowlands Scottish professional soldier.

The small number of the reinforcements caused widespread dismay among Dundee's followers, and his position was increasingly desperate. He was in grave danger of being trapped between Mackay and Argyll's forces to the west. If Dundee marched against Mackay, Argyll might invade Lochaber in his absence; if, on the other hand, Dundee moved against Argyll, Mackay would be free to pursue his plan of entering Lochaber and garrisoning Inverlochy. Dundee leaked rumours that his intention was to invade Argyll, although Mackay believed that the Jacobite commander intended to return to Strathspey.

KILLIECRANKIE

Dundee had been expecting the main force of at least 5,000 men from Ireland to arrive on 29 July. He intended to fill the intervening time with a recruiting drive in Atholl and Mar, where he had not, so far, campaigned. While Lord John Murray of Atholl was a Williamite supporter, many of his people were not, and, as Dundee approached, Murray found himself defied at his own castle of Blair by his factor, Patrick Stewart of Ballechin. Lord Atholl established a loose blockade of the castle, and received a message from General Mackay that the latter was on his way to restore the situation. The men of Atholl found themselves caught in the middle, as Dundee wrote to them on 10 July, ordering them to join his forces and threatening to treat as traitors any who refused.

Mackay had left Edinburgh on 22 July, and reached Perth on the 25th. Dundee, meanwhile, had broadcast his intention to call a general rendezvous of the clans on 28 or 29 July. But this was intended to mislead Mackay into thinking that he would remain inactive until then. On 23 July Dundee marched suddenly from Glen Roy with those men he had, amounting to about forty horse and 2,000 foot. Moving across the Spey through Badenoch, Dundee entered Atholl on 26 July, with Lord Murray's supporters falling back before him to the Pass of Killiecrankie. The Jacobite forces encamped around Blair Castle.

Mackay had discounted Dundee's threat to Atholl when he arrived at Perth, his main objective still being to march to Inverlochy and establish a fort there. He had with him one battalion each of the foot regiments of Hastings, Leven and Kenmure, making a total of 3,500 foot, along with the troops of horse of Annandale and Belhaven. His artillery consisted of three antiquated 'leather' guns dating from the Civil War period, and the expedition brought along with it no fewer than 1,200 baggage horses.

Dismissing a report that Dundee was approaching Blair Castle, Mackay set out from Perth on 26 July and halted for the night at Dunkeld. Here he encountered a discomfited Lord Murray with news of Dundee's advance and, in response, Mackay sent Lieutenant-Colonel Lauder with 200 firelocks to hold

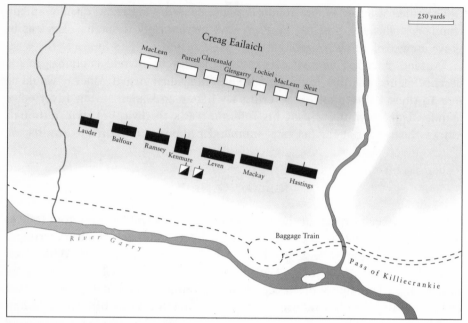

Killiecrankie, 27 July 1689

the head of the Pass of Killiecrankie and, confident that the Highlanders would not be able to stand up to cavalry, sent for six troops of horse that he had left at Perth. Resuming his march next morning, before the horse could arrive, Mackay was joined by Robert Menzies's Highland Company, although Murray warned that the Atholl men were not to be relied upon. Murray clearly felt that it would be dangerous for Mackay to proceed further, at least until his cavalry reinforcements arrived.

However, Mackay disregarded what he saw as Murray's overcaution and, placing Hastings's Regiment of Foot and Annandale's Troop of Horse in the rear to guard the baggage train, set off through the pass. Dundee was preparing to attack Lauder's detachment at the head of the pass when, early in the afternoon, he learnt of the approach of Mackay's main force. The Jacobite commander called a hasty council of war. The regular officers, including Cannon, argued that the Highlanders were too few and too exhausted to risk battle, and urged that an engagement should be avoided until the promised reinforcements from Ireland had arrived.

Dundee, however, strongly suspected that the troops from Ireland would never appear, and the Highland chiefs took the regulars' caution as a slur on the courage of themselves and their men. In the end it was the advice of Lochiel, the most respected of them, that the army should fight now that tipped the balance. Dundee's officers urged that he should not personally take part in the fighting, but he, probably aware that he was known to the

Highlanders as 'Dark John of the Battles' and knowing how much store the clansmen placed on courage and personal leadership, demanded his right to 'one day's work at the harvest'.

While skirmishers were sent forward to occupy Mackay's attention, Dundee led his main force at a fast pace, despite the burning heat of the afternoon, north around the Hill of Lude and back across a pass to the east of it, and deployed on the steep slopes below Craig Eaillach. He may have hoped to attack Mackay's column while it was still on the march, but the government commander, realising his danger, deployed his men to their right as they debouched from the mouth of the Pass of Killiecrankie, on the broad Urrad Plateau, facing a rocky slope up which the government troops began to advance.

The length of the plateau caused Mackay concern for the safety of his flanks. He placed Lauder's fusiliers 'on a little hill wreathed with trees' in order to secure his left, but remained seriously worried about his right flank, and decided that his only option was to extend his line to cover it. Accordingly, Mackay made most of his regiments double their files to their front, forming three ranks instead of six, and anchored his right on a stream near to the mouth of the pass. But he had no units left to form a reserve, and was concerned both by the rocky ground sloping upwards to his front and the River Garry to his rear.

From left to right his units were deployed as follows. In the wood on the left flank were Lieutenant-Colonel George Lauder and his 200 fusiliers of the Scottish Brigade; next, forming two divisions each three ranks deep, was Brigadier Balfour's Regiment. With Balfour in overall command of Mackay's left wing, his regiment was led by Major James Fergusson. To the right of Balfour's Regiment was Brigadier George Ramsey's Regiment. The two units each probably totalled about 500 men and, deducting the 200 men detached under Lauder, made 800 in all. This division was separated from the rest of the army by a 100yd-wide bog, on the far side of which was deployed Viscount Kenmure's Regiment. It had been raised only at the end of April, and consisted entirely of raw recruits, which may have been why Mackay had left it in six-deep formation. This unit also probably totalled about 500 men.

Kenmure's Regiment, considering its lack of experience, was dangerously isolated, with another gap between it and its neighbour to the right, the Earl of Leven's Regiment. The gap was inadequately filled by Mackay's three leather guns, and, a little way behind them, two troops of horse, both militia units, accompanied by Mackay himself. Leven's Regiment was notable for having allegedly been fully recruited within two hours in March, and now totalled between 600 and 700 men. Unlike Kenmure's, it was evidently regarded as sufficiently well trained to be deployed in three ranks.

Both of Mackay's remaining regiments were veterans. The General's own Regiment was led by Lieutenant-Colonel James Mackay, and probably numbered between 500 and 600 men. Next to it was Edward Hastings's Regiment, 600 strong and the only purely English unit serving with Mackay. On the far right, probably under the cover of trees, was the Highland Company of Captain Robert Menzies of Weem, around 80 men.

In all, Mackay had about 3,500 foot and 100 horse, of whom around half could be termed experienced. Although he had extended his line so far that it was for the most part deployed in only three ranks, this formation was possibly the best with which to meet a 'Highland charge'. As the English forces were to discover half a century later, on the battlefield of Culloden, a three-rank deployment enabled the delivery of devastating musket fire. The real weakness lay in the fact that the gaps between some units were too wide. The most serious of these was the interval between Ramsey's and Kenmure's Regiments. The bog was by no means impassible, and meant that Balfour's men were effectively isolated from the rest of the army. The six-rank deployment of Kenmure's Regiment increased its vulnerability, and there was also a 150yd gap between it and Leven's Regiment. Kenmure's Regiment, forming the centre of the army, was effectively isolated from the rest of it.

The Jacobites were drawn up in three bodies on Orchil Ridge, just out of musket range of the enemy. The bulk of Dundee's men were massed in the centre, with weaker wings on either side, about 200yd away. Dundee's plan was to smash through Mackay's weak centre by force of numbers. The Jacobite right, fronting Balfour's men between Orchil and Letton, seems to have consisted only of Sir John MacLean's Regiment of about 300 men. The centre contained, from right to left, Purcell's Dragoons, with 300 to 400 men, next to them the MacDonalds of Clanranald and Glengarry, possibly around 600 strong. Then came Sir Evan Cameron of Lochiel with around 240 men. The left wing was formed of Sir Alexander MacLean's Regiment of 200 men, a mixture of Highlanders and Irish regulars. Next to them, on the extreme left of the army, were around 700 men under Sir Donald MacDonald of Sleat. The whole force was probably deployed four deep, with about forty horse under Sir William Wallace of Craigie acting as reserve.

A prolonged pause, lasting most of the afternoon, ensued. Mackay made what was, in the circumstances, a less than inspiring speech, warning his men that, if they ran away, the Highlanders would slaughter them all. The Jacobites, meanwhile, directed a constant barrage of yells and threats towards their opponents, but for the moment made no other move. There are various theories regarding Dundee's delay in attacking. Possibly, remembering the rough handling that he had received in his only other pitched battle, at Drumclog in 1679, he might have been hesitant about committing raw troops in an attack, or he might have been waiting for dusk to reduce the accuracy of enemy fire.

Mackay saw no advantage in delay, and his leather guns opened up in an attempt to sting Dundee into attacking while it was still daylight. The guns appear to have done little damage, possibly because they had been undercharged with powder in an attempt to prevent them from bursting. It may be, however, that the fire of the leather guns provoked Dundee into attacking. Some of Lochiel's men attempted to occupy a couple of cottages nearer to the enemy, but were driven back by musketry from the nearest of Mackay's men. It was now early evening and, possibly because he feared that the rough handling suffered by Lochiel's men would cause the rest of his army to lose heart, Dundee ordered a general attack. It was around 8 p.m. when the battle began. The full weight of the Jacobite centre headed downhill towards Kenmure's Regiment. If they advanced at a full run, it would have taken the Highlanders around two minutes to cover the 400yd between them and Mackay's men. But this could be done only at the cost of losing whatever formation they possessed and arriving short of breath. In most cases the advance took rather longer, and must have begun at a walk before breaking into a run in its final stages.

With most of Dundee's men massed in the centre, their intended targets were Kenmure's and Leven's Regiments but, possibly because they came under heavy fire, Lochiel's men veered away to their left and joined Sir Alexander MacLean in attacking Mackay's Regiment. This exposed Lochiel's men to flanking fire from Leven's Regiment, which probably accounted for the 120 Camerons who fell at Killiecrankie. With half its men down, Lochiel's force must have been effectively destroyed before it even reached the enemy lines. Indeed, the overall Highland attack seems to have been slowed enough by concentrated fire for Mackay to consider counter-attacking with his two troops of horse.

Seeing Mackay's intentions, Dundee led his own two troops of cavalry forward in a charge that silenced any of the leather guns that were still in action, and caused Lord Belhaven's militia troop to rout. Some of the fleeing troopers bolted through the ranks of Kenmure's Regiment, throwing those raw soldiers into disorder. Annandale's troop of horse followed suit, leaving Mackay alone, except for a servant, in the face of the enemy. Half of Leven's Regiment broke in similar panic, and Kenmure's wavering men found themselves under attack by all three regiments of the Jacobite centre (Purcell's, Clanranald's and Glengarry's), totalling around 1,200 men and outnumbering Kenmure's by two to one.

The centre of the government army collapsed as Kenmure's men broke in panic-stricken flight towards the baggage train and beyond it into the mouth of the Pass of Killiecrankie. Kenmure's lieutenant-colonel, John Fergusson of Craigdorroch, fell, and half of the Regiment were killed or fled. Leven's Regiment was also hard hit by the Jacobite onrush. The remainder of Mackay's men held on a short while longer. The General's own Regiment was attacked by Sir Alexander MacLean and MacDonald of Sleat, probably joined by the remnants of Lochiel's men. Most of Mackay's Regiment joined in the general panic, although Lieutenant-Colonel James Mackay and some of his officers, with a few pikemen, held out for a short time longer. Two of them, Captains George Connon and Alexander Lang, were killed, together with six subalterns.

Mackay wrote of his Regiment that all the captains were 'either killed or do bear the marks of their good behaviour'. However, Balfour's Regiment, Mackay claimed, never fired a shot. The government forces on the left, because of the lie of the ground, could see little of what was happening elsewhere, other than the disturbing sight of the Highland Charge sweeping Kenmure's Regiment away. Balfour felt that, in the circumstances, his best option was to retreat, and at first he did so successfully. However, once he reached the edge of the plateau and his men tried to descend the slope, which was covered with bushes and trees, order rapidly broke down. Sir John MacLean's Regiment, with some Atholl men who had now joined in the fight, closed in. In hand-to-hand combat, Brigadier Balfour was cut down by three Highlanders, while at least two of his captains were killed trying to escape across the river.

On the whole, however, Balfour's Regiment does not seem to have suffered as heavily as Ramsey's, which had seven of its captains killed, with only two junior officers taken prisoner. Seeing the way events were turning, Lieutenant-Colonel Lauder's fusiliers made off.

George Ramsey, once across the river, found that only about 200 of the Scottish Brigade remained with him, most of them having thrown away their weapons in order to run faster. Mackay, meanwhile, had joined 'a small heap of redcoats' on the right, consisting of the Earl of Leven and his officers and a mixture of men of several units. He could see that Hastings's Regiment was still intact and advancing back to its original position. It was obvious to Mackay that his only option was to retreat and save what part of his army he could. Without being molested further, he led his survivors back across the River Garry and joined Ramsey, and during the night withdrew westwards over the hills.

Part of the reason for Mackay's escape was that Dundee had been brought down by a musket shot, probably fired by one of Leven's men, quite early in the action. Accounts differ over the details, probably because amid the smoke and confusion nobody was clear exactly what happened. But Dundee appears to have been injured seriously, probably mortally, by a musket shot in the stomach. He was found by some of his men, who started to carry him away but were driven off by the fire of Leven's men. A letter supposedly written after the battle by Dundee was almost certainly a forgery, with Dundee dying before his body was stripped during the night by some Camerons. The Earl of Dunfermline took over temporary command, but was unable to organise another attack on the retreating enemy.

Losses on both sides had been high. The Jacobites claimed that Mackay had lost 1,200 casualties in the battle and as many more in the pursuit, which, allowing for fugitives who later rejoined their units, is probably roughly correct. But the Jacobites themselves had lost 700 men, something like a third of those engaged, with losses falling particularly heavily on the clan gentry.

The greatest loss, of course, was the death of John Graham, Earl of Dundee. He has been awarded a probably inflated place in Jacobite hagiography. He was no more than a competent general, and it is hard to see how, if he had survived, he could have carried out the triumphant march on Edinburgh that his admirers often visualised. Jacobite losses had been too great and its army too small for that to have been feasible, even for a commander as capable as Dundee's kinsman, the great Montrose. But 'Dark John of the Battles' would probably have inspired new supporters and presented a continuing serious irritation to the Williamites in Scotland for some time to come. As a leader, he would prove irreplaceable and, without him, as events would prove, Jacobite hopes in Scotland were slim indeed.

SIX

● ● ● ● ● ●

Stalemate in Ireland: July–December 1689

THE BATTLE FOR ULSTER

Fierce fighting was continuing elsewhere in Ulster. The other principal Protestant garrison, at Enniskillen, adopted a much more active strategy than its counterpart in Derry. Enniskillen, consisting of about eighty thatched houses, was in a strong, natural defensive location, situated on an island at the junction of the Upper and Lower Lough Erne, protected on one side by a lake and on the other by a river and a marsh.

The defenders, under the half-Swedish Gustavus Hamilton, proved aggressively active, their cavalry raiding across South Donegal. A leading role was played by 25-year-old Thomas Lloyd, a former cornet in Richard Hamilton's Dragoons. Lloyd was described by a contemporary: 'A good sort of man, he was vigilant, careful, active, of a great soul, very observing, slipped no opportunity that offered to gain his end, and besides a man of unwearied industry and good intelligence, and for his personal valour, few went beyond him.'[1] He was an excellent leader of irregular horse, and quickly gained the soubriquet of 'Little Cromwell'.

The main weakness of the Protestants at Enniskillen was their need to hold the line of the Erne from Ballyshannon to Lower Lough Erne in order to ensure supplies. It could be readily threatened by Jacobite forces based at Sligo. At the end of January 1689 the Enniskillen forces consisted of one regiment of foot, formed from twelve companies 'armed chiefly with pikes and scythe-blades attached to poles'.[2] However, news of James's arrival in Ireland resulted in eight more regiments of horse, dragoons and foot being raised.

When Richard Hamilton advanced on Derry, he detached a small force under Piers Butler, Lord Galmoy, to deal with Enniskillen. Galmoy was a hardline Jacobite, who attempted to intimidate his opponents into surrender. He threatened to hang the minister of Enniskillen and exterminate the entire population of the town, but his threats lost most of their credibility following an unsuccessful attempt to take the Williamite outpost of Crom Castle on Upper Lough Erne. His artillery apparently consisted only of two light pieces of ordnance of the type known as 'leather guns'. They were, according to a Williamite writer:

> two cannons made of tin, near a yard long in the chase, and about eight inches wide, strongly bound with small cord, and covered with a sort of buckram, near the colour of a cannon. These two mock cannon he drew towards Crom with eight horses apiece, making a great noise as if they were drawn with much difficulty. As soon as they came before Crom, he threatened to batter the castle with these two great battering guns, and had the vanity to fire one of them which burst and had like (as 'twas said) to have spoiled the gunner.[3]

Enniskillen's determination to resist was strengthened when Galmoy executed two captured Williamite officers, and allowed his men to mistreat their bodies, using their heads as footballs. Having failed in his objective, Galmoy withdrew into Cavan, but the danger to Enniskillen was far from over.

Next to arrive in the area was a force of 2,000 men commanded by the celebrated Patrick Sarsfield, one of the glittering figures of Jacobite mythology. A former regular army officer, who had fought in the only skirmish of note during William's march on London in 1688, the young Sarsfield evidenced considerable ability as a cavalry commander. He had accompanied James from France and was promoted to brigadier-general on the urgings of Tyrconnel and d'Avaux, although against the inclinations of the King, who remarked that Sarsfield had 'nothing in his head'.

Sarsfield was ordered by Tyrconnel to take 2,000 men to secure Sligo, doing so without opposition on 1 May. His next objective was to gain control of the stretch of the River Erne between Lower Lough Erne and the sea and sever the supply route to Enniskillen. Leaving a garrison in Sligo, Sarsfield headed for the Williamite outpost at Ballyshannon. The garrison commander, Captain Henry Folliat, briskly rejected Sarsfield's summons to surrender.

The Jacobites were well into hostile territory, with Protestant forces under Sir James Caldwell holding the various crossings of the River Erne, including that at the village of Balleek. In the mean time, in Enniskillen, Gustavus Hamilton had prepared a force of 1,000 men under Thomas Lloyd to relieve Ballyshannon. Their route ran through Balleek, to the south of which was a large bog, which the road crossed by means of a narrow causeway.

Lloyd reached Balleek to find that Sarsfield had broken down the bridge that led on to the causeway, and built a barricade manned by musketeers, keeping his cavalry further to the rear on firm ground. Lloyd had the advantage in numbers, but was uneasy on seeing the enemy position.

He decided that his only option was to attack across the bog, encouraged by a local man's disclosing a route across it. As the Williamite advance began, the Jacobite musketeers on the causeway, about to be outflanked, panicked and, as some of Sir James Caldwell's men came across the Erne by boat in support of Lloyd, fled in a rout that continued until they were back in Sligo.

What became known as 'the Break of Balleek' was an ignominious beginning for Sarsfield, who lost heavily in the pursuit. Although the strategic importance of the action was minimal, so long as Sarsfield continued to hold Sligo it was an important moral victory for the Enniskilleners. Sarsfield attempted to renew his threat to Enniskillen by occupying Manor Hamilton, about 17 miles from the town, and sending out his cavalry on renewed raids along the Erne. He failed to intimidate Sir James Caldwell, who responded to a summons with the comment that he 'would defend the river while I had a man to stand by me'.[4]

At the same time, Lloyd was making his own raids, striking to within 30 miles of Dublin, causing widespread panic in the Irish capital, and carrying back with him to Enniskillen some 3,000 cows and oxen, 2,000 sheep, and 5,000 horses loaded with corn, malt and meal. Even hostile observers were struck by the greater discipline of Lloyd's men compared with Sarsfield's troopers.

Fears that the Williamite fleet being prepared for Derry might relieve Enniskillen caused the Jacobites to make a renewed effort to take the latter town. This time the task was entrusted to the Duke of Berwick, who, with troops detached from the army before Derry, made a good beginning when he took an enemy outpost at Trillick, about 12 miles from Enniskillen. But, after initial skirmishing, Berwick concluded that Enniskillen was too strong to take by assault, and instead ordered Sarsfield to make a renewed attempt to cut off its supplies by making another advance on Ballyshannon, while Berwick's men advanced to join him along the north side of Lough Erne. However, although Sarsfield, with about 3,000 foot and 200 horse, marched to within 5 miles of Ballyshannon, Berwick failed to join him. Learning that the English relief fleet had by now arrived in Lough Swilly, the Duke rejoined the main Jacobite army before Derry.

Sarsfield was apparently unaware of Berwick's departure when he sent a message to Major-General Anthony Hamilton at Belturbet, suggesting that they should join forces. Remaining confident that he could take Ballyshannon and, eventually, Enniskillen, Sarsfield next contacted Justin MacCarthy, newly created Viscount Mountcashel, suggesting cooperation between both of them and Berwick.

NEWTOWNBUTLER

Mountcashel, however, had received orders from James to act independently against Enniskillen. He had about 4,000 men, including three regiments of foot, sixteen troops of cavalry and dragoons and eight guns. Mountcashel's force included some of the rawest troops in the Irish army, and, even after it had been reinforced by Anthony Hamilton's Dragoons and an undisciplined force of Ulster Gaels led by Connacht Mor Maguire, it was distinctly inferior to its opponents.

Gustavus Hamilton in Enniskillen sent 500 men to reinforce Ballyshannon, while Mountcashel advanced towards the Williamite garrison at Crom Castle. This could easily have been bypassed while Mountcashel continued on his way to Enniskillen, but instead the Jacobite commander decided to try to capture it by storm. The result was a costly repulse under a hail of enemy fire, and Mountcashel, who, reportedly, had spent the battle on a nearby hill, peering short-sightedly at the action and howling with rage, settled down to contemplate a new attempt next day.

Meanwhile, several ships from England had reached Enniskillen, bringing with them supplies and a number of officers, including a professional soldier, Colonel William Wolseley. Gustavus Hamilton was unwell and delegated command to Wolseley, who reorganised the Enniskilleners into one regiment of horse, two of dragoons and three of foot.

On 31 July the Williamite cavalry under Lieutenant-Colonel Berry marched out of Enniskillen, followed by Wolseley with the foot. Their objective was Mountcashel's force at Crom. Learning of the enemy approach, Mountcashel sent Anthony Hamilton's Dragoons to intercept Berry's Horse. The opposing forces met near the village of Lisnaskea, and Berry's men made a skilful feigned withdrawal, leading the Jacobite dragoons into a carefully placed ambush. Hamilton's men were routed and chased from the field, while Berry joined Wolseley's force.

Mountcashel with the Jacobite foot now took up position near the village of Newtownbutler. The Jacobites fired the village itself to deny the enemy cover, and took up a strong defensive position on a hill to the south, dominating the Enniskillen road below, which ran across a causeway through a bog, at the end of which Mountcashel positioned his artillery. With an advantage in numbers of two to one, the Jacobites seemed to have cause for optimism.

Anxious to settle matters quickly, in case Sarsfield's men arrived, Wolseley decided to attack. He marched through the village and down to the bog, which had partially dried out owing to recent dry weather, allowing the Williamites to march across it. Colonel Zachariah Tiffin's foot were on the right, with Thomas Lloyd's on the left. Advancing steadily, despite heavy Jacobite fire, the Williamite foot reached the causeway and captured the enemy guns. Their advance was followed by that of Wolseley's Horse, at the sight of whom Mountcashel's entire force broke and fled.

Mountcashel with a few of his officers took refuge from the rout in a copse, but then ill-advisedly charged the captured guns. He was brought down, seriously wounded, by the fire of the Williamite guards, and taken prisoner.

As well as seven guns and large quantities of arms and ammunition, the Jacobites lost between 1,000 and 2,000 dead and about 400 prisoners, together with a number of foot colours. Wolseley admitted only to two officers and twenty men dead, and between forty and fifty wounded.

The disaster at Newtownbutler ended Jacobite hopes of taking Enniskillen. Sarsfield pulled back to Sligo, and the morale of the Enniskilleners was further boosted by news of the relief of Derry. Following up his victory, Wolseley sent a detachment under Zachariah Tiffin to reinforce the garrison of Ballyshannon, and Tiffin's son-in-law, Lieutenant-Colonel Gore, persuaded a Jacobite prisoner he knew, in exchange for a pardon, to go into Sligo and spread reports of the approach of a massive force of Williamites.

This proved too much for dwindling Jacobite morale; with his men deserting, Sarsfield had no option but to abandon Sligo to be bloodlessly reoccupied by Gore, although Sarsfield succeeded in convincing King James that he had evacuated the town only in the face of overwhelming numbers.

The Jacobites' failure at Derry, their defeat at Newtownbutler and now the loss of Sligo, had forced King James's men firmly onto the defensive. And they faced the threat of a massive Williamite army from England.

SCHOMBERG'S CAMPAIGN

William had been planning an expedition to Ireland since early summer. The new king had little faith in the loyalty of the remnants of James II's regular British army, and sent most of them over to Flanders to fight the French, where they would be out of harm's way. To subdue the rebellion in Ireland he would employ Dutch and Huguenot professional soldiers and new levies raised in England.

To command the expedition, and conduct what he intended to be a short, decisive campaign, William appointed one of Europe's leading professional soldiers. The Duke of Schomberg was half German and half English, and in a career spanning over half a century had served in many European armies. He was appointed a Marshal of France in 1677 but, being a Huguenot, left that country after the Edict of Nantes to take service with the Elector of Brandenburg. In 1688 the latter lent the old mercenary to William of Orange to assist him in what proved to be a virtually bloodless invasion of England. Schomberg had impressed William, not least for his hostility towards Catholic monarchs such as Louis XIV and James II, and he seemed a safe and competent choice to command the expedition to Ireland.

Schomberg was described by a contemporary as 'of middle stature, well-proportioned, fair complexioned, a very sound hardy man of his age, and sat a horse the best of any man; he loved constantly to be neat in his clothes, and in conversation he was always pleasant . . . .'.[5] However, an amiable personality was not enough to ensure success and, at the age of 74, Schomberg was arguably past his best as a commander in the field. Preparations for his expedition were beset by delays. The main problems were shortages of shipping and supplies, blame for which was ascribed to the incompetence of John Shales, commissary-general at Chester. Schomberg supported this condemnation, although he himself was increasingly fussy and prone to delay.

The first wave of his expedition, consisting of Schomberg himself with ten regiments of foot, left the anchorage of Hoylake, near Chester, on 12 August, escorted by a naval squadron under Commodore George Rooke. Landfall was made in Ulster next day, at Bangor Bay. The ships then returned to Hoylake to pick up the remainder of the expeditionary force, whose arrival gave Schomberg a total of 14,000 men. Although his cavalry did not arrive until the end of the month, Schomberg's force was more than sufficient to overawe the few hundred Jacobite troops in the area, who hastily withdrew towards Newry. The Williamites occupied Bangor and the nearby village of Belfast without resistance, and prepared to move against the nearest Jacobite garrison at Carrickfergus, held by two regiments.

If Schomberg were to achieve the decisive victory expected of him, he would have to move quickly, for the campaigning season was already well advanced. The defenders of Carrickfergus proved defiant. The first of Schomberg's men arrived on 20 August, and within two days twelve regiments of foot, with some artillery, were building siege works around the town. Operations proceeded slowly, with the Williamites commencing a heavy bombardment of the town. Schomberg refused to grant terms to the garrison for a week. It was not until 27 August that the Duke reached agreement with Carrickfergus's governor, MacCarthy Mor. By then about 200 Williamites and 150 Jacobites had become casualties.

While the siege had been in progress, Schomberg had been joined by 500 Enniskilleners, who made an initially poor impression on English observers:

> some without boots and pistols, others with pistols, but without carabines, some with one pistol and a carabine without a sword, others without all, with only a fowling-piece or firelock, most of their horses small and poor, yet such have been the courage and actions of these men as is scarce credible, especially the routing of 3,000 men under McCarthy. These brave men the general made welcome and will soon be better armed and accoutred.[6]

The arrival of Schomberg caused a major crisis of confidence in the Jacobite high command. The French envoy, d'Avaux, had little faith in the Irish troops, apart from the cavalry. In September he complained to Louvois that there were few reliable Irish general officers and that 'there is no order or discipline in the army'. An English Jacobite, John Stevens, was serving as a lieutenant in the Lord Grand Prior's Regiment of Foot, and noted that most of the officers recruited in the spring and early summer were quartered near to their homes 'the better able to muster all the rabble of the country, which when they was to march towards the enemy either he had no right to command or else they deserted . . . I am an eye-witness that regiments that mustered 700 and upwards at home came not into the field or even to Dublin 400 strong'.[7] Many officers followed the customary practice of the time of falsely inflating their muster rolls in order to claim pay for non-existent soldiers:

> What was worst of all, the people, greedy of novelties and ignorant of the dangers and hardships attending the military life, flocked to be soldiers as if the whole business had been to live at ease and rifle their enemies; but when they perceived how dear they were to buy their bread and liberty, rather than expose their lives or undergo the labours and wants a soldier is often exposed to, they deserted in vast numbers . . . our men were newly brought from the mountains . . . the most of them had never fired a musket in their lives. A people used only to follow and converse with cows, so hard to be made sensible of the duty of a soldier or be brought to handle their arms aright, that it was difficult to make any of them understand the common words of command, much less to obey them. Besides their natural uncouthness, they are stubborn and conceited, to be governed with rigour and severity, not to be wrought upon with leniency and gentleness, for by experience I have found they not only fear, but respect and love the officer much more that beats them daily without mercy than him that cherishes and carries a light hand over them. They will follow none but their own leaders, many of them men as rude, as ignorant, and as far from understanding any of the rules of discipline as themselves. This was the utter ruin of the army . . .[8]

He added that:

> These officers had seen and knew no more than their men, and consequently understood as little how to exercise or train them, every one thought himself qualified enough to bear a commission if he could march before his men, and repeat by rote the words of the common exercise. For want of arms most of the army was taught the little they learnt with sticks . . . many regiments were armed and sent upon service who had never fired a shot, ammunition being kept so choice that they were never taught to fire, and it is hard to guess when these men were upon action whether their own or the enemy's fire was more terrible to them.[9]

By early September Williamite forces in Ireland totalled over 20,000 men. There seemed to be little prospect of halting an advance on Dublin by Schomberg. D'Avaux reported that some Jacobite regiments now mustered only 200 men,[10] and that the Jacobite foot totalled no more than 6,000 to 7,000 men, a third of them unarmed, while for those men fortunate enough to have muskets, no more than four rounds apiece were available.[11] It was feared that any advance by Schomberg would trigger a Protestant uprising in Dublin, and orders were given for a militia to be formed consisting of all male Catholics between the ages of 16 and 60, while in coastal areas deemed vulnerable to attack, all livestock was to be driven away inland.

The French generals with James concluded that it would be impossible to hold Dublin, and advised that the Irish capital be abandoned and the army pulled back to Athlone to attempt to hold the line of the Shannon. For once, however, King James was made of sterner stuff, telling d'Avaux that he 'was resolved not to be tamely walked out of Ireland, but to have one blow for it at least'.[12] He quashed a proposal that Dublin be burnt, and at the head of his guards marched north to Drogheda, where he arrived on 26 August. Tyrconnel was instructed to hasten the reorganisation of the army, while the Duke of Berwick began a scorched-earth operation along the probable route of Schomberg's advance.

It was not until 2 September that the Williamite forces at last marched southwards from Belfast. Schomberg made slow progress. He found that the town of Newry had been razed to the ground by Berwick and, with supplies almost impossible to obtain on the line of march, was forced to rely upon what could be carried by sea from Belfast and landed at Carlingford. The Jacobites made no attempt to hold the favourable defensive position of the Moyry Pass, between Newry and Dundalk, but this was the only piece of good fortune to cheer Schomberg. As his men trudged southwards in wet and windy weather, supply problems increased. There was a serious shortage of bread, and the Duke was forced to send his artillery horses back to Belfast to collect supplies. Foraging soldiers seized and devoured some 2,000 sheep belonging to the Jacobite Lord Bellew. The unfortunate animals gained a posthumous revenge when large numbers of Williamite troops were struck down by 'fluxes'. Among them was Jean-François Morsier, a Swiss soldier serving in one of the Huguenot regiments. He recounted:

The prevailing sickness was the bloody flux, caused by the bad food, which was almost entirely limited to oat-cakes, which are small cakes of the thickness of your little finger, made from oat-flour dried in front of the fire, and the drink of fresh beer and water from a stagnant bog, in some places well-water which the soldiers brought in to sell in the camp at half a sou the bottle. My sickness got so bad that I could not bear it any longer, being tormented by a burning fever from which I could get relief only by putting my head and forehead against the wet tent, for it rained continually. So I was sent to a castle at Karlinfort, where the sick were. All the places were taken; I had to go into a pigeon-loft at the top of the house; two or three cadets and soldiers did their best to clean it up and we slept on the floor.[13]

On 7 September Schomberg's advance ground to a halt just to the north of Dundalk, where the Williamites encamped on 'a low moist ground under great hills'.[14] They were astride the road between Newry and Dundalk, about a mile to the north of the latter. The Williamite army was deployed with a view to defence, rather than continuing its advance. D'Avaux believed that the Williamites could have marched on at least as far as Drogheda, as James had forbidden a continuance of the scorched-earth policy any further south than Newry, and the Plain of Louth was rich in grass, wheat and oats.

Schomberg, however, resisted the urgings of some of his officers to renew his advance. On 15 September he wrote complacently to King William: 'Some of the colonels wish to go to Ardree and talk about giving battle as if it were only a trifle. I do not think it will be to your majesty sense to quit this position where we can always maintain communication with Belfast.'[15] King James, meanwhile, had established his headquarters at Knockbridge, 5 miles from Dundalk, where, for their first night, James and his staff stayed awake, expecting an enemy attack. D'Avaux discovered the Jacobite sentries all asleep and could not understand why Schomberg did not attack.

But the elderly Williamite commander was so worried by his lack of supplies and by the obvious deficiencies of his army that he had concluded that he had no option but to stay on the defensive. With much of the ground too soft to pitch tents, the army was crammed into a few areas of firmer terrain, overcrowding adding to its health problems. The raw English recruits, in particular, had little understanding of proper sanitation arrangements, while the Dutch and Huguenot troops built themselves adequate wooden shelters and huts. Throughout the autumn, deaths from disease – most probably pneumonia – mounted steadily. The Williamite chronicler, George Storey, wrote: 'I was forced to go and dig potatoes, which made the greatest part of a dinner to better men than myself; and if it was so with us it may easily be supposed the poor soldiers had harder times of it.'[16]

On 21 October Schomberg shifted camp to what was hoped would be better ground, but Storey noted little improvement:

we had 67 that were not able to march to fresh ground, whom we put into those huts, leaving the surgeon with an officer and twelve men purposely to attend them: The Chaplain likewise went to see them once a day; but always at his going, found some dead. Those that were alive, seemed very sorry when the others were to be buried, not that they were dead, (for they were the hardest-hearted one to another in the World) but whilst they had them in their huts, they either served to lay between them and the cold wind, or at least were serviceable to sit or lie on.[17]

Von Rosen was certain that Schomberg faced serious problems and persuaded James to offer battle. The opposing armies were roughly equal in size: James had 20,000 men to Schomberg's 19,000, but the latter had considerably more experienced troops. Schomberg, however, declined the challenge and allegedly lay down on a little hill and went to sleep. For his part, James decided that the enemy position was too strong to attack and withdrew behind the River Fane, where the Jacobite army remained for the next two weeks.

John Stevens had been unimpressed by the Jacobite troops he first saw outside Drogheda in September, noting that many of them were 'almost naked or at best very ragged and ill-shod. The only creditable and hopeful part of the army were the horse, who were for the most part good men, well armed and mounted, and their number not very great.'[18] Stevens felt that the Jacobites were generally comfortable in their quarters:

Whilst the army continued encamped in this place it suffered no want of anything that was necessary. There was plenty of forage for the horse . . . The Country abounded with straw and corn which served both to lie upon and cover our huts wherewith we supplied the want of tents, there being very few in the army, and even such as had them made huts as being warmer and drier. The army was punctually paid, and the brass money passed as current and was of equal value with silver, which made the camp so plentiful of provisions that I have seen a good carcass of beef sold for eight [shillings] and commonly for ten or twelve, good mutton for twelve or thirteen pence a quarter, goose for six or eight pence a piece, and so proportionately of all sorts of proven. At the headquarters French wines and brandy were at twelvepence the bottle, and at several sutlers throughout the camp at one shilling and sixpence. The scarcest thing was ale, and yet no good want of it at threepence per quart.[19]

D'Avaux painted a gloomier picture and certainly, after the army had pulled back to Ardree, with continuing heavy rain flooding trenches and tents, conditions worsened.

Both sides had had their fill of the vile weather and disease. Schomberg maintained his position: 'I do not see why we should risk anything on our side. We have one little river before us and they another.'[20] Early in November James effectively ended the campaign by withdrawing most of his forces into winter quarters around Dublin. Schomberg was busy finding excuses for his failure, and to William blamed everyone except himself: 'The officers are incapable, but the sickness and laziness are worse still. The colonels take so little care of their regiments that half the pikes are broken, and so are half the firelocks and muskets.'[21]

A few days after James had pulled back to Dublin, Schomberg ordered a retreat to Lisburn. Thousands of his sick died on the way. Storey wrote: 'All the roads from Dundalk to Newry and Carlingford were full of nothing but dead men who, even as the wagons jolted, some of them died and were thrown off as fast.'[22]

James officially took the view that the setbacks that had befallen the Williamite army, costing it a third of its total strength, were the judgement of God. In England, many placed the blame on Schomberg, although the unfortunate commissary-general Shales was made the official scapegoat and arrested, but eventually released without punishment. As for Schomberg himself, 'It has cast such a mist upon him that the remainder of his life will not be able to dissipate.'[23]

King William decided that in the spring he would have to take command personally in Ireland.

SLIGO

While the deadlock at Dundalk continued, fighting had flared up again in Ulster. After the loss of Sligo, the only remaining Jacobite garrison of note was at Charlemont. Sarsfield, ordered to strike quickly to retake Sligo before Schomberg could reinforce the garrison, was provided with 3,000 men from the main field army, and recruited another 2,000 men on his march from Athlone.

Sligo was garrisoned by Zachariah Tiffin and was used by Thomas Lloyd as a base for his continued raiding. However, Lloyd felt that he would be unable to hold Jamestown against Sarsfield's approaching brigade, and unsuccessfully sought Schomberg's permission to evacuate it. A German-born professional soldier was given command at Jamestown, while Lloyd himself assumed control at Sligo, but failed to make adequate preparations. Sligo's defences consisted of an earth wall, which the garrison was too weak to defend, the castle, in too great a state of disrepair to be defensible, and a strong fort, which Lloyd failed to provision or to arm adequately.

Sarsfield's first move was to send detachments to cut off Sligo's links with Boyle and Jamestown. Lloyd attempted to strike back on 13 October, but on Curlew Mountain ran into an ambush by a Jacobite detachment under Captain Ulick Burke. Defeated, with some loss, Lloyd had no alternative but to fall back into Sligo. The Williamite outposts at Boyle and Jamestown were abandoned as their garrisons unsuccessfully tried to withdraw to Sligo.

Sarsfield knew that he must strike quickly at Sligo before Lloyd could be reinforced, while Lloyd made another attempt on 15 October, at Ballydare, to block the Jacobite advance. He hoped to hold a bridge over the river, but Jacobite cavalry were shown a nearby ford by a local man, and Henry Lutterell took a mixed force of horse and foot across in an attempt to cut Lloyd's retreat. 'Little Cromwell' learnt of the danger and pulled back towards Sligo, from where Russell's men from Jamestown were marching to reinforce him. Lutterell found himself trapped between the two Williamite forces, but with seventy cavalry troopers he launched a spirited charge that routed Russell. Both he and Lloyd withdrew to Sligo.

Sarsfield and the main Jacobite force wasted no time in following up this success. The inadequately manned outer defences of Sligo were quickly overrun. Russell and Lloyd, with their horse, made a hasty escape towards Ballyshannon, leaving only about 400 foot of La Melloniere's Huguenot regiment to hold the town. Seeing the castle to be indefensible, the Huguenot commander, Saint-Sauveur, withdrew to the fort, hoping to defy Sarsfield – who had no artillery – long enough for relief to arrive.

The resourceful Sarsfield brought up a 'sow' – basically a siege tower of the kind commonly employed in medieval times. '[O]ne remarkable stratagem made use of by the Irish for the storming of the fort was, they built a box of timber as high as the wall with stairs through which they might ascend to the top of the wall without danger.'[24] However, not only was it not bulletproof, but the defenders managed to set the 'sow' alight by means of lowering a man in a basket to ignite some bundles of straw previously thrown over the wall around the siege tower.

Sarsfield settled down to blockade the fort, and on the third day the defenders, virtually without supplies, asked for terms. On 22 October, colours flying and drums beating, the Huguenots marched out, granted safe passage to Ballyshannon, while their officers were entertained to a meal by Sarsfield.

Sligo's defences were strengthened, and the capable Henry Lutterell was installed as governor. Thomas Lloyd's reputation was shattered by the debacle at Sligo. He died from dysentery, soon after being ordered to join the main army at Dundalk. Sarsfield was firmly established as a Jacobite hero.

SEVEN

• • • • • • • • • • •

The End of the Highland Army: Dunkeld and Cromdale

Following its costly victory at Killiecrankie, command of the battered but elated Highland army was assumed by Brigadier General Alexander Cannon. A native of Galloway, Cannon was a professional soldier who had served in Holland with the Anglo-Dutch Brigade until, after a dispute with William of Orange, he had returned home in 1687 and become colonel of the Queen's Regiment of Dragoons. Cannon, described by Mackay as 'an old, inactive Man',[1] was neither an inspired nor an inspiring leader, with no skills in the delicate art of commanding Highlanders. But no more suitable commander was available, and Cannon at least began in a position of advantage. Mackay's army was temporarily out of action, and its main supply base at Perth was vulnerable to attack.

But Cannon missed his opportunity. Despite the distractions of the booty taken at Killiecrankie, the Highland army, exceptionally for a clan force, actually increased its strength after the victory. Starting off after the battle with about 1,500 men fit for action, Cannon was reinforced by over 1,500 clansmen, attracted by news of the Jacobite victory. But the confusion of the government forces proved to be short-lived. Mackay, after rallying his forces at Stirling on 29 July, reoccupied Perth, in the process routing a small force of Athollmen whom Cannon had belatedly dispatched there to collect supplies.

Cannon correctly rejected the advice of the clan chieftains to invade the Lowlands. For an army lacking horse and faced by the relatively formidable government cavalry this would have been courting disaster. But Cannon was wrong to dismiss the Highlanders' alternative plan of marching along the southern edge of the Highlands to recruit in hitherto untried areas. Instead, he reverted to Dundee's unfruitful attempts to recruit from the Gordons of Aberdeenshire, and turned north-eastwards.

Marching on a parallel course, Mackay reached Aberdeen on 10 August. Here he hoped to concentrate a strong force of horse to drive back the Highland army, which he possibly overestimated at 4,000 foot and 150 cavalry. Cannon gained few of his anticipated recruits, and the disgruntled clan chieftains now proposed a direct attack on the government forces. This notion was, correctly, rejected by Cannon and the other regular soldiers, but the result was a further lowering of morale among the clansmen, some of whom began to drift away. It was urgent to find some means of restoring their enthusiasm, and an opportunity quickly presented itself.

Among the new units raised by the government in the spring of 1689 was the Earl of Angus's Foot, later called the 'Cameronians' after Richard Cameron, a leading preacher who gave his name to one of the most extreme of the Covenanting sects. The Earl of Angus was a youth of 18, and actual command of the regiment was exercised by the regiment's 28-year-old lieutenant-colonel, William Cleland.

Cleland was initially better known as a scholar and poet than for any military ability. Described by Mackay as 'a sensible, resolute man, though not much of a soldier',[2] he had been credited with a major part in the small Covenanting victory at Drumclog on 1 June 1679. He was involved in Argyll's unsuccessful rising of 1685 and, along with several other future officers of Angus's Foot, was forced to seek refuge in Holland.

Angus's Regiment, with 1,200 men in ten companies, had an establishment twice as large as any of the other units commissioned by the Scottish Convention. Its formation initially encountered a good deal of opposition from the General Meeting of the Covenanting sects, who were suspicious of any cooperation with the regular army and known 'malignants' such as Hugh Mackay. Its members tried to set strict, and indeed impractical, restrictions before agreeing to the formation of the new unit. All recruits were to be reliable in their religion, with the right of veto over the appointments of their non-commissioned officers and officers, who, if from a regular army background, were thought likely to hold suspect religious views.

As well as objections to the suitability of some officers, there were demands for 'an elder in every company, with the respect and esteem due to persons of their character, who may with authority reprove officers, without respect of persons'. Also likely to be difficult to impose on hardbitten regulars were severe penalties for 'fornication . . . and all lascivious, filthy and unchristian talking, swearing, cursing, mocking of godliness, drinking of healths and all drunkenness etc.'.[3] Unsurprisingly, Cleland and his officers refused to have any truck with these proposals, which were eventually replaced by a much vaguer declaration against 'Popery and Prelacy'.[4]

The first muster of the regiment on 14 May listed 40 sergeants, 60 corporals, 36 drums and 1,147 'sentinels' (privates). Few of the officers had a regular army background, although a number, including Cleland and Major James Henderson, had seen action in the Covenanter insurrections. Most of the remainder also came from the Covenanter areas, including Captain John Blackadder, son of a leading preacher.

When the regiment arrived at its first quarters, in Dunblane and Doune, the men had only those weapons they had brought from home. But on 20 May the Governor of Stirling Castle was instructed to issue them with two barrels of powder, ball and 400 pikes, while 400 muskets were to be supplied from Edinburgh, with an additional 200 sent by boat from Leith. Most of the firearms were apparently matchlocks, and no swords or bayonets were available until later in the year, although forty halberds for sergeants were supplied. Angus's Foot went to war wearing their civilian clothes, for apparently no uniforms were issued until after October, when a contract was made with Edinburgh merchants to supply the regiment with 1,200 red coats and the same number of felt hats.

In July Angus's Foot made a brief foray into Lochaber, but were recalled on news of Killiecrankie and quickly fell into disputes. The men were semi-mutinous, discontented with some of their officers, and angry over arrears of pay. The Duke of Argyll recommended that the two battalions of Angus's be reduced to one, saying that 'there may be some service to be had of them; but the other half, both officers and soldiers, are madmen, not to be governed, even by Master Shields, their oracle'.[5] (Shields was the regiment's self-appointed minister.) The mutineers in turn complained that Cleland had appointed 'profane officers', and had forced them to make an unnecessary march on the Sabbath. They also, apparently with some cause, alleged that Cleland and Major Henderson had retained money sent for the men's pay and had also kept back funds intended to buy clothing and shoes.

These problems were evidently sorted out sufficiently for the regiment to return to duty, although it continued to be regarded with suspicion and exasperation by the authorities. Indeed, suspicions were later expressed that the Cameronians were deliberately set up for what happened next.

The Convention in Edinburgh feared that Mackay's move north-east in response to Cannon's march would open the way for other Jacobite forces to advance through the unguarded Pass of Killiecrankie and fall on Perth. To counter this possibility, on 12 August Cleland was ordered to move his regiment from its quarters at Dunblane and Doune and garrison the small town of Dunkeld. The intention was for the Cameronians to be reinforced by Lanier's cavalry from Perth and Angus, but a delay by Mackay in issuing the necessary orders, probably a genuine oversight, although subsequently viewed with dark suspicion by the Cameronians, left the regiment dangerously isolated.

DUNKELD

Although Dunkeld was a potential death trap in case of a major Jacobite attack, in mid-August the likelihood of this seemed remote. The Athollmen were now beginning to submit to the government, and Cannon, his army

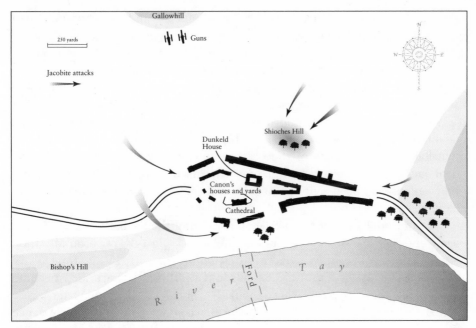

Dunkeld, 21 August 1689

believed to be on the point of disintegration, was supposedly far away. Unfortunately for the Cameronians, this over-optimistic assessment ignored the mobility of the Highlanders.

Dunkeld stood on the north bank of the River Tay, about 15 miles north-west of Perth. A ring of hills overlooked the town, and there was also rising ground nearer to hand, including a hill by the river to the east of the town. From the foot of this hill the main street of Dunkeld ran westwards to the Town Cross, from where a side street called Scots Raw branched off to the north-west, while the principal thoroughfare continued to the south end of Dunkeld cathedral. This was a half-ruined building, although its main walls remained intact. Clustered around it were the large houses formerly belonging to the clergy, some of them facing the cathedral across the main street, their gardens sloping down to the Tay, while others formed an irregular semi-circle to the north of the graveyard. Here was situated Atholl House, the splendid town residence of the Marquis of Atholl, forming a square around a central courtyard. Its north-eastern face, on Scots Raw, was hemmed in by smaller buildings. To the east of Atholl House, Shioches Hill, a narrow, steep area of ground split up by ditches, ran north of the buildings opposite the Cross, while from the west end of the cathedral a road led down to the Tay, where the foundations of an old bridge formed a ford.

Angus's Regiment arrived in Dunkeld late on Saturday 17 August, and camped between the cathedral and Atholl House. Its actual strength was probably between 700 and 800 men, plus officers and non-commissioned officers. Companies probably averaged between seventy-five and eighty men. There was not yet a grenadier company, and the proportion of musketeers may have been below the recommended ratio. Many of the men may have been armed with halberds or similar pole-type weapons, or had cut down their pike lengths for greater ease of use in confined conditions. The mood of the soldiers had not been improved by their being assigned to what they considered to be a death trap, and they were met with hostility by the townsfolk, to which some of the Cameronians responded by looting houses. Local Jacobite sympathisers fomented the discontent by alleging that the Cameronians had been sent to Dunkeld with the express mission to 'burn and kill all before them'.[6]

At 9 a.m. on 18 August, regardless of its being the Sabbath, Cleland's men began entrenching themselves in the ditches or 'yard dykes' around Atholl House, 'the old breaches whereof they made up with loose stones, and scaffolded the dykes about'.[7] The wisdom of these preparations became apparent at about 3 p.m., when about 300 local Jacobite supporters were sighted in the hills above the town. The newcomers sent in a flag of truce with an uncompromising ultimatum: 'We, the gentlemen assembled, being informed that ye intend to burn the town, desire to know whether ye come for peace or war, and do certify that if ye burn any one house, we will destroy you.' Cleland responded firmly: 'We are faithful servants of King William and Queen Mary, and if you, who send these threats, shall make any hostile appearance, we will burn all that belongs to you, and otherwise chastise you as you deserve.'[8] At the same time, Cleland sent urgently to Perth for reinforcements.

Early on 19 August, in response to his plea, two troops of horse and three of dragoons under the Earl of Cardross arrived, together with some additional arms and ammunition. Next day, Cardross, as senior officer, decided to dislodge the growing numbers of local Jacobites who were lurking in the surrounding hills. At about 8 a.m., leaving a garrison of 150 men to hold Atholl House, he mounted a sortie in force upstream along the Tay. A good deal of indecisive skirmishing followed, in which the government forces claimed to have killed some thirty rebels at the cost of only four men to themselves. But the same evening large numbers of enemy troops were seen to be massing in the hills. Against all expectations, Cannon and the Highland army, estimated at 4,000 strong, had arrived. Dunkeld seemed destined to be the death trap that Cleland's men had feared.

On 17 August, as Mackay complacently awaited tidings of the Jacobite army's disintegration, Cannon and his men slipped away from their quarters at Strathbogie in the first of several 'extraordinary long marches', crossing the River Dee that night. Mackay, unwilling after his previous experience to pursue the Highlanders into the mountains, made a long detour south by way of Aberdeen, and by 22 August had still reached only Drumlithe, over 50 miles from Dunkeld.

Cannon had initially been planning a morale-boosting raid into enemy territory. But when reports reached him from the rebels around Dunkeld, he saw the opportunity for a desperately needed success. He ordered the Highland army to march on Dunkeld.

News of the approaching Jacobites reached Colonel Ramsey, commanding government forces in Perth. He sent Lord Cardross instructions to withdraw to Perth, but – most probably intending his orders to apply to them as well – omitted to mention the Cameronians.

The result was another acrimonious dispute. Cleland's somewhat paranoid followers mutinied, declaring that they would go with the horse rather than stay and be butchered in 'an open, useless place'. This was a reasonable enough reaction, and it is difficult to see why Cleland, unless motivated by exasperation or wounded pride, chose to dig his heels in and announce his determination to stay and fight. He and his officers, blaming the reluctantly departing Cardross for 'the blood and loss of that regiment', offered to shoot their own horses as security against their abandoning their men, who, probably with rather less enthusiasm than claimed in contemporary accounts, agreed to stay. As the enemy closed in, their situation appeared desperate.

The Jacobite forces at Dunkeld probably totalled around 4,000 men, the bulk of them being the men of the Highland army. Its exact composition is uncertain, but it included most of those who had fought at Killiecrankie. Among them were Sir John MacLean's Regiment of about 300 men, the MacDonalds of Clanranald and Glengarry, some 600 strong, and Sir Alexander MacLean's Irish regiment of 200 men, said to be the best in the Jacobite army. Since Killiecrankie they had been reinforced by various other contingents, including a number of Athollmen, some MacGregors under the father of the celebrated Rob Roy, Appin Stuarts, Glencoe MacDonalds and the followers of MacNeill of Barra. Also present were Purcell's 400 dismounted Irish dragoons, and four troops of horse, totalling about 150 men. The Jacobites had captured a number of firearms at Killiecrankie, but they probably remained in fairly short supply, and the average clansman was a poor marksman. As at Killiecrankie, the Highland army would have to rely upon getting to grips with the enemy as quickly as possible, when, in hand-to-hand fighting, their superiority in numbers might outweigh discipline and firepower. Unfortunately, Highland tactics were ill-suited for the kind of street fighting that would be involved at Dunkeld.

Cleland briefly considered making another sortie against the enemy massing to the east of Dunkeld, but wisely thought better of it. He decided to stay on the defensive and so force Cannon to commit his men in the kind of attack on a prepared position that would minimise his numerical advantage.

For their part, Cannon and his regular officers made their decision to attack without any proper consultation with the clan chieftains, at least one of whom, Sir John MacLean, protested in vain against the plan.

Cleland had no reason to be overconfident. His main defence lines around Atholl House and the cathedral included low garden walls or 'dykes' to provide cover, but there were breaches in them, in places they were 'not four feet high' and might easily be crossed by a determined assault. Equally worrying was a shortage of powder and shot, although attempts were made to replenish the latter by melting down lead from the roof of Atholl House. Cleland hoped to break the force of the enemy attack by means of small 'combined arms' skirmishing parties, which would make a staged withdrawal on the main defences.

Fighting began at about 7 a.m., when the Jacobite guns 'advanced down to the face of a little hill, close upon the town'. These were the light leather guns captured from Mackay at Killiecrankie, now positioned on Gallowhill just north of the town, and intended to cover the first major assault, which was launched at the same time. Coming from the eastern end of Gallowhill, it was headed by 100 men in back- and breastplates and pot helmets, carrying targes and armed with swords. These may have been from Sir Alexander MacLean's Regiment, so equipped in order to reduce the effect of enemy fire. They advanced towards a government outpost on Shioches Hill, and were followed by the remainder of MacLean's Regiment and probably Purcell's Dragoons, many of them armed with snaphaunce flintlocks to provide covering fire. These were the nearest to regular troops that Cannon possessed, and behind them, ready to exploit any success, came a larger force, with two troops of horse to their left, which, according to one account, were used to drive on reluctant clansmen.[9]

Stationed on Shioches Hill was a detachment of Cameronians under Captain William Hay and Ensign Lockhart. Lockhart and twenty-eight men were posted at the foot of the hill behind a stone dyke, and it was they who bore the brunt of the first enemy attack. 'And after they had entertained them briskly with their fire for a pretty space, the rebels forced the dyke, and obliged them to retire, firing from one little dyke to another, and at length to betake themselves to the house and yard dykes.'[10] Hay and his main force also fell back, without casualties, apart from Hay himself, who suffered a broken leg, perhaps by falling from a dyke.

At about the same time fighting began at the eastern end of Dunkeld. The small picket of Cameronians stationed there made only a token resistance before firing the houses and falling back on a barricade established at the Town Cross. This was defended by Lieutenant Stuart with twenty men, who now attempted to fall back on Atholl House. Most of them made it, although Stuart himself was overwhelmed and was killed as he attempted to regulate the retreat.

More and more Highlanders were now pushing forward through the outskirts of the town. Captain Blackadder of the Cameronians described how the attackers 'came running on like desperate villains, firing only once, and then came on with sword and target'.[11] This is a classic description of the famous Highland Charge, and it is instructive to compare it with the explanation given in 1724 by General Wade: 'They generally give their fire at a distance, they lay down their Arms [muskets] on the ground and make a Vigorous attack with their Broadswords.'[12] But whatever potential for success the Highland Charge had on open ground against an opponent with shaky morale, it was largely ineffective in close-quarters street fighting against opponents without any means of escape who were fighting for their lives.

Nevertheless, the considerable Jacobite advantage in numbers was beginning to make itself felt. On the western edge of the town, the picket of twenty-four men under Lieutenant Forrester and Ensign Campbell that had been holding some 'little dykes' was initially threatened at a distance by two troops of horse that Cannon had sent across Bishop's Hill with orders to secure the ford over the Tay. Although Forrester's men were able to hold them off, the attackers were reinforced by large numbers of foot, and the Cameronians were forced to make a fighting retreat to the cathedral, several men being trapped in houses and killed.

The Jacobites now launched a simultaneous assault at four points on the shrinking defensive perimeter. One party, although coming under heavy fire, deployed under cover of the river bank and stormed from the rear the houses to the south of the cathedral. Then, led by the Appin Stuarts, they launched a ferocious assault on the cathedral itself, which was filled with townspeople who had neither joined the Jacobites nor fled Dunkeld before fighting began. The cathedral was held by about 100 men, who eventually repulsed the assault, but by now the defenders of Dunkeld were hard-pressed on all sides:

> All the outposts being forc'd the rebels advanced most boldly upon the yard-dykes all round, even upon those parts which stood within less than forty paces from the river, where they crowded in their multitudes, without regard to the shot liberally poured in their faces, and struck with their swords at the soldiers on the dyke, who, with their pikes and halberds, returned their blows with interest. Others, in great numbers, possessed the town houses, out of which they fired within the dykes, as they did from the hills about.[13]

The defenders had been pushed back to their inner line, a small area including the cathedral, Atholl House, and a steadily dwindling number of clergy houses (only three of which were still held at the end of the battle).

As the Jacobite snipers homed in on their targets, Cameronian losses began to mount. At about 8 a.m., Lieutenant-Colonel Cleland, directing operations

in the open, was fatally hit in the head and liver; at about the same time
Major Henderson was mortally wounded, and three captains were more or
less severely wounded. Command now passed to the senior captain, Munro, a
professional soldier.

The Jacobite assault was beginning to lose some of its impetus. The
clansmen were becoming bogged down in a mass of struggling men around
the ditches and were suffering heavily from enemy fire. One of their poets
wrote later: 'the stalwart young men fell . . . felled by bullets fired by
cowherds.'[14] The bulk of these losses would have fallen on the elite of the
clan forces, the gentry and *caterans*. To add to the Jacobite discomfiture,
Cannon had chosen to direct the attack from the rear, and this decision,
although justified both by orthodox military thinking and by the recent fate of
Dundee, infuriated the clansmen, who compared Cannon unfavourably with
his predecessor, cursing 'a devil of a commander who was out of sight of his
enemies'.[15]

Cannon does not seem to have considered a change in tactics, probably
because the bulk of his men were neither armed nor trained sufficiently well
to fight in any other way. Nor did the Jacobite artillery prove effective.
Although the guns were light enough to have been fairly easily manhandled
close enough to Atholl House to blast holes in its flimsy defences, no attempt
was made to do so. One reason may have been that Cannon had failed to
obtain enough ammunition for them of the right calibre, so that by 9 a.m.
they seem to have fallen silent. Nevertheless, though with rather less intensity
than previously, fighting continued until about 11 a.m. Blackadder recalled:

> In all which time, there was continual thundering of shot from both sides,
> with flames and smoke, and hideous cries, filling the air. And, which was
> very remarkable, though the houses were burnt all around, yet the smoke
> of them and all the shot from both sides, was carried everywhere outward
> from the dykes upon the assailants as if a wind had blown every way from
> the centre . . .[16]

The Cameronians were running short of ammunition, despite stripping
lead from the roof of Atholl House and melting it down in hollows in the
ground to make shot. Enemy snipers in nearby houses were particularly
troublesome, and at about 9.30 a.m. Munro counter-attacked, ordering
sorties by small parties of men armed with firepikes to burn the houses.
Particularly savage fighting followed: some Highlanders were killed outright,
others – sixteen in one case – were locked in blazing houses to burn to death,
'which raised a hideous noise from the wretches in the fire'.[17] The clansmen
retaliated in kind.

By about 11 a.m., his ammunition running dangerously low, Munro was
preparing for a last stand at Atholl House: 'And if they should find themselves

overpower'd there, to burn it, and bury themselves in the ashes.'[18] But, quite suddenly, the Jacobites began to withdraw. The reasons were later the subject of heated recrimination. Some Jacobites placed the blame on Cannon, although other reports said that the clansmen, with little stomach for continued hand-to-hand fighting amid the blazing buildings, refused their officers' pleas to continue the attacks against 'mad and desperate men' and 'Devils'. This latter explanation seems most likely, while the Jacobites were also probably running out of ammunition.

Cannon's men withdrew to the hills north-west of Dunkeld: 'Whereupon they within beat their drums and hallooed after them with all expressions of contempt and provocations to return.'[19] Then, singing psalms as they did so, the Cameronians set to work repairing their defences in preparation for an anticipated renewal of the attack. But in the afternoon unexpected assistance arrived in the shape of Lord Cardross and his horse, who had pleaded to be allowed to return. The sight of the government cavalry was too much for the Highland army, which may also have been aware that Colonel Ramsey was approaching with additional reinforcements from Perth. The Jacobites made off up the Tay valley, abandoning some of their dead and a good deal of booty.

The Cameronians admitted to losing two officers and fifteen other ranks dead, with about thirty wounded. In fact, as they were unsure of their own exact strength at the start of the action, actual losses may have been slightly higher. Whatever the exact tally, Dunkeld for a time ended the military effectiveness of Angus's Regiment. Quarrels and dissension continued, and it was said of the rank and file that 'their heads are blown up with such notions as renders them intolerable. They are worse than they were in every way.'[20] General Mackay, in any case no friend to the regiment, withdrew it temporarily from active service.

The number of Jacobite losses is also uncertain. They carried many of their casualties away with them, and government estimates of around 300 dead may therefore be rather low. The MacLeans and Appin Stuarts, among the best of their units, suffered particularly heavily. One of the most influential of Cannon's commanders, Sir Alexander MacLean, was seriously wounded. Cannon endeavoured to minimise his defeat by claiming that he successfully stormed Dunkeld, forcing the survivors of the garrison to take refuge in the cathedral and a large house. King James at least was convinced, sending his congratulations on the 'victory'.

The Highlanders, however, were not deceived, and were further demoralised by news of the Jacobite failure before Derry and the landing in Ulster of Williamite forces under the Duke of Schomberg. On 24 August Cannon, with little option, had given his men permission to disperse to their homes in order to bring in the harvest. Although the chieftains had promised to remuster their clans in due course, they agreed to provide only a force totalling 1,810, and the time and place were left unspecified.

In the interim, events continued to go against the Jacobites. The always lukewarm Athollmen submitted to the government, and Mackay placed a garrison in Blair Castle. The Jacobite leadership was torn by dissension between the regular army officers and the clan chieftains led by Glengarry, while Cannon and the Earl of Dunfermline reportedly lurked at Inverlochy, consoling themselves with aqua vita. September passed with no sign of the promised remuster. The only significant activity was a number of raids into the Lowlands by the young Rob Roy Macgregor, and these were little more than attempts to gain supplies to enable the clans to survive the winter. Cannon wrote in despair to James's Secretary of State, the Earl of Melfort, begging for supplies 'for otherwise I know not what shall become of all of us here'.[21]

Mackay was in considerably better shape. On 28 August, with a powerful force of seven regiments of foot, two of horse and two of dragoons, he had advanced without opposition from Perth to Blair Atholl. Soon afterwards torrential rain brought active operations to a close, and, in order to ease supply demands, Mackay sent most of his English forces home. Brigadier Lanier, who had always detested his Scottish experiences, to his great relief was sent to Ireland. Mackay still had to maintain garrisons in a semi-circle around the Highlands, together with several field forces. But, in a further sign of the decline of James's support in Scotland, large numbers of Jacobite sympathisers in the Lowlands were making their peace with the authorities in Edinburgh.

As winter approached, the Jacobites in the Highlands continued their desperate raids in search of sustenance. The Williamite garrisons were too small to prevent incursions that penetrated as far as Kintyre and, in December, even caused a flurry of panic in Glasgow. These failed entirely to relieve the shortages. Some of the regular officers died of hunger, or were reduced to trying to barter their uniform buttons for food.

Jacobite hopes were revived for a time by the failure of Schomberg's autumn campaign.[22] James promised that in the spring he would send the Earl of Seaforth to raise the northern clans, together with a contingent of French troops under the Duke of Berwick. In the meantime, Cannon was to hold the clans together through the winter and stay on the defensive. Despite his instructions from James, Cannon was planning a renewed northern campaign with the objective of taking Inverness, but proved unable to persuade any additional clans to muster, with waning enthusiasm further dampened by shortage of food and money.

While Colonel Leslie at Inverness had to face no more than a few uncoordinated raids, Mackay had reverted to his scheme of garrisoning Inverlochy and then pacifying the Highlands. In the meantime a major effort would be made, if necessary employing bribery, to persuade the chiefs to make terms.

On 24 January 1690, in an effort to revive his faltering cause in Scotland, King James dispatched an Aberdeenshire professional soldier, Major-General Thomas Buchan, to join Cannon, who was also promoted to Major-General. Buchan brought with him ammunition and money, and some professional officers. But he did not bring the Duke of Berwick or any French troops, whom the chiefs had been keenly expecting. At a council of war held at Inverlochy in January, some of the clan leaders argued that, as James had broken his word, they were free to make terms for their own preservation. However, they were rallied by Lochiel, who pointed out the dishonour involved in submitting while James still maintained an army in Ireland and had supporters in England.

Buchan had continuing problems in raising the Highlanders. Many potential supporters preferred raiding in their own interests, and provisions remained a major problem. It was eventually agreed that for the present each of the Jacobite clans should provide Buchan with 100 men, so that he at least had the basis of a raiding force, and Buchan organised a foot regiment of his own, using regular officers and Irish soldiers. He eventually seems to have mustered a total of 800 to 900 men, according to Mackay, who described them as: 'the very worst men among the Clans, the chiefs never venturing their best but where they go themselves'.[23]

CROMDALE

After a raid into Strathnairn, which solved the immediate supply problem, Buchan, accompanied by Cannon and Dunfermline, moved to Upper Strathspey. Here, on 29 April, a council of war decided that next day they would move on to Glenlochy, separated from low-lying ground by the wooded hills of Cromdale which would protect them from cavalry, while they recruited from the Grants and other potential supporters in the north-east.

Buchan was overconfident, feeling his campsite to be safe from attack, even though he knew that enemy forces from Inverness were marching against him. He assumed that any attackers would come through the hills to Ballachastell. The Spey was fordable in the area in only three places, the principal one near Cromdale church, at a point where the river bent to the north-west. The other two crossing points were nearer to the Jacobite camp. Buchan placed guards of 45 men at each, with a reserve of 240 men under a lieutenant halfway between them and the main camp. The remainder of the army was encamped in scattered quarters around Cromdale and the area of Lethendry House to the east. Keppoch, however, had quartered his MacDonalds about half a mile north-east of Dalchapple, where a steep hill provided some refuge from attack. The main weakness of Buchan's deployment was that if his outposts were attacked by mounted troops his own dismounted men would not be able to react in time.

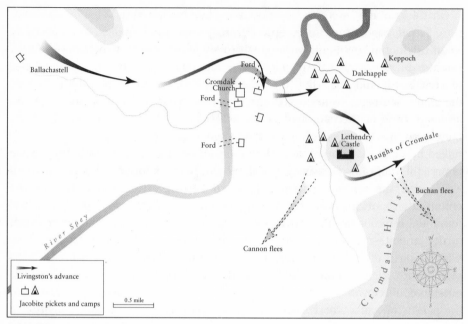

Cromdale, 1 May 1690

Colonel Livingston had left Inverness on 27 April with 400 of Leslie's Regiment, six companies of Grants, Mackay's Highland Company, his regiment of dragoons and two troops of horse; in all, a total of about 800 foot and 400 horse. Livingston learnt of Buchan's location at around noon on 30 April and set off southwards over the hills, at 2 a.m. reaching Ballachastell, where he gave his men a brief rest, having first ensured that none of the locals escaped to give warning to the enemy.

As he closed in, Livingston apparently sent 200 men to create a diversion near the Cromdale church ford, taking the remainder to the lower ford. The guards here were possibly distracted by the skirmishing at Cromdale church, and Mackay's Highlanders and two troops of dragoons crossed the ford without being spotted. At the same time Livingston, with four more troops of horse and dragoons and some Grant foot mounted behind them, bore down on the Scottish camp. The result was total confusion among the surprised Jacobites, many caught still asleep. Buchan hastily ordered some troops, possibly from his own regiment, to hold Lethendry Castle. Highland resistance elsewhere was patchy; Cannon and many of his men fled in their shirts or naked. The MacLeans made a brief stand at the foot of the Hills of Cromdale but, finding themselves unsupported, fled when they were about to be surrounded. Only the sudden descent of mist over the hillsides prevented many of the fugitives from being hunted down.

Livingston re-formed his men on the plain, while Keppoch's MacDonalds seized their opportunity to escape. The sixty men holding the castle, probably from Buchan's Regiment, were surrounded after government troops hurled some grenades among them. Livingston claimed that between 300 and 400 of the enemy had been killed, and about 100 captured, although Buchan claimed his actual losses were much lighter. His own Regiment, however, seems to have been virtually destroyed. The Royal Standard and much of the commanders' correspondence were taken.[24]

Cromdale was the effective end of the Highland army. Some of the Jacobite prisoners starved to death at Aberdeen, while others remained in prison until 1693. Buchan was now regarded as 'the most ungrateful ruffian living to the Highlanders', and had no prospect of raising another force. While the rebel areas in the Western Highlands suffered from seaborne raids by government forces under a Major Ferguson (who committed similar atrocities to those which made his grandson notorious in 1746), Mackay marched with little resistance to Inverlochy and began constructing Fort William. This was completed in eleven days.

By now the Jacobites were reduced to carrying out scattered raids, while even such hitherto committed chieftains as Keppoch and Lochiel were putting out feelers for terms and allowing their tenants and clan gentry to make their own individual settlements. Patchy Jacobite resistance continued into 1691, with the Earl of Breadalbane eventually brokering a deal by which the remaining diehard Highlanders were to submit by 10 October in return for what were effectively generous bribes to their chieftains. Most did so although, in a tangled web of confusion and double-dealing, the MacDonalds of Glencoe failed to comply in time, resulting in February 1692 in the infamous 'Massacre'.

In March 1692 Buchan and Cannon were given passes to leave the country for France. Although there would be vague plans for them and other Jacobite officers to head a Scottish insurrection as part of James's invasion of the British Isles that year, these schemes came to nothing. With the exception of the handful of Jacobite diehards who held out on Bass Rock into 1694, King James's war in Scotland was over.

EIGHT

• • • • • • • • • •

The Road to the Boyne: January–July 1690

PLANS AND PREPARATIONS

As the campaigning season of 1689 came to an end, all those involved in the War of the Three Kingdoms might reflect on a year of mixed fortunes.

Observers differed as to James's mood as the year ended. To some he appeared despondent, while others felt that he displayed an air of unjustified confidence. Such optimism was not shared by some of his closest advisers. Ultimately the Stuart cause could survive only by carrying the war across the Irish Sea into Scotland and England. In Scotland the Jacobite cause was crumbling; in England Stuart supporters remained disorganised and unable to act.

Tyrconnel warned that the Irish army would face a stern test the following summer, and throughout the winter he wrote repeatedly to Mary of Modena, in France, urging her to press for massive military supplies to be sent to Ireland. As well as the 8,000 firearms already dispatched, he asked for a further 6,000 matchlocks and 5,000 flintlocks, 12,000 swords, 2,000 carbines and the same number of cases of pistols and holsters.

Preparations for the coming year's campaigning were less than energetic. Some attempts were made to put Dublin into a state of defence, with trenches and palisades, and guards on the bridges, but there was little prospect of the Irish capital holding out against serious attack.

James and Tyrconnel had become increasingly frustrated by the French. They felt the best opportunity for landing in England or Scotland had now gone, although they argued that a squadron of French frigates sent to the Irish Sea could obstruct Williamite convoys. For the moment, however, they were pinning their hopes on promised French reinforcements.

French aims differed sharply from those of James and his supporters. As early as June 1689, King Louis had written to d'Avaux telling him that the best way for James to increase his support in Scotland and England was by success in Ireland. 'In a word, he should not cross with troops to England at least until he has a significant number of armed supporters who have declared for him, strong enough to resist the troops of the Prince of Orange on their own.' A seaport should be secured, while the French navy should be able to ensure the safe crossing to the British mainland of James and his army. 'As soon as this happens, I will be the first to urge this enterprise upon him.'[1]

For Louis, James's Irish adventure was ultimately a diversion. Tyrconnel had no illusions about the game that the French were playing, commenting that the Jacobites were 'only destined to serve a present turn and be sacrificed at last to our enemies'. French troops would come only at a price. Louvois demanded that reinforcements should be matched by an equal number of Irish troops sent to France. The latter would be under the command of Lord Mountcashel, who had recently escaped after his capture at Newtownbutler. James was unenthusiastic about the exchange, but eventually five regiments of foot, totalling 5,387 men, were selected. D'Avaux complained to Louvois that 'two-thirds of [the officers were] very bad'. When the Irish troops disembarked at Brest observers were horrified; they were 'without shirts, without shoes, most of them without hats, shockingly dirty and generally speaking, devoured with vermin'.[2] Some of the worst recruits were rejected, and the remainder were reorganised into three regiments, Mountcashel's, O'Brien's and Dillon's, which, re-equipped, served with distinction under Mountcashel in Savoy and Catalonia.

The French contingent sent to Ireland was headed by the Marquis de Lauzan, a friend of James whom he had specifically requested as replacement for the detested von Rosen. Lauzan, however, was a vain, ambitious courtier-soldier with little military experience. D'Avaux, who was now on poor terms with James, left on the convoy that had brought Lauzan and his contingent into Cork on 12 March. The reinforcements consisted of 6,000 infantry which, after they had been filled out with some Irish troops, formed five regiments. Three of them were French, one Walloon; the remainder, consisting of two battalions of Zurlauben's Regiment, were German. Many of the latter were former prisoners of war, and also Protestants – whose employment upset James. Also dispatched was an artillery train of twelve guns, plus gunners, a number of engineers, a medical team, wagon makers, and a large quantity of arms and ammunition. The Jacobites complained that many of the firearms were of poor quality.

The Williamites were also preparing for action. William would reluctantly take command himself. He told the Duke of Bavaria: 'I am terribly embarrassed to be obliged to go to Ireland, where I shall be, as it were, beyond all knowledge of the world. If I can reduce that kingdom quickly, I shall then have my hands free to act with much more vigour against the common enemy.'³ He also felt that a quick conclusion to the Irish war was needed to dampen Jacobite opposition in England.

During the spring a steady build-up of the Williamite forces continued. Included were 6,000 infantry and 1,000 horse from Denmark under a professional soldier, the Duke of Württemberg-Neustadt. The Jacobites, reviving memories of past invasions of Ireland, made much of William's bringing in the 'old invaders'. Throughout April and May, English, German and Dutch troops and supplies arrived. In place of the discredited John Shales two new commissary-generals, William Robinson and Bartholomew van Honnrigh, a Dutch merchant who had traded in Dublin, were appointed, and provisioning was placed in the capable hands of the Perira brothers, Amsterdam Jews with long experience in supplying the needs of continental armies.

Tyrconnel continued to lament the lack of French frigates to interrupt William's convoys, while the Royal Navy's Sir Cloudesley Shovell felt that twenty enemy vessels could have devastated the English supply routes. Shovell made several raids on Jacobite harbours, including one in May when he captured a twenty-gun Jacobite frigate in Dublin harbour under the impotent gaze of James and his troops.

On land, Schomberg was first to move. In Ulster, the Jacobites still had garrisons at Cavan and Charlemont in County Armagh, although Sarsfield evacuated the former in March. This left Charlemont as the only remaining Jacobite garrison in Ulster. It was held by a small garrison under the colourful Colonel Tadhg O'Regan.

As spring began, Schomberg commenced operations at Charlemont. Guards were posted near the town on the River Blackwater, and prisoners taken in skirmishes informed the Williamites that O'Regan was short of supplies. Shortly afterwards, a relief force of 500 men succeeded in running some supplies into the garrison, but as the relieving troops were then unable to get out again, their value was small.

Schomberg granted O'Regan generous terms by which the garrison would be allowed to march to Dundalk with their arms and provisions, apart from seventeen cannon and a mortar. Some 800 men marched out, accompanied by a surprisingly large number of women and children. Schomberg was curious as to why so many were present, and was told 'that the Irish were very hospitable and that they all fared alike, but the greatest reason was the soldiers would not stay in the garrison without their wives and mistresses. The Duke replied that there was more love than policy in it.'⁴ Schomberg was equally taken with the old hunchback O'Regan when he made his appearance:

Old Teagle, the governor, was mounted upon an old stoned horse, and he was very lame with scratches, spavin, ring-bones, and other infirmities, but withal so vicious that he would fall kicking and screaming if anybody came near him. Teague himself had a great bunch upon his back, a plain red coat, an old weather beaten wig hanging down at full length, a little narrow white beaver cocked up, a yellow cravat string (but that was all on one side) his boots with a thousand wrinkles in them, and though it was a very hot day yet he had a great muff hanging about him, and to crown all, was almost tipsy with brandy. Thus mounted and equipped, he approached the Duke with a compliment, but his horse would not allow him to make it a long one, for he fell to work presently, and the Duke had scarce time to make him a civil return. The Duke smiled afterwards and said, Teagle's Horse was very mad, and himself very drunk.[5]

For some reason O'Regan was regarded as a great hero in Jacobite circles, and knighted by King James.

The fall of Charlemont left the Jacobites without any significant garrison in Ulster, and both the main field armies began to prepare for the coming campaign. The Jacobite forces were gradually concentrated around Dublin, although neither side could begin active operations until there was sufficient grass to feed the thousands of horses.

The Jacobites now had to decide on their strategy for the coming campaign. James had two main options: either to seek battle, in the hopes of gaining a decisive victory, or avoid it by securing fortifications with his infantry and using his cavalry to attack enemy communications. The French favoured the second option, coupled with a scorched-earth strategy. They again proposed that Dublin be burnt and the Jacobites pull their main forces back behind the line of the Shannon, leaving behind a number of garrisons, in the hope that these would occupy the Williamites long enough for the French to gain the upper hand at sea. Tyrconnel also favoured this course, telling James, 'whoever has time has life'.[6] The King, however, dismissed the burning of Dublin as being 'too cruel'. He also felt that it was important for his credibility that he should continue to hold one at least of his three capitals, and that Dublin was important logistically, supplying as it did around a third of the army's needs.

Although overall the Jacobite troops were better equipped and, in some cases, better trained than in the previous autumn, not all were well prepared for battle. Stevens noted that in Sir Michael Creagh's Regiment of Foot, ten muskets were imperfect for every one in good condition. However, Tyrconnel, although otherwise doubtful of Jacobite prospects, felt that 'our men are in good heart, we have a great many brave men at the head of them that will, I am persuaded, not quit their master or their friends on the day of trial'.[7] James had about 25,000 troops in his main field army, including a number of weak, newly raised regiments, with an average of only four rounds per musket. The artillery train consisted of around a dozen guns, mostly 6-pounders, and a few mortars.

Having decided on a defensive strategy, James had to try to anticipate enemy plans. Initially he pushed his forces northward to bar the routes south and south-east from Ulster. Other troops were stationed in and around Dundalk, and 3,000 men under Patrick Sarsfield were sent to Finea in County Cavan, which was one of the routes that the Jacobites anticipated the enemy might take. The other was near to the coast, via Newry and the Moyry Pass and on to Dundalk.

Schomberg's preference was for an initial advance by a strong detachment westwards to Athlone, cutting the Jacobite line of retreat across the Shannon, and then for another force to strike at Kells while the main army advanced on Dublin. However, this strategy would have been a logistical nightmare. In any case, the final decision would now rest with King William.

On 11 June William sailed from Hoylake with a convoy of 300 troop and supply ships. Aboard them, as well as a large quantity of supplies, were 15,000 additional troops. William was greeted in Carrickfergus and Belfast by celebratory bonfires. At Loughbrickland in County Down, while leaving Schomberg nominally in command of the army, William reviewed his troops. Meinhard Schomberg, son of the Marshal, was put in command of the horse and the Dutch Count de Solms commanded the foot. The army totalled about 35,000 men, 10,000 more than their opponents. The best were the Dutch contingent, which included nine regiments of horse and two of dragoons, with three battalions of Dutch Guards, totalling 2,000 men, and five other Dutch regiments of foot. The Danish contingent consisted of three horse and eight foot regiments. There were three German regiments and two of Huguenots. The English contingent, whose loyalty William suspected, totalled some 13,300 men, including two troops of horse guards, eight line cavalry regiments, four of dragoons and twenty-three foot battalions.

William was generally at ease in the company of his soldiers and was greeted warmly. As Storey relates:

That afternoon his majesty, Prince George [of Denmark, married to the queen's sister, Anne], the general, the duke of Ormond and all the great men came to the camp at Loughbrickland. The king had given orders before his coming that we should remove our camp from the south side of the town to the north west, that his majesty might take a view of the regiments as they marched: the weather was then very dry and windy which made the dust in our marching troublesome: I was of opinion, with several others, that this might be uneasy to a king [mainly because of William's asthma] and therefore believed that his majesty would sit on horseback at a distance in some convenient place to see the men march by him. But he was no sooner come than he was in among the throng of them and observed every regiment very critically. This pleased the soldiers mightily and every one was ready to give what demonstration it was possible both of their courage and duty. The king and prince had their moving houses [timber pre-fabricated buildings] set up and never after lay out[side] the camp during their stay in Ireland.[8]

William was generally acknowledged to be better as an inspirational leader in battle than as a strategist, where Schomberg might have usefully complemented him. But the King had lost faith in the old duke and made little effort to consult him. His revised plan was for the bulk of the army to advance directly, via Newry, on Dundalk, while a detachment under Lieutenant-General Alexander Douglas took a longer route via Armagh.

James had hoped to block the enemy advance at the Moyry Pass, a naturally strong, defensive position, where the road south ran along a narrow causeway across a bog. The King seemed uncharacteristically confident and energetic, spending 18 to 20 hours a day in the saddle. However, reports of Douglas preparing to move from Armagh, plus difficulties in keeping the army supplied so far from Dublin, led Lauzan to fear that the Jacobites might be outflanked by Douglas if they remained at the Moyry Pass, and he urged James to pull back southwards, abandoning Dundalk.

APPROACH TO THE BOYNE

So it was that the Williamites arrived at the Moyry Pass on 22 June to find only a small Jacobite force led by Lieutenant-Colonel Dempsey. A brief action ended indecisively, each side claiming to have inflicted about thirty casualties on the other, Dempsey being mortally wounded. But the skirmish convinced James that the enemy was too strong to be held at this point, and, with the decision to abandon Dundalk, the only feasible defensive position this side of Dublin was along the line of the River Boyne, about 30 miles north of the capital.

The Williamites entered Dundalk without opposition on 25 June. The Duke of Württemberg-Neustadt prophesied to the Danish Secretary for War: 'The army is assembled here. The enemy yield everywhere, if they go on like this, we shall soon be in Dublin!' Possibly the least happy man in the army was William himself. The vast clouds of dust stirred up by his army as it marched in the hot, dry weather were aggravating his asthma.

On 27 June the Jacobites began to pull back towards Drogheda. By 30 June they were taking up position along the southern bank of the Boyne. The French still favoured a retreat across the Shannon, while Tyrconnel doubted both the ability of the Jacobite troops and the willingness of the French to support them. But James was adamant. He would not be pushed out of Ireland without fighting a battle, and the line of the Boyne, fighting in defence of the only British capital city in his hands, seemed as good a place as any.

For William, the growing evidence that the Jacobites were going to stand was excellent news. A decisive victory would give him Dublin and perhaps bring the war in Ireland to a swift conclusion. Throughout the morning of 30 June, columns of Williamite troops pressed on southwards towards the Jacobite positions on the Boyne.

THE BATTLEFIELD

As the French generals and Tyrconnel had observed, the Boyne was not a good defensive position. Contained in the loop of the river a few miles to the west of Drogheda were three settlements, Oldbridge, Sheephouse and Donore. Each consisted of a handful of cottages and cabins. A lane led uphill from the crossing of the Boyne at Oldbridge to Donore, and then south-eastwards to the small village of Platin, which lay astride the Drogheda–Duleek road. The bridge over the Boyne at Duleek was vitally important to the Jacobites because, if it were taken, the enemy could move into the rear of the Jacobite army and cut off its retreat to Dublin. The Boyne had a number of fords in this area; most vulnerable was the vital Oldbridge Ford. This was crossable at all but the highest tides, and indeed was the best crossing place of the Boyne between Drogheda and Slane. Furthermore, a deep ravine would allow an attacking force to approach under cover to within 200 to 300yd of the ford. The Boyne at this point, and down to Drogheda, was tidal, and therefore the time of low tide was important. On 1 July it would be at its lowest – about knee-deep – between 9.30 and 10 a.m. Other fordable points, further downstream, were at Drybridge and Mill Ford, close to Grove and Yellow Islands.

The Williamite forces began to deploy on the northern bank of the river, which was significantly higher than the south bank, meaning that Oldbridge and the Jacobite forces there would be well within range of William's guns. And the Williamites had a distinct advantage in artillery, with thirty-six heavy pieces against fifteen or sixteen Jacobite light guns. The Jacobites had established some makeshift defences in Oldbridge, mainly consisting of earth barricades and loopholes for musketeers knocked into the walls of houses.

James planned to counter-attack as the enemy crossed the river, and so would have been well advised to concentrate his artillery at Oldbridge, but instead he moved one battery away before the fighting began. Once across the river, the Williamites would still be at a disadvantage, having to advance up the hill from Oldbridge to Donore. On the plateau at the summit the Jacobites had occupied a ruined church and walled graveyard, and this position was further strengthened by a bastion-shaped earthwork and smaller 'sconce' covering the approach from Oldbridge.

PRELIMINARIES

Mainly because of its multiple fordable points and its twisting course, with lower banks on the south side, the Boyne was not a good defensive position. The majority of the Jacobite senior officers knew this, and it appears that at a council of war held on the previous evening virtually all those present urged the King not to make a stand here, but to continue his retreat. James, however, claimed that to abandon Dublin without a fight would cause the Irish to 'desert him by degrees', while his honour and prestige would not bear a repeat of the debacle of 1688, and that he was not prepared again to lose all 'without a stroke'.

William was eager for a quick resolution and had pushed the advance, despite very hot weather, at such a pace that his men were exhausted. James had expected his opponent to take four days to march a distance that the Williamites actually covered in half that time. William probably hoped to fight on 30 June, but although his vanguard approached the river at dawn, it took until at least 3 p.m. for all of his army to deploy.

For some reason difficult to understand, although he claimed implausibly that it was to accustom them to being under fire, William drew up two battalions of his Dutch foot and large numbers of horse and dragoons on open ground, leaving them exposed to the fire of the Jacobite artillery for much of the day. This apparent disregard for the lives of his men was a habit of William's. He was to do the same later in the year at Limerick.

Williamite observers admitted that the Jacobites seemed to be deployed 'very advantageously', with the bulk of the army drawn up in two lines, the second one 'a convenient distance' behind the first, where it could provide ready support. A small reserve was placed in the rear of the second line. The only variation to the normal pattern was a regiment deployed forward as a kind of 'forlorn hope' towards Oldbridge. Because some units were hidden in folds in the ground, William was uncertain of the exact strength of the forces facing him, and he feared the Jacobites might have concealed reserves, possibly hidden behind Donore Hill. By the time a deserter eventually provided the Williamites with a reasonably accurate estimate, it was too late in the day to attack.

During the late afternoon an artillery exchange took place between the Jacobite guns and the Williamite batteries sited opposite Yellow Island and further to the east, during which William almost became a casualty. He had ridden down to Oldbridge Ford to investigate the crossing point more closely and had continued for about 200yd upstream, when he was struck a glancing blow by a canonball. Williamite Secretary at War Robert Southwell reported that the Jacobites brought down two 6-pounder guns to aim at the King.

They began to fire and presently one of the balls past so close to his Majesty's back upon the blade of his right shoulder, as to take away his outward coat, chamois waistcoat, shirt and all, and to draw near half a spoonful of blood. The thing was indeed skin-deep, yet it looked as if it were burnt and discoloured big as the palm of one's hand. This accident happened about two o'clock in the afternoon but without other emotion in his Majesty than he rose a little upon his stirrups.[9]

Other accounts suggested that the king was picnicking with some of his staff in sight of the enemy when the shot was fired: 'He said nothing, only these words in Dutch "t'hoot met nadeer" that is to say, "it needs not to come nearer."'[10] William then retired to have his wound dressed.

A French artillery officer with the Oldbridge batteries had ordered the guns to open fire at the group of enemy officers, probably not realising that William was among them. It is tempting to speculate on the effects if William had been killed. Command would have devolved on Schomberg and it is questionable whether, in the political uncertainty that would have followed, he would have persisted in attacking the Jacobite army. Queen Mary, as joint ruler with William, would have succeeded as sole monarch. Though a daughter of James, she had little sympathy with his ideas, and William's political backers would have rallied to her. On the wider European scene, however, without William's unifying efforts the Grand Alliance would almost certainly have collapsed, perhaps creating further opportunities for the French and Jacobites.

When rumours of William's death reached their lines, carried by a deserter, the Jacobites were ecstatic. In Paris the news, speedily dispelled, led to a brief outburst of wild rejoicing. William took prompt steps to reassure his own troops by riding through their ranks. Most of them were deployed around the village of Mellifort, whose location behind a ridge meant that next day the Williamites could march unseen to any of the crossing points of the Boyne.

A council of war was held that evening, and William's commanders were divided in their views. One group, headed by Schomberg, wanted to make a feint frontal attack, while sending the bulk of the army in a flanking move, crossing the Boyne further to the west at Slane, and then moving behind the Jacobite right in order to cut their line of retreat to Dublin. Schomberg felt that the Jacobite position was too strong to be attacked frontally, and only an outflanking move could dislodge them. An alternative plan was put forward by Count Solms. He wanted a concentrated frontal attack at Oldbridge by the entire army. There were obvious disadvantages to this proposal, not least that it would involve an assault uphill against the strongest part of the Jacobite position. Schomberg's plan had a good deal to recommend it. But William had lost faith in the old Marshal, and in the end the meeting settled on a compromise. Lieutenant-General Douglas would take about 8,000 foot 2 miles upriver at dawn and cross the Boyne via the ford at Slane. This force would attack the Jacobite left flank while William led the frontal assault at Oldbridge.

The plan was not settled upon without some debate. General Meinhard Schomberg (son of the Marshal), who would be with the flanking force, wanted it to set out at midnight. This was rejected by William, who did not want the flanking force actually to get in rear of the Jacobite army, fearing that this would render it very vulnerable. He also visualised a three-pronged assault, in which Williamite cavalry would cut the Oldbridge–Donore road to prevent several thousand Jacobite foot stationed in Drogheda from intervening. His intention was that Schomberg and Douglas should cross at Slane at 5 a.m., and that the attacking forces should eventually converge around the centre of the enemy position. However, probably because of fears of treachery, William did not reveal the details of the plan until next morning. This resulted in considerable confusion over both the size and departure time of the flanking force.

Agreement was more easily reached on the identifying field sign to be worn by the Williamite troops. The potential for serious confusion was even greater than was usual in battles fought in the age of black powder. The opposing armies wore a wide variety of uniforms and coat colours, with red coats on both sides. It was decided that the Williamites should wear the distinguishing badge of a green bough or other plant or piece of paper in their hats. The Jacobites had settled on a white field sign.

Although James felt fairly confident in the strength of his position at Oldbridge and Drybridge, regarding it as a 'tolerable good post', he was aware of the danger of the Jacobite army being caught in the large loop that the Boyne formed backing on to the Donore Hill. If the Williamites made a flanking attack the Jacobite line of retreat could be cut. So James ordered Sir Neal O'Neill's dragoon regiment to hold the crossing of the Boyne at Slane. As it would prove, this was too weak a force for the responsibility placed on it.

OPENING MOVES

Dawn on 1 July broke mistily, which was advantageous for William's flanking force. But this benefit was partly eroded by the confusion that ensued. It seems that there were actually two separate detachments of flanking troops. The first detachment consisted of General Meinhard Schomberg's two cavalry brigades, the dragoons of Eppinger's Brigade and Trelawney's Brigade of Foot, accompanied by five guns. This force set off at about 5 a.m., and was followed four hours later by an additional detachment under the Earl of Portland. A total of around 10,000 men were involved.

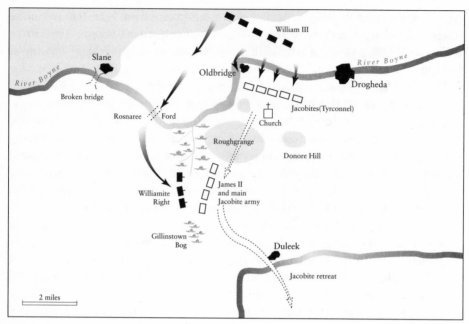

The Boyne

The bridge at Slane proved to have been broken down by the Jacobites, so that Schomberg moved further downstream to cross the Boyne at the ford at Rosnaree. Fighting began at about 6 a.m., as the Williamites encountered O'Neill's 480 dragoons. O'Neill's outposts on the high ground on the south bank of the river gave warning of the enemy approach, but Schomberg led a force of dragoons down to the ford, and in a short action drove the Jacobites back, supposedly for a distance of 2 miles. In fact resistance by the Jacobite dragoons, some of whom seem to have fought on horseback as cavalry, was stiffer than Williamite accounts gave them credit for. The Jacobites seem to have resisted for about two hours, and 'did wonders', not breaking until their commander received a mortal wound from a shot in the thigh.

The scale of Jacobite resistance was sufficiently worrying for William to dispatch the second contingent of troops, under Douglas, to reinforce Schomberg. This meant that something like 12,000 men, a third of William's total strength, were now engaged in the flanking move. A considerable proportion were in fact wasted, as it would take three hours for Douglas to link up with Schomberg.

However, William's errors were counterbalanced by those of King James, who was unaware that what he believed to be his dangerously open left flank was in fact protected by a deep ravine that would block the approach of any flanking force from Rosnaree. In his council of war the previous evening, James had decided to move at least part of his left wing eastwards to cover the Rosnaree Ford, leaving the bulk of his foot at Oldbridge. The move did not begin until dawn, amid confusion in which many of the Irish troops assumed that it was the beginning of a retreat.

When the action at Rosnaree began, James concluded that William was preparing to cross there in strength in a bid to cut the Jacobite line of retreat to Dublin. His reaction was to send the front line of his left wing, consisting of Lauzan's 7,000 French infantry regiments and two regiments of horse under Sarsfield, to counter the threat. For a time both Lauzan and Douglas were marching on parallel courses on opposite banks of the Boyne. When he reached the high ground overlooking Rosnaree, Lauzan

saw that the dragoons that I had left at the bridge of Slane had been pushed back and that the enemy had already crossed the ford this side of Slane and that they were passing in columns, cavalry, infantry and cannons, either making for Dublin or for our rear. The King came there and ordered us to adopt battle line, moving my left to make space on my right, resting on the river. Then I could either shadow the march of the enemy towards Dublin, or attack there, as soon as Milord Tyrconnel, who commanded the left wing, arrived.[11]

BATTLE FOR OLDBRIDGE

James, seeing Douglas's detachment moving to reinforce Meinhard Schomberg at Rosnaree, concluded that William had committed the bulk of his army in an enveloping movement, and made a hasty decision to send almost two-thirds of his army westwards to counter it. As a result only 7,000 Jacobites remained at Oldbridge to confront over half of the allied army – almost 20,000 men. Originally the Jacobites had posted only two foot regiments, those of Clanricarde and the Earl of Antrim, at Oldbridge, but these had been reinforced by five more infantry battalions, including one from James's Guards, three cavalry regiments, those of Tyrconnel, John Parker and Hugh Sutherland, two troops of the Lifeguard under the Duke of Berwick, and Dongan's Dragoons. In all, Tyrconnel had about 1,500 horse, 800 dragoons and 4,000 foot, with Richard Hamilton in overall command of the latter.

The Williamite artillery opened fire against Oldbridge at about 8 a.m., but it was two hours later before the tide was low enough for the allied foot to begin to cross. During this time the allied forces were moving slowly towards the river in preparation for a two-pronged attack. The first force advanced through what would later be known as King William's Glen, which concealed their approach from the enemy on the far bank of the river. The second column, mainly cavalry, which was advancing towards the ford at Drybridge, also proved difficult to spot.

So far, the errors of the two commanders in committing such a large proportion of their forces in operations to the west had to some extent cancelled each other out, but James had, ultimately, fatally compromised himself by leaving such a small number of troops at Oldbridge. The Jacobite redeployment had almost been completed when the attack at Oldbridge began. Fortunately for James, Meinhard Schomberg had been slow in pressing his advantage after securing the Rosnaree crossing, so that both forces arrived at the Roughgrange ravine at the same time.

While this was happening, the Jacobite right wing horse and the two infantry brigades on the right of the first line were moving down the slope closer to Oldbridge Ford. They were not intended to hold the position indefinitely, but to act as a rearguard while the guns and baggage began pulling back towards Dublin, after which the right wing was to join the remainder of the Jacobite army to face what was seen as the main enemy threat.

As the early morning mist cleared, the day grew hotter, the troops marching to Roughgrange sweltering amid the dense clouds of dust raised by their progress.

It quickly became apparent to Tyrconnel, left in command of the right wing, that the allies were about to launch a full-scale attack on Oldbridge. Proceedings opened with a heavy artillery bombardment of the Jacobite positions. William's plan was to follow this softening-up attack with an assault by his best troops, the Dutch Guards and the Enniskilleners. The attack was headed by the Dutch, led by their grenadier companies. As the Dutch crossed the river the Jacobites at first held their fire. The Dutch Guards

> were the first that took the river. The Irish had lined the houses, breastworks and hedges beyond the river with my Lord Tyrconnel's Regiment of Foot Guards and some other companies. They had posted also seven regiments of foot, about 150yd backwards, who stood drawn up behind some little hills, to shelter them from our cannon, which played all this while; besides these, were two troops of guards, four troops of my Lord Tyrconnel's and four troops of Parker's Regiment of Horse, posted in the same manner . . . The Dutch beat a march till they got to the river's side and then the drums ceasing, in they went, some eight or ten abreast being presently almost up to the middle of the stream, for they stopped the current by their sudden motion and this made it deeper than usual.[12]

Another eyewitness wrote that: 'The enemy did not fire until our men were towards the middle of the river, and then a whole peal of shot came from the hedges, breastworks, houses and all about, yet we could not perceive any fall but one, and another staggered.'[13]

The Dutch Guards did not reply to the enemy fire, but pressed on and climbed the further bank of the river, their fifers striking up 'Lillibullero'. As they crested the bank, the Irish, according to one account, 'rose up from behind the walls and gave one fire upon them and ran away'.[14]

Tyrconnel ordered Colonel William Dorrington with James's Regiment of Guards to reinforce the troops already in Oldbridge, with the rest of the foot deployed on the south bank of the Boyne to the east of Oldbridge. Some of the Irish infantry may indeed have fled fairly quickly, but this did not apply to all of them. Many of the raw recruits had been shaken by the ferocity of the allied artillery bombardment as it 'played furiously upon the Irish trench, beat it down in several places and killed some men in it; they also fired one round at the slated house with such effect that they fled out of it in great precipitation, our artillery all the time continuing their thunder so vehemently against the trench that the soldiers did not peep over it'.[15]

De Morsier, a Huguenot serving with the Dutch Guards, described the opening moments of the action. At 9 a.m. the troops were just beginning breakfast when the order came to stand-to. The no doubt grumbling Guardsmen were forced to:

drop everything and form up in battle order. Not knowing what was happening we marched straight away, leaving our baggage behind and tents standing; only our little band marched, while the rest of the army watched us defile.

We came to where we had been posted the day before and went down by a sunken road below the hills on the river bank: I asked many times what did our manoeuvre mean and if we were going to attack the enemy in this formation. My lieutenant replied that he knew nothing, others replied likewise. At length we went on and the hautboys were called for but could not be found anywhere. Coming even further downhill we saw without any more doubt that we were going to attack, and our twisting road straightened out so that the enemy could now see us. As we did we doubled pace and fell into a big ditch half-filled with mud and had great difficulty in pulling ourselves out. We had a chance to wash when we jumped into the river to face the enemy on the other side blazing away with their muskets in a terrific fire. That did not hold us back and we fell on them, as much with musket fire as with bayonets, and drove them off. Our French [Huguenot] battalions and others followed us close while the King had a battery of cannon fire on the enemy army.[16]

The Irish did not break as quickly as he suggests, but held their ground for about fifteen minutes, until the Dutch Guards came close to them, and then made an orderly withdrawal, rallying in a field of corn to the south of Oldbridge. The Duke of Berwick suggested that Clanricarde's Regiment of Foot did not break until it had suffered 150 casualties. Led by Richard Hamilton, the remainder of the Irish foot, who had been sheltered to some extent from enemy fire by a hedge, counter-attacked, although it is unclear when exactly this happened. One account suggested that it took place when only a third of the Dutch Guards were actually across the river.

The Irish closed to within a pike's length (about 16ft) of their opponents, and were received with heavy musketry. The contest continued for up to a quarter of an hour, the Dutch being engaged by at least one battalion of the Royal Guards. Major Thomas Arthur of its First Battalion ran a Dutch officer through the thigh before being mortally wounded. It seems most likely that the Royal Guards were the only Irish foot actually to close with the enemy, while most of the remainder hung back. According to one account:

> the Dutch left the village and formed themselves about the middle of the field of battle. Upon this a much superior number of Irish foot soldiers came against them with a great shout. As they came on they were much galled by our artillery, and several times put into disorder. When they approached within the usual distance, they stood a great while, until the Dutch and they had fired three or four discharges at one another, and then retreated into the smoke, which saved them from being cannonaded as they went off.[17]

Once the village itself had been cleared, some of the Dutch went in pursuit of Clanricarde's men, driving them from the second line of hedges, while the remainder of the Dutch Guards deployed to their left, closer to the river. The Ulster foot probably crossed close behind the Dutch, while the Huguenot regiments of Melloniere, Caillemotte and Canbon began to cross about 100yd downstream. Soon afterwards, the Nassau Brigade also crossed nearby.

The Irish infantry in the vicinity had now effectively shot their bolt. The Dutch Guards and the leading Huguenot battalion, with around seventy casualties, had suffered fairly severely at the hands of the Irish Guards. The Irish counter-attack had been mounted in the face of heavy enemy artillery fire. Hardly surprisingly for such inexperienced troops, some of the Irish had faltered and not closed with the enemy. A French officer, Boisseleau, noted: 'our Irish never experienced fire before and that took them by surprise . . . I led them three times to the attack. The truth is that the enemy was stronger and their firepower heavier.'[17]

The Jacobites were even more inferior in firepower than the relative numbers engaged on each side might suggest, for many Irish units were very short of muskets in good working order. The Williamites may have had as much as a four to one advantage in musketry. But the Irish Guards' loss of about 100 men bears witness to the hard fight that they put up.

With the infantry beaten, any chance of turning back the allied troops now rested with the Irish cavalry. It was customary for French cavalry of the period to fire their pistols or carbines as they attacked, in an attempt to unhorse opponents and cause confusion in their formations; after that they 'charged home', sword in hand. English and Dutch cavalry often relied rather more on firepower. At the Boyne the Jacobite cavalry seem to have followed French tactics.

As the first of the Irish cavalry bore down on them, the Dutch Guards hastily formed up to meet them. They were given little time, as the Jacobite cavalry took advantage of hollows and folds in the ground to approach, undetected, as close as possible. Some accounts suggest that the Dutch formed square, and that their defences were strengthened by stakes, pointed at both ends, and known as 'Swedish Feathers', planted in the ground to form a hedge against the attackers. It is more likely the Dutch remained in line and relied on musketry and bayonets.

William himself was reportedly alarmed, exclaiming:

'my poor guards, my poor guards, my poor guards' as the enemy were coming down upon them but when he saw them stand their ground and fire by platoons, so that the horse were forced to run away in great disorder, he breathed out, as people used to do after holding their breath upon a fright or suspense, and said he had seen the guards do that which he had not seen foot do in his life.[19]

At this stage the Irish cavalry seem to have made three or four attacks, showing such bravery in the face of heavy fire that their opponents, in most cases probably unfairly, accused the troopers of being drunk on brandy. Drunk or sober, the Irish Jacobite cavalry were formidable opponents. They numbered among their commanders very experienced officers, including some English and Scottish regular soldiers. The English included Dominic Sheldon, who was in overall command of the horse engaged, and three of the four cavalry colonels present, Parker, Sutherland and the Duke of Berwick.

The cavalry attacked in loose formation, riding up close to the enemy, sword in hand. In such situations the outcome rested largely on a test of will. If infantry retained their formation, and kept up a steady fire while presenting a wall of bayonets or pikes, there was not usually a great deal of harm that cavalry could do them, and the horsemen could only mill around, ineffectively stabbing at their opponents while they and their mounts were shot down. If, however, the infantry lost their nerve and their formation, they rapidly became a panic-stricken mob, easy prey to their mounted pursuers.

In order to bring this about, cavalry had to create a gap in the infantry formation that could then be exploited.

Morsier was involved in the encounter between the Jacobite horse and the Dutch Guards:

We had more to do with King James Lifeguards who tried to knock us down, the musketry covered us with such a dense pall of smoke that the King on the ridge, could not see us and said (so Monsieur Bolens de Collambert a Swiss halberdier, has said to me) 'My regiment is entirely beaten!' And an instant later, when the smoke cleared he exclaimed: 'Thank God, I see them again.'[20]

According to another account:

At the first push the first rank only fired and then fell on their faces, loading their muskets again as they lay on the ground; at the next charge they fired a volley of three ranks, then, at the next, the first rank got up and fired again, which being received by a choice squadron of the enemy . . . they fell upon the Dutch as having spent all their front fire, but the two rear ranks drew up in two platoons, and flanked the enemy across, and the rest, screwing their swords [bayonets] into their muskets, received the charge with all imaginable bravery and in a minute dismounted them all.[21]

The Dutch Guards had been deployed in a wheatfield with ditches and ridges, all of which hindered cavalry attacks. The Dutch were able to fire both frontally and from their flanks, and kept up a steady platoon fire. The Irish cavalry, on the other hand, stood their best chance of success in their first charge, with steadily diminishing prospects thereafter. The first critical attack was reportedly led by Tyrconnel himself, at the head of his Lifeguard. But when this was repulsed, the vigour of succeeding attacks was much less. By the end of the engagement with the Dutch Guards, Jacobite horsemen were failing to close with the enemy, but retiring after firing a few pistol shots.

The brunt of the fighting was undertaken by Tyrconnel's, Parker's, and the Guards' Regiments. Of these, Parker's Regiment seems to have suffered most with only 30 of its 300 men unscathed at the end of the battle. Sutherland's Regiment, on the other hand, an Irish unit with a Scottish commander, held back from the first charge and came off lightly.

Although the Dutch Guards had succeeded in holding their ground, other troops fared worse. Hanmer's English Regiment of the Nassau Brigade and the Brandenburg Brigade were hit by a Jacobite cavalry squadron about 200yd downstream of Oldbridge. Forty of the attackers broke right through the enemy ranks, while others closely engaged Hanmer's Regiment, although only three of the latter are listed as killed. The Huguenots, however, suffered a rough handling. Richard Hamilton had attempted to counter-attack them with some foot but, finding himself deserted, took command of a squadron of cavalry and made a renewed assault. Caillemotte was mortally wounded and was carried off the field still calling out to his men: 'A la gloire, mes enfants! A la gloire!' Callinet's regiment seems actually to have been broken.

Losses were far from one-sided. The Irish Guards cavalry suffered heavy losses from enemy fire while attempting to rally in Oldbridge, possibly after breaking through the Dutch Guards, while a few horsemen may actually have reached the north bank of the Boyne before being shot down. Out of Hamilton's squadron of sixty men, only six or eight were still fit for action.

While the Jacobite cavalry were being rallied, the Duke of Schomberg crossed the river to try to reorganise the broken Huguenots. He called out: 'Allons, Messires, voilà vos persecuteurs!' But then he and his staff found themselves surrounded by about forty Jacobite troopers.

> Tyrconnel's Guards, seized with fury and mad to strike blows of desperation suddenly returned to the charge and with an overpowering impetus broke and pierced right through La Melloniere's Regiment and tried to block those still in the water from crossing. But however great their activity and bravery, most of them were soon killed and the survivors to remove themselves from such a hot spot made a small detour, a caracole, and pushed close to the village where Monsieur de Schomberg was. Unhappily they came across his path and slashed him twice with sabres on the head and then, most say, shot him with a pistol.[22]

The Jacobites claimed that Schomberg was killed by a shot fired by Guards trooper Brian O'Toole, although others suggested that the fatal shot was fired accidently by a member of La Melloniere's Regiment.

When news of Schomberg's death reached William, the King reacted with marked indifference, although not as brutally as when he heard of the death of George Walker, the Derry clergyman who had been joint governor during the siege. Walker had accompanied some of the Enniskilleners into action and had been killed, causing William to remark: 'Fool that he was, what had he to do there?'

Some of the Enniskillen units had been heavily engaged; St John's Regiment, crossing the Boyne to support the Dutch Guards and Caillemotte, repulsed a flank attack by Irish cavalry. George Hamilton's (ex-Thomas Lloyd's) and Zachariah Tiffen's Regiments were also among the first units to cross the Boyne:

> It was not until the attackers were in the middle of the stream that they became aware of the danger of the enterprise on which they were embarked. Up till then little more than half of the hostile army had been

seen, now whole regiments of horse and foot seemed to start out of the ground, and a wild shout of defiance rose from the Meath shore.[23]

In all there seem to have been three or four major cavalry attacks. The first was the frontal attack on the Dutch Guards; second were the assaults on Hamner's and Calliemotte's Regiments, during which some Jacobite troopers may have got as far as Oldbridge. Third came the attack on the flank of St John's Regiment, which was not pressed home and may have been followed by a fourth, equally hesitant, attack. Despite the ferocity of the fighting, Williamite losses seem to have been light. Most severe were those of the Dutch Guards, who lost 100 men, although some of these fell in the infantry engagement. Hanmer lost three, St John about a dozen, and eighteen of Caillemotte's Regiment fell.

Even after their charges had petered out, the presence of the Jacobite cavalry prevented the allies from advancing without the support of their own horse. Meanwhile, at around 11 a.m., further downstream, at the eastern end of Yellow Island, 7,000 Danish troops were also crossing the river. They met no real opposition, but the water here was deeper, indeed believed by the Jacobites not to be fordable. The Duke of Württemberg, commanding the Danish troops, later reported to William:

Some squadrons at once appeared to dispute the crossing and charged us. We replied with a great volley which so astonished them that they retired. Where Your Majesty's Guards crossed the water was so deep that it came up to their armpits. While we were marching out of the water a squadron of dragoons came up and charged the Guards. I allowed only the grenadiers and some platoons to charge.[24]

The Danes held their muskets and ammunition over their heads in order to keep them dry, and suffered only three men wounded from the enemy fire. The dragoons who opposed them were probably Lord Clare's 'Yellow' Dragoons (so called from the colour of their coats), who seem to have been fairly quickly repulsed. Another attack was made by Tyrconnel's and Galmoy's Regiments of Horse, which broke a few of the Danes, although the majority held their ground.

As more Williamite troops crossed the river, widening their bridgehead, the Jacobites were becoming overstretched. Their infantry were beaten, and the cavalry, despite energetic efforts by Sheldon and the Duke of Berwick, whose own 200-strong Lifeguard suffered almost 100 per cent casualties, had largely shot their bolt. The French artillery officer at Oldbridge, Captain Laisne, believing that the situation was now hopeless, ordered his guns to be limbered up and was escorted from the field by some of the 'Yellow' Dragoons. Some Danish cavalry had crossed to the left of their infantry, but were routed by a charge by Dongan's Dragoons, although Walter Dongan himself was killed by a cannon shot during the action. Once across the river, the Danish infantry had time to re-form and easily repulsed two ineffective cavalry attacks.

It was now about noon, and the battle had been raging for almost two hours. A force of about 1,200 cavalry under Godert de Ginkel, the Dutch professional soldier who had gained William's confidence by his ruthless suppression of a mutiny of English troops at Harwich in the previous year, was supposed to cross the river at Mill Ford in order to support the foot, but had been delayed, possibly because Ginkel wanted the Irish cavalry, so far as possible, to be engaged elsewhere before he attempted to climb the steep southern bank of the river. William, meanwhile, realised that the battle had reached a crisis which required his own intervention if it were to be resolved in the allies' favour. He still had 1,000 horse and 6,000 foot in reserve, and decided to lead them across himself.

WILLIAM'S ATTACK

William's crossing was less romantic than his admirers have often suggested. He almost certainly rode a brown rather than a white horse, he became stuck in the mud, and then suffered an attack of asthma. He was eventually brought ashore on the southern bank of the river by an Enniskillen trooper.

However, William quickly recovered and got his own cavalry into action against a dwindling Jacobite force that probably totalled no more than around 1,000 horse and dragoons. The allies launched a poorly coordinated attack on Donore Hill, which proved to be both confused and hard fought. De Bostaquet, a trooper in Schomberg's Regiment of Horse, took part:

> the king having passed the river, placed himself at the head of our squadron and told Belcastel to charge in support of a squadron of Enniskilleners. The commander of that squadron did not press forward and the said Belcastel made us advance, withholding our fire, so that we advanced on the enemy sword in hand. The enemy had spread thirty or forty grenadiers along the length of a ditch who fired, we admired the King's coolness as he passed between them and us, sustaining the volley without breaking his horse's pace. The ditch impeded our passage to the extent that it would have been impossible to cross in formation without breaking it down. However Belcastel had us pass the obstacle wherever we could. He found a gap on our left where le Sieur de Moliens and myself entered. I was saluted by two pistol shots that missed me. He sent Enniskillens after us. I would have stabbed one who appeared near me except he shouted out that he was an Enniskillener. I recognised him from

the green mark he wore in his hat . . . Happily I was dragged from this skirmish by two of these Enniskilleners, who appeared between the two cavaliers who had fired on me. We clashed with the enemy in a melee and broke them but Belcastel, the commander of our squadron, being seriously wounded, Varenques struck down from behind, the wind and the ground being against us, our squadron retreated in disorder . . .

The king rode up to us and admonished us for charging so clumsily. M de Gatigny, his chief aide, told me some time afterwards that we had worked ourselves into a state of fury at the enemy and even though he cried out to us several times to halt in the name of the King we had rushed on . . . My comrade Vervillon was killed there, Hubac and several others killed and wounded. God protected me; my doublet was pierced in two places . . .[25]

Much of the confusion seems to have been caused by the Enniskilleners. William found himself in the midst of them and made strenuous efforts to rally them:

It was about a mile further on the top of the hill [Donore] where were some old walls, that the enemy had well lined with firelocks. Here his Majesty led up some Dutch troops, but before they had got in, the Inniskilleners had made an assault on the other side, and did very bravely at first, but espying another great party whom they took for the enemy, just ready to surround them, they began to fly, and did actually put in disorder the Dutch horse and all others that stood in their way. The place was unfortunately full of holes and dung pits, and the passage narrow, but above all the dust and smoke quite blinded them. His Majesty was here in the crowd of all, drawing his sword and animating those that fled to follow him. His danger was great among the enemy's guns that killed thirty of the Inniskilleners on the spot. Nay one of the Inniskilleners came with a pistol cocked to his Majesty till he called out 'what, are you angry with your friends?'[26]

The already dire confusion increased when the Enniskilleners and a Danish regiment charged each other by mistake. A sharp clash took place to the left of Donore in a narrow lane, where Ginkel in a 'sharp dispute' lasting half an hour eventually pushed back some opposing Jacobite horse led by Sheldon.

The Irish horse seem to have mounted a final rearguard action near Platin Castle, about a mile south of Donore. Apparently the Enniskilleners made another botched attack, and Richard Hamilton, commanding the Irish force, led a counter-attack, but pressed it too far.

General Hamilton, in order to favour the retreat of the Irish and French Foot, drew up a Body of Horse very artfully near Plattin Castle, in an

James II, c. 1690. (*Getty Images*)

William III by Godfrey Kneller. (*National Gallery of Ireland*)

King Louis XIV by Hyacinthe Rigaud. (*Getty Images*)

Richard Talbot, Earl and Duke of Tyrconnel, Lord Lieutenant of Ireland, by John Bullfinch. (*National Gallery of Ireland*)

Scottish Royalist and Jacobite John Graham of Claverhouse. (*Getty Images*)

Sir Cloudesley Shovell by Michael Dahl, 1702. (*National Maritime Museum, London, Greenwich Hospital Collection*)

Patrick Sarsfield, Earl of Lucan, attributed to Hyacinthe Rigaud. (*National Gallery of Ireland*)

Godert de Ginkel by Godfrey Kneller. (*National Gallery of Ireland*)

William III of Orange (left) and Frederick, Duke of Schomberg, *c.* 1675. (*Getty Images*)

Koning Iacobus .II. belegert Londonderry   Le Roy Iaques .II. assiege Londonderry
                                                              Adr. schoonebeck exc. s

King James II Besieges Londonderry, engraving by Adriaan Schoonebeck. (*Getty Images*)

James II, former King of England, and the Earl d'Avaux defeated by the Protestants at *Enniskillen*, etching, Dutch School. (*National Gallery of Ireland*)

General view of Dunkeld Cathedral, situated on the banks of the Tay. (*Crown copyright reproduced courtesy of Historic Scotland*)

The Battle of the Boyne by Benjamin West, 1690. (*Getty Images*)

The Battle of Barfleur, 19 May 1692, by Richard Paton, eighteenth century. (*National Maritime Museum, London, Greenwich Hospital Collection*)

The Battle of the Boyne by Jan Wyck. (*National Gallery of Ireland*)

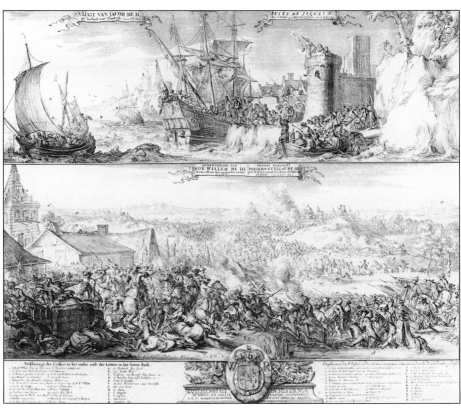

The Battle of the Boyne below the Flight of King James II from Ireland on 12 July 1690, etching by Romeyn de Hooghe. (*National Gallery of Ireland*)

John Churchill, 1st Duke of Marlborough. (*Getty Images*)

Edward Russell by Thomas Gibson, *c.* 1715. (*National Maritime Museum, London, Greenwich Hospital Collection*)

Following page: *The Celebrated Battle off Cape La Hogue.* (*Royal Naval Museum*)

Athlone Castle. (*Courtesy of Athlone Town Council, Heritage Island, Dublin*)

The Celebrated BATTLE off Cape LA HOGUE
in which Admiral Rook burnt the French Admiral's Ship called
Rising Sun, with Twelve other large Men of War, May 20. 1692

Grainger inv. et sc.

enclosed field, into which there was only one entrance, through a gap made by Pioneers. The other eight troops of Inniskilling Horse, commanded by Col. Wolseley, not thinking it necessary to wait for help, and being desirous to be sharers of the transactions of that day, went on with a resolution to attack this party though under very great disadvantage.[27]

Thanks to a mistaken order, the Enniskilleners were disordered, and Hamilton took advantage of this with a counter-charge. However, William was approaching with his main cavalry force and quickly drove the Jacobites back. Hamilton was captured and was near to being summarily dispatched until spared by William, who scornfully reminded him of his parole-breaking.

THE END OF THE BATTLE

Meanwhile a stand-off continued at Roughgrange. At about noon King James received word from Tyrconnel that the latter was under heavy attack, and could not follow the rest of the army to Roughgrange. The King's reaction was to attack the enemy in front of him 'forthwith', but Sarsfield and Brigadier Thomas Maxwell pointed out that it would be impossible to cross the ravine with the enemy so close. At this point, while the Jacobites hesitated, the dust created by Douglas's approaching column was sighted. James concluded that the enemy were moving to cut him off from Dublin and that the only way of avoiding this was to get back to Duleek before them.

The army moved off in two columns, based on the two lines into which it had been formed. The French foot led the first column. The retreat was harassed by enemy horse, but it was because of a failure of morale that the formation began to break up. The second column speeded up and began to crowd into the first. As the troops approached Duleek, Lauzan became convinced that the army was about to be caught between the jaws of a pincer attack. He urged James to escape with a cavalry escort.

The King's departure proved a fatal blow to the Jacobites' already faltering resolve. The rout started when Berwick's Horse charged some Irish foot, including the Grand Prior's Regiment, mistaking them for the enemy. Stevens described how:

The Lord Grand Prior's whereof I served was then in Duleek lane, enclosed with high banks, marching ten in rank. The horse came on so unexpected and with such speed, some firing their pistols, that we had no time to receive or shun them, but all supposing them to be the enemy (as indeed they were no better to us) took to their heels, no officer being able to stop the men even after they were broken, and the horse past . . . looking about

I wondered what madness possessed our men to run so violently nobody pursuing them. What few men I could see I called to, no commands being of force, begging them to stand together and repair to their colours, the danger being in dispersing; but all in vain, some throwing away their arms, others even their coats and shoes to run the lighter . . . I thought the calamity had not been so general until viewing the hills about us I perceived them covered with the soldiers of several regiments, all scattered like sheep running before the wolf, but so thick they seemed to cover the sides and tops of the hills.[28]

About half of the Irish foot, around 5,000 to 6,000 men, broke, in many cases abandoning their arms and equipment in their flight. But about three-quarters of the army escaped intact, mainly because of the Williamites' hesitant pursuit. A significant role was played by the French infantry, especially Zurlauben's Regiment, who not only presented a firm front as rearguard, but also prevented many Irish from quitting their ranks by threatening to shoot them.

The Battle of the Boyne was the only occasion that William and James met in battle, and the only full-scale battle in which James ever personally commanded. William had proved himself an excellent leader in battle, although his skills as a general were less impressive. James, however, had failed on both counts. His old paralysis and indecision, together with what could be represented as a degree of cowardice towards the end, had been only too apparent. He had been comprehensively out-thought and out-fought by the enemy.

The Battle of the Boyne was a major success for William, but it was not the decisive victory he had hoped for. Jacobite losses probably amounted to around 2,000 men, including 800 dead, but the Irish army had not been destroyed. William had lost his best chance of a quick victory.

NINE

· · · · · · · · ·

The Irish Recovery

THE RETREAT

King James himself brought the news of defeat to Dublin. Outstripping his fleeing troops, James, escorted by his Lifeguard, rode into the Irish capital the same evening and, reportedly 'in a manner stunned',[1] retired to the Castle, where no meal had been prepared for his unexpected return. A meeting of the Privy Council was called that night, at which James allegedly denounced his Irish troops, who had 'basely' fled. 'Henceforth I am never more determined to head an Irish army, and do now resolve to shift for myself, and so, gentlemen, must you.'[2]

Next morning, in a repetition of the panic that had overcome him in 1688, and suffering from the same symptomatic nosebleeds, James rode out of Dublin. Although he had not given up hope of regaining his English throne, he had abandoned the possibility of doing so via Ireland. On 4 July he embarked on a French ship in Kinsale and sailed for Brest, never again to set foot in his British kingdoms.

James was not greatly missed by the majority of his Irish subjects. To the soldiers he was henceforth known as *Seamus an chaca* – 'James the beshitten'.[3]

It seemed unlikely that James's cause in Ireland would long survive his departure. Throughout the evening of 1 July, the Irish army was dissolving. John Stevens noted that when the Duke of Berwick halted the troops still with him, although the colours of five or six regiments were present, no more than 100 men mustered under them. Next morning Stevens and his companions marched towards Dublin, 'we scarce the shadows of regiments'.[4] The Jacobites halted outside Dublin, the colours being planted on high ground to act as a rallying point. By the end of the day the Lord Grand Prior's Regiment mustered a total of 100. By now Tyrconnel and Lauzan, left in command with Berwick following James's flight, knew that the only hope of prolonging resistance and rebuilding the army lay in retreating to the west and defending the line of the River Shannon.

It was doubtful how much of the army would get there. When the order to march west arrived, Stevens's men began to defect, so that within quarter of an hour only twenty were left with the colours. The Lord Grand Prior's Regiment had joined Lord Kilmallock's Foot, which was still intact as it had been in Dublin throughout the battle. But

The whole day was a continual series of alarms, the greatest reached us within less than two miles of the Naas, where Kilmallock's officers attempting to draw up their men to line the hedges, the confusion and terror of the soldiers who had never seen the enemy was such they were forced in all haste to march away. It was ridiculous to see the brother of the traitor [O'Donnell] who had the name of lieutenant-colonel reformed in our regiment, pretend to take authority upon him here. And order us to line the hedges, when at that time our whole strength was but six musketeers, eight pikes, four ensigns and one lieutenant besides myself . . . For our comfort no enemy was within twenty miles of us, but fear never thinks itself out of danger. We followed Kilmallock's men with such speed it had been hard for an enemy to overtake us, and that regiment though till then untouched was in such a consternation that when they came to the Naas they were not 100 strong.[5]

Stevens and an ensign lost touch with the remnants of the regiment and, having spent the night in exhausted sleep on the floor of an empty house, attempted, both riding on one lame horse, to catch up with their comrades. But the horse was commandeered by some of Tyrconnel's officers. Left on foot, Stevens and the ensign

attacked a village with design to force away a horse under the colour of pressing, but in reality was not much better than robbery. But the women of the village, setting up the cry, soon gave the alarm to all the men that were abroad, who flocking in with their roperies and half pikes had put us to the rout again, but that I had my leading staff which being longer than their weapons terrified and made them give way where I came, but whatever was gained I was forced to loose to protect my companion, who having no weapon but his sword, was too hard set, and doubtless had he been furnished with a half pike we had got the better of the whole village and forced away two horses. As the case stood we were obliged to quit our pretensions and march off without horses, but not without some peals of curses for our good intentions, and the good bangs I had given some of the men in the skirmish.[6]

Stevens and his companion eventually reached the rallying point at Limerick on 11 July.

LOST OPPORTUNITY

There is little doubt that if William had acted rapidly in the days immediately following the Boyne he could have broken Jacobite Ireland. He occupied Dublin without resistance on 4 July, but Williamite elation over the victory at the Boyne was tempered on 8 July when news of the French naval victory at Beachy Head arrived. The King feared that an invasion of England might follow, and this caused further delays. William also lost what might have been his best chance of bringing the war to a quick conclusion when he issued an uncompromising declaration which, intended to drive a wedge between the Irish leadership and the rest of the population, in fact offered so little that it actually stiffened resistance. This uncompromising approach made most of the Irish, whatever their view of King James, determined to fight on in the hope of at least securing better terms.

William's declaration also helped damp down dissension among the Jacobite leadership, now gathered at Limerick, their de facto capital, which, with a peacetime population of 12,000, was the third largest town in Ireland. Tyrconnel claimed that Limerick could only hold out against a determined attack for three days. With memories of the sack of Drogheda by Cromwell in 1649, Tyrconnel was anxious to avoid Limerick suffering a similar fate. However, his proposal to seek terms met with a storm of protest from the army officers, headed by Patrick Sarsfield. They were able to cite William's own uncompromising declaration as evidence of the need to fight on in order to at least gain better terms, and for the moment their views carried the day.

The French commander, Lauzan, was principally concerned to extricate his own troops from what he deemed to be a lost cause. He retired with the bulk of his men to Galway to await ships to carry them back to France, and proposed that the best of the Irish regiments should accompany them.

Although distracted by the news of Beachy Head, William still hoped to conclude the Irish war before the end of the year. The Scottish professional soldier Major-General James Douglas was ordered to capture the town of Athlone and its bridge over the Shannon and to open a road into Connaught.

FIRST SIEGE OF ATHLONE

In the meantime William was engaged in mopping-up operations designed to complete his control of the province of Leinster and the eastern Irish seaboard. His immediate objective, after finding that the enemy had evacuated the port of Wexford, was the town of Waterford. Major-General Percy Kirke, the rather questionable hero of the relief of Derry, was tasked with taking Waterford. It was less well defended than Kirke believed, and Colonel Barrett, its governor, asked for terms on 23 July and, after some negotiation, was allowed to take his men to the nearest Jacobite garrison at Mallow.

Waterford harbour was still dominated by Duncannon Fort, the last remaining Jacobite garrison in Leinster. Its governor, Colonel Michael 'Brute' Burke, at first was defiant, but the arrival of Sir Cloudesley Shovell and his naval squadron, with the threat of bombardment from the sea, changed Burke's mind, and he surrendered, being allowed to march with all arms and possessions to Limerick.

William now handed over command to Count de Solms, who was to march on Limerick, and left for Dublin. But, learning en route that there was no sign of the French following up their success at Beachy Head, he decided to resume command and conclude the Irish war himself. There were disquieting signs that this was not going to be so easy as William anticipated. On arriving before Athlone on 17 July, and summoning its garrison to surrender, Major-General Douglas met a firm rebuff.

The Governor of Athlone was a remarkable veteran soldier, Colonel Richard Grace, now aged about 70. Grace's career spanned the English Civil War, during which he had fought in Prince Rupert's Regiment of Horse at Marston Moor, as a guerrilla leader in Ireland against Cromwell, and in command of Irish troops in the service of Spain.[7] Grace remained a devoted supporter of the House of Stuart, and in 1689 raised one of the first regiments of foot for the Jacobite army. He commanded a brigade of foot (consisting of his own, Art and Hugh MacMahon's Regiments) in the Boyne campaign, was evidently able to extricate them relatively intact, and was sent to garrison Athlone.

Athlone consisted of two walled towns, the 'English' town on the eastern bank of the River Shannon and the 'Irish' town on the western side, in Connaught. They were linked by a stone bridge. Grace, with only 1,500 men, and with the defences of Athlone in some disrepair, decided against trying to hold the 'English' town and, breaking down two of the arches of the bridge, retreated to make his stand in the 'Irish' town and Athlone Castle.

Major-General Douglas had around 3,000 men and an artillery train consisting of two 12-pounders, ten lighter guns and two small mortars. It was a barely adequate force, and its chances were further reduced by a shortage of ammunition and by low morale. Grace's response to the Williamite summons has passed into Irish legend. He fired his pistol over the head of Douglas's emissary and retorted: 'These are my terms, these only will I give or receive, and when all my provisions are consumed, I will eat my old boots.'[8]

Grace had good reason for confidence. Unable to cross the Shannon, Douglas could not isolate the defenders of Athlone, and although he commenced an artillery bombardment his guns were too few and too light to make any impression on the Jacobite defences, which Grace had strengthened by earthworks covering the western end of the bridge. Grace's infantry brigade was supported by nine troops of dragoons and two of horse, with Sarsfield's redoubtable cavalry likely to attack any Williamite detachments that managed to cross the Shannon.

After a week, Douglas's chief gunner had been killed, several of his pieces had been put out of action, and his ammunition was exhausted without result. He had suffered between 300 and 400 casualties, and his force was further stricken by sickness and lack of supplies. The final blow to Douglas's hopes came on 24 July, with a report that Sarsfield was approaching with 15,000 horse to raise the siege. Greatly exaggerated though the rumour was, it was enough to cause Douglas to abandon the siege and pull back to join William and the main army, now before Limerick.

ADVANCE ON LIMERICK

William was not overly concerned by the failure to take Athlone. Once Limerick fell, he expected resistance in the remainder of Ireland to collapse.

It was natural for William, having taken the decision to remain in Ireland, to take charge of operations against Limerick. The defences were said to be in a state of disrepair, a view shared by Lauzan, who reported gloomily to Paris that Limerick could be taken by a bombardment of roasted apples. The defence of Limerick had been placed in the charge of Major-General Boisseleau, an expert in siege warfare, and one of the few French officers still on good terms with their Irish allies.

Like Athlone, Limerick consisted of two separate walled towns, the 'English' and the 'Irish', on opposite banks of the Shannon, linked by Ball's Bridge. The medieval defences were unlikely to withstand prolonged bombardment, but as the Irish army rallied outside Limerick, Boisseleau made use of its plentiful manpower to dig a ditch in front of the wall of the 'Irish' town, and construct a number of redoubts and other outworks.

John Stevens had rejoined the Lord Grand Prior's Regiment on 12 July, 3 miles outside Limerick. Even with other stragglers who had already reached the town, the regiment initially totalled no more than 200 men, some with arms 'fixed', some with inoperable arms, and some with no weapons at all. Most of the officers had lost all of their possessions during the retreat from the Boyne. Stevens, like many others, was 'left almost naked, not having so much as a shirt to change. In which condition being a stranger and without friends, I continued for many days, for money was as scarce as clothes, and what we had only brass, which was then of little or no value, till I met an Englishman who had but three suits, yet taking compassion on me, gave me one.'[9]

Two days later Stevens's Regiment was reviewed by its brigade commander, Brigadier-General John Wauchope, a Scottish professional soldier. Although it now mustered around 300 men, only half had serviceable muskets, a situation mirrored in most of the other regiments. Many had thrown away their weapons during the retreat, and Wauchope considered shooting some of them as an example, but it was decided that there were simply too many unarmed men for this to be effective. In most cases two badly understrength regiments had to be brigaded together to form a viable unit. The Lord Grand Prior's was brigaded with Lord Slane's Foot.

During the following days, Stevens and his men laboured in continuing hot weather on the defences of Limerick.

Sarsfield and the other senior Irish commanders, unlike Tyrconnel and Lauzan, were optimistic. To defend Limerick de Boisseleau had a regiment apiece of horse and dragoons, and twenty-eight infantry battalions, although the latter were so weak that they totalled only 14,000 men. There were about 2,500 cavalry under Sarsfield in County Clare, and a number of troops in other garrisons. Further up the Shannon were a large number of poorly armed Ulstermen operating more or less independently under Hugh Balldearg O'Donnell, a descendent of the great 'Red Earl' who had fought against Queen Elizabeth.

William, meanwhile, was approaching Limerick. The march proved difficult, partly because Berwick had repeated his effective scorched-earth strategy. Crops were burnt, roads were blocked, and parties of Jacobite horse and the irregular guerrillas known as rapparees harassed Williamite detachments and outposts. In theory, the Williamite forces were under strict discipline. Looters who were brought to the King's attention were hanged: 'The King is very strict and will suffer none to plunder, so that this part of the army will be very poor because we are forced to be honest', wrote one disgruntled soldier.

William had about 25,000 men, but no guns heavier than field pieces. The siege train of heavy guns had been sent separately to Kilkenny, to await William's order to proceed to Limerick. The effects of Berwick's destruction were clearly visible from Limerick: 'the devastation spread on all sides, and quite round might be seen some villages, and many farms, and considerable gentlemen's country houses, in flame'.[10]

On 8 August the Williamite vanguard came in sight of the defences. William was not well informed of enemy strength, other than that the bulk of its troops were in Limerick and Galway, and that Sarsfield, with a cavalry force whose numbers popular report exaggerated, was on the loose. On the day that they appeared before Limerick, the Williamites dispatched a summons to surrender to Boisseleau. This was part of the normal etiquette of siege warfare, as was Boisseleau's equally polite rebuff. William remained confident that as soon as his siege train arrived, Limerick's fate was sealed.

'SARSFIELD'S RIDE'

It was already late in the campaigning season to undertake a major siege, and the Jacobites hoped to prolong resistance until bad weather and supply difficulties forced William to abandon his operations for the year. Tyrconnel believed that this might be achieved by a dogged defence of Limerick, but there were other, more aggressive proposals. Berwick suggested unleashing all the cavalry in a massive raid on Dublin, and there may have been an abortive scheme to kidnap William himself. But the most promising opportunity presented itself the day after the siege began, when a French gunner deserted from the besiegers and came through the Jacobite lines with news that William's heavy artillery train, under his comptroller of artillery the great Dutch siege engineer Wilhelm Meesters, was on the march from Cashel to join the besieging army.

This was Sarsfield's opportunity. He set off the same day to Clare Castle to obtain Tyrconnel's permission to lead his horse in an attack on William's siege train. With Tyrconnel's agreement, Sarsfield wasted no time in mustering as many cavalry as were readily available.

On the evening of 10 August Sarsfield and some 600 horse crossed the Shannon at Killaloe and headed eastward into the Silvermine Mountains.

The Jacobites were spotted by a local Protestant landowner, who hastened to the Williamite camp with the news. However, his report was dismissed by everyone except Meinhard Schomberg, who unsuccessfully suggested that a cavalry regiment should be sent to reinforce the escort of the artillery train. William himself was sceptical, although eventually the one-eyed, generally uncooperative Sir John Lanier was told to take a cavalry force to locate Sarsfield. Although the order was issued on the morning of 11 August, Lanier had still not moved by the afternoon.

During the day Sarsfield received reports from his scouts that the artillery train, stretching along 2 miles of road, was on the move from Cashel, where it had spent the previous night. As the day drew on, it became clear that the enemy were taking no precautions against attack, and at dusk they went into camp for the night near ruined Ballyneety Castle.

Sarsfield knew that he must act quickly before the small escort of the artillery train was reinforced. Silently, the Jacobite horse closed in.

The train consisted of around 100 carts and wagons, and eight 18-pounder guns. The only troops actually with the civilian drivers and wagoners were a dozen fusiliers and a few artillerymen. The main escort, consisting of eighty troopers from Colonel Edward Villier's Regiment of Horse, was bivouacked some distance away, and its commander, Captain Thomas Poultney, had failed to post sentries or send out patrols. Only ten guards were on duty, and their main concern was to keep an eye on the horses that had been loosed to graze.

At around midnight Sarsfield, with about 500 men, fell on the camp. It was said that the Williamite watchword that night was 'Sarsfield'. When challenged, Sarsfield replied with his own name, and when again questioned, further into the camp, supposedly replied: 'Sarsfield is the word! And Sarsfield is the man!'

In any event, the surprise was complete. The guards fired wildly while the men in the camp blundered around in total confusion. Sarsfield's troopers swept down on Poultney's men as they desperately tried to dress and form up, and chased them into the woods. The wagoners attempted to hide, while Wilhelm Meesters resourcefully hid himself in a bed of nettles, where he remained for the duration of the raid.

Sarsfield ordered his men to burn the entire contents of the camp. Gunpowder, bombs, tools and match were set alight or exploded. The guns, under the reluctant direction of a captured artilleryman, were overcharged with powder and then placed vertically with their muzzles in the ground and fired. In the event, the resulting explosions burst only two of them.

The sound and sight of the explosions alerted Williamite detachments as far away as Limerick. Lanier, still inactive in camp, was ordered to ride at once to try to salvage the train or at least to intercept Sarsfield. Once again, he proved dilatory, not getting under way until after midnight, and then taking a circuitous route towards Ballyneety. He then made the assumption that Sarsfield would return the way he had come, and spent the night vainly waiting at Killaloe.

At dawn English troops reached the smoking ruins of the camp at Ballyneety. As well as broken and dismounted guns, and burnt-out wagons, there were about fifty bodies, mostly those of unfortunate wagoners and gunners, although some Williamite reports claimed that they included women and children caught up in the mêlée. To William, however, the material losses were far more serious. About 1,000 wagons and their contents had been burnt. Among the losses were 120 barrels of gunpowder, together with large quantities of match and other munitions. Around 3,000 canonballs had been scattered around, although many of these could be recovered. Thousands of tools needed for entrenching work had been broken or stolen, and boats intended for a pontoon bridge over the Shannon had been burnt, while 500 artillery horses had been driven off.

Sarsfield and the majority of his troopers evaded enemy attempts to intercept them, and got back safely across the Shannon. 'Sarsfield's Ride' had two major effects. Firstly, although most of William's siege guns could be salvaged, the vast quantities of other material and munitions destroyed could not be quickly replaced, delaying an assault on Limerick when time was critical. Secondly, the successful outcome of the raid acted as a major boost to Jacobite morale. In Limerick and across Ireland, what had seemed to be a lost cause suddenly revived, with increased attacks on Williamite convoys and outposts and growing numbers of rapparees in what had hitherto been seen by William's forces as 'pacified' territory.

THE GREAT ASSAULT

William was determined that siege operations against Limerick should continue, even if they lasted all winter. Parties of troops dug trenches and prepared emplacements for the heavy guns that were not yet available, while the Jacobites attempted to delay the work by gunfire and skirmishing. The Irish could not afford heavy casualties, and gradually pulled back within their main defences, after fighting several small skirmishes amid the thick hedgerows on the outskirts of the town, during which allied soldiers could hear their opponents 'with their damned Irish brogue on their tongues' and retorted: 'ye toads, are ye there? We'll be with you presently.'[11]

William concentrated his efforts against the south-west and north-east-facing sections of the defences, and on 17 August attacked two small outlying forts. One attack was directed against a redoubt on the south side of the town, near St James Gate, whose garrison held out until ordered to withdraw. Another assault fell on one of a line of redoubts opposite the south-eastern angle of the defences, which was held by a detachment of the Lord Grand Prior's Regiment, who fled without firing a shot.

Next day, with his siege guns remounted, and fresh supplies of powder and ammunition, William was able to commence his bombardment. As usual, the King tried to encourage his men with displays of personal leadership, riding forward to inspect their front-line positions, on one occasion narrowly escaping being hit by a shot fired by a Jacobite 24-pounder.

On the afternoon of 20 August the Williamites made a determined attack on a Jacobite outpost known as the Yellow Fort, which lay to the south of the Irish town, at the edge of some boggy ground. It was held by a detachment of the Irish Guards under Colonel Fitzgerald, to whom the attackers, a force of Brandenburgers and Danes, were ordered to give no quarter. The fort fell on the third attack, only one prisoner being taken, although a number of the defenders managed to escape.

A prompt counter-attack was launched by Lord Kilmallock's Horse, supported by dismounted dragoons and foot. The fort was briefly retaken before a counter-charge by Williamite cavalry drove the Irish out again, partly, so Stevens claimed, because of the poor performance of the Irish foot. The Williamites claimed to have killed 300 of the enemy, for their own admitted loss of around 79 dead and 192 wounded.[12]

With the Yellow Fort in their hands, the besiegers were able to bring their guns closer to Limerick's walls. On 22 August, after Boisseleau had rejected another summons to surrender, the siege artillery concentrated its fire against a tower at the southern angle of the walls, known as the Black Battery, bringing part of it down. The same night, in a move designed to sap civilian morale, a mortar bombardment of the town began.

Throughout the following day the bombardment continued. By now the eastern section of the medieval walls was suffering significant damage, and fragments from the wall and from shot that broke against it were falling in the trenches manned by the defenders, inflicting numerous casualties. The next night Wilhelm Meesters moved some of his guns to within 100yd of the walls. It seemed that the defences of Limerick would quickly crumble before the onslaught.

But next day, 25 August, the hitherto fine weather broke with torrential rain, which flooded the trenches with up to 2ft of water and left the siege guns unable to fire until the afternoon. With time running out, William redoubled his efforts the following day, in continuing heavy rain, and a breach was made

> in the southernmost part of the east wall near twenty paces wide, and though somewhat high yet easy of ascent, the vast quantity of rubbish beaten from the upper part of the wall and tower having almost filled the counterscarp so that there was no difficulty in mounting. Their cannon also levelled the glacis of the covered way and, having beat down the palisades, opened a plain passage to the breach and that gave a fair invitation to assault the town.[13]

The following day, William called a council of war to consider his next move. Some officers wished to delay an assault until the breach was widened, but with continuing rain, and insufficient ammunition for another two days of battering the defences, there was little option. If an assault were to be made at all, it would have to be that day. During the morning continued firing had widened the breach to around thirty paces across. It was clear to Boisseleau that an assault was imminent and, unable to repair the damage because of the continuous heavy enemy fire, he built an inner wall or hornwork behind the breach, with guns covering it.

William's plan of moving troops up close to the breach in readiness to assault had been adopted by the besiegers. Led by a 'forlorn hope' of grenadiers, the attackers were to advance to the edge of the counterscarp and there hold their ground. The attack began at 3.30 p.m. on 27 August, the rain having for the moment stopped. Led by 100 Huguenot officers, 500 grenadiers raced towards the Jacobite defences under heavy fire, backed by an intensive bombardment from their own guns. Storey, who was watching, described how: 'In less than two minutes the noise was so terrible that one would have thought the very sky ready to rend in sunder. This was seconded with dust, smoke and all the terrors that the art of man could invent to ruin and undo each other.'[14] The grenadiers, fired up by the rage of battle and perhaps hoping to get clear of enemy fire, did not halt as ordered when they reached the edge of the counterscarp, but waded on through the wet ditch beyond and began to scale the breach.

Stevens, with troops including the Lord Grand Prior's and Boisseleau's Regiments, was drawn up in the street behind the hornwork, awaiting orders to relieve its defenders. They had just been ordered to man the walls near St John's Gate:

but before we could reach it, our governor, Major General Boisseleau, came running and ordering us to the left, led to the breach . . . we perceived the breach possessed by the enemy, a great number came down into the retrenchment made within it, and above twenty of them were got into the street. Having heard no firing of small shot before, we at the first sight thought they had been our guards retiring out of the counterscarp, they being all in red coats, till we discovered the green boughs in their hats, which was the mark of distinction worn by the rebels, whereas ours was white paper. Besides an officer on the breach brandishing his sword called upon his men to follow, crying the town was his own. Our guards, who were in the counterscarp, upon the first appearance of the enemy abandoned their post without firing a shot, flying with such precipitation that many of them found their way through our dragoons, who were posted on the right of them, towards St John's Gate. These dragoons behaved themselves with much bravery presenting their pieces upon such of the guards as had not passed through them, which obliged many to stand, as did some of their officers ashamed of the infamous flight of their men. With those few that stood by them the dragoons made good their post during the whole time of the action.[15]

Meanwhile, wave after wave of Williamite foot, some eight battalions of them, all disregarding orders to halt at the counterscarp, crowded forward after the grenadiers. Led by the Green Regiment of Brandenburgers, the attackers pressed forward through the breach, entering the killing ground which had been prepared by Boisseleau. The grenadiers, whose leading officer, Captain Farlow, seen by Stevens urging on his men, had been shot down, and the Brandenburgers came under heavy fire from three sides, musket fire, canon loaded with small shot, and grenades all being directed against them. Some of the grenadiers broke through and charged towards the main square. All were brought down, the defence being augmented by unarmed soldiers and women hurling stones. 'Meanwhile', wrote Stevens:

the Grand Prior's Regiment had well lined the retrenchment within the breach, and being undeceived that the enemy and not our own men were those that rushed in so impetuous, the word was given to fire, which was performed so effectually that a considerable number of the rebels dropped, and our men renewed their charges with such vigour that in a very short space they had not left one enemy within the breach, though still nothing daunted they pressed over, fresh men succeeding those that were killed or wounded. This sort of fight was continued near an hour, our battalion alone making good their ground against that multitude of enemies which being still backed with new supplies was all that while insensible of its losses . . . Our continual firing having made a great slaughter among the rebels, and they beginning to abate of their first fury, M de Beaupre, a

Frenchman and lieutenant-colonel to Boisseleau our Governor, leaped over our retrenchment making to the breach. Most men strove to be foremost in imitating so good an example, so that being followed by a resolute party he soon recovered the top of the breach. Here the fight was for some time renewed and continued with sword in hand and the butt end of the musket. Our other men upon the walls were not idle this while, some firing and others casting stones upon the enemy beneath, which did no small execution but the greatest havoc was made by two pieces of cannon playing from the citadel and two others from the King's island, as also two others from the Augustine chapel near Balls Bridge, which last scoured all along our counterscarp then filled with rebels, and the other four swept them in their approach on the south and east sides. The enemy thus cut off on all sides came on faintly, and a barrel of powder which lay near the south-east tower accidentally taking fire and blowing up some that were near it, the rest conceived it had been a mine and fled, neither fair words nor threats of officers prevailing to bring them back.[16]

The counter-attack described by Stevens was assisted by a sortie made by Colonel Mark Talbot's Regiment of Dragoons via St John's Gate, which took the Williamite foot and the Danish Green Regiment in the rear, completing their rout. The Brandenburgers had been ordered to storm the Black Battery but, as they advanced, a magazine, or the barrel of powder referred to by Stevens, exploded, throwing the attackers into confusion.

Fighting seems to have continued for about three and a half hours, and it was not until around seven in the evening that William admitted defeat and ordered a withdrawal. An eyewitness saw that:

Our men drew off, some were brought off dead, and some without a leg; others wanted arms, and some were blind with powder especially a great many of the poor Brandenburgers looked like furies with the misfortune of the gunpowder . . . the king stood nigh Cromwell's fort all the time and, the business being over, he went to his camp very much concerned, as indeed was the whole army, for you might have seen a mixture of anger and sorrow in everybody's countenance.[17]

The repulse cost the Williamites almost 3,000 casualties, including many officers, compared with an admitted Jacobite loss of around 100, although the actual figure may have been nearer 500.

On 28 August a truce was observed while William's men carried off their wounded. William had failed. A council of war on 29 August overruled the King's wish to make another assault, this time led by William himself, feeling that another failure would cause a general uprising in Ireland. On 30 August the frustrated and angry King ordered the siege to be raised, and on

5 September, leaving Count Solms in command, he sailed from Dublin for England.

The Jacobites had won their greatest success of the war, largely thanks to Sarsfield's raid. Failure at Limerick ensured that the quick victory that William had hoped for was no longer possible.

MARLBOROUGH'S CAMPAIGN

In an age of political intrigue, John Churchill, Earl of Marlborough, was one of its greatest practitioners. As a career soldier, Churchill had displayed his military potential fighting for King James in the Monmouth Rebellion of 1685. Three years later, he demonstrated his eye for the political main chance in his well-timed defection to William just after his landing in England – a desertion that did much to convince James of the futility of military resistance.

Although rewarded, Marlborough was mistrusted by his new masters. Indeed, it was not long before he was putting out discreet feelers to the court of the exiled James. In the summer of 1690 Marlborough was one of the council of nine left by William to advise Mary when he went to Ireland. In August Marlborough proposed to the council that he should make a landing with 5,000 men on the coast of Munster in order to capture the key ports of Cork and Kinsale.

At a time when, following the defeat at Beachy Head and the burning of Teignmouth, England seemed to be under imminent threat of French invasion, Marlborough's plan did not meet a favourable reception from Queen Mary, who in any case distrusted him. Marlborough was supported by the Secretary of State, the Earl of Nottingham, and Admiral Edward Russell, who persuaded Mary to put Marlborough's scheme to William. The King was attracted by the plan, which would make use of some of the troops already brought back from Flanders and Ireland during the invasion scare, together with some marines – the first occasion on which this term was officially used. But with artillery in Ireland in short supply following Sarsfield's raid, Marlborough would have to rely on naval artillery support, and he was told that he would have to provide his own munitions. The only additional help that William was willing to offer was some cavalry, and to ensure that the main Jacobite forces did not interfere with Marlborough's operations.

This was the 40-year-old Marlborough's first independent command, and he set to work with all his customary vigour and drive. In a fortnight's feverish activity he extracted the required munitions from the parsimonious officials at the Tower of London and the magazines at Portsmouth and Plymouth, including no less than 13,000 grenades for the expected storming operations. On 25 August he was given a warrant to embark eight regiments of foot. Three, those of Trelawney, the Princess of Denmark and Hastings, had fought at the Boyne, while the remainder had been with Marlborough in Flanders in the previous year. On the same day the Board of Admiralty was instructed to land the 2,000 men of the two marine regiments at such points as Marlborough should direct.

Marlborough's force was embarked at Portsmouth by 30 August, aboard an imposing armada of English and Dutch warships. Adverse winds prevented the expedition from setting sail until 17 September, by which time William was back in England. With the failure of the operations against Limerick, the King had instructed Count Solms that his main task for the remainder of the year should be to assist Marlborough. Before Marlborough reached Ireland, Solms had been replaced by Godert de Ginkel, who was told to provide Marlborough with heavy siege guns and an additional 5,000 men, as well as posting cavalry with the aim of preventing the Jacobites – in particular Sarsfield's cavalry – from interfering with Marlborough's operations.

The expedition took five days to arrive off Crosshaven, at the mouth of Cork harbour, after a stormy voyage that prostrated Marlborough with seasickness. He had asked Ginkel for a contingent of English troops under the experienced professionals Kirke and Lanier, but Ginkel, perhaps jealous that any success might be a purely English achievement, or because he had lingering doubts regarding the loyalty of an all-English force under English commanders, replied that neither Kirke nor Lanier, nor their men, could be spared. Instead he would send eight heavy guns, with 4,000 foot under the German General Tettau, and 1,000 horse and dragoons under Major-General Schravemoer, under the overall command of the Duke of Württemberg, who, with eight years' seniority over Marlborough, could theoretically assume command of the whole operation.

On arriving off Crosshaven on 21 September, Marlborough, evidently unaware of the potential command complications, sent a message to Tettau and Schravemoer to join him before Cork. Marlborough's own expedition had already fired its first shots in anger on 22 September, when the fleet forced its way past the small fortification known as Prince Rupert's Tower that lay at the entrance to the harbour, before a landing party of seamen occupied the fort and dismounted its eight guns. On 23 September, Marlborough, with about 6,000 men, landed at Passage West, about 9 miles from Cork, on the western side of the great harbour, and began to march on the city.

Cork, with a pre-war population of 20,000, was defended by medieval walls, in places 50ft high and 10ft thick, but the suburbs of Cork had spread out well beyond them, and the defensible area consisted of an oblong about 700yd long and 250yd wide, situated on an island in the River Lee, with gates at each end leading to bridges over the north and south branches of the river. Opposite the south-western corner of the walls, on a rocky outcrop above the South Channel, was the recently strengthened Elizabeth Fort, armed with brass guns. But this in its turn was dominated by Cat Hill to its south-east. Cork's great weakness was that it was commanded by high ground on both sides of the river, which, prior to the war, the military engineer Thomas Phillips had considered to render the town indefensible.

The Jacobites had obtained Marlborough's plans from a captured courier even before the expedition landed, but the Duke of Berwick, now in overall command following the departure of Tyrconnel and Lauzan, made no effort to secure Jacobite communications between Limerick, Cork and Kinsale. Berwick shared the view that Cork could not be held, and sent instructions to evacuate the town to its governor, Colonel Roger MacElligott. MacElligott was a long-time professional soldier who had served in the Low Countries before being sent over to England with the Irish contingent in 1688. Interned by the Williamites on the Isle of Wight, MacElligott had escaped to France before returning to Ireland with James. He now commanded about 4,500 men drawn from seven regiments.

MacElligott chose to ignore Berwick's instructions. He would stand and fight. In an attempt to address some of the weaknesses of Cork's defences, he began to construct outworks on Cat Hill to the south of the city and below Shandon Castle on the north side. This was a serious miscalculation. MacElligott's best chance of delaying Marlborough would have been to concentrate all available troops in more easily defensible Kinsale.

Marlborough's vanguard appeared before Cat Hill on 24 September, skirmishing with some enemy dragoons stationed there. On the Williamite side, Ensign Crammond noted that 'we had some popping from the hedges, but without loss'. Next morning, as sailors from the fleet began dragging up heavy guns to bombard Cork from Cat Hill, it was discovered that the Irish dragoons had withdrawn to Elizabeth Fort. At the same time, Schravemoer and Tettau were closing in on the north, occupying the high ground overlooking the city without opposition, as the Irish also abandoned Shandon Castle with a large quantity of munitions, firing the suburbs as they withdrew into the old city.

On 25 September ships arrived from Waterford with large quantities of munitions and other supplies, and eight heavy guns, while boatloads of troops were brought up river to threaten Cork from marshy ground to the east of the city.

Although resistance had been lighter than expected, the Williamites felt that Cork's inner defences were still strong enough to cause problems. There was an exchange of letters between Schravemoer and MacElligott, in which the Dutchman urged Cork's governor not to fire any more of Cork's suburbs. MacElligott replied defiantly that he was not afraid of his attackers and would decide for himself what he burnt, although he tempered his response with the gift of a jar of wine.

On 26 September the attackers continued to close in, with Marlborough's men moving forward through the burnt-out southern suburbs and bombarding Elizabeth Castle, while the Dutch and Danish horse to the south-west occupied Gill Abbey. The potential command problems between Marlborough and the Duke of Württemberg were resolved by an agreement that each should command on alternate days.

When he occupied Gill Abbey, Schravemoer was met by the pro-Williamite Dean of Ross, who pointed out that the tower of nearby St Finbar's cathedral would make an excellent vantage point from which to fire on Elizabeth Fort. Two files of musketeers under Lieutenant Horatio Townsend were sent to occupy the tower and duly opened fire on Elizabeth Fort, killing its commander. The defenders replied to such effect that the tower shook, but Townsend took the precaution of removing the ladder leading up to its top, forcing his men to stay in position.

At the same time, Elizabeth Fort was coming under heavy fire from Marlborough's batteries, consisting of two 24-pounders and three 18-pounders. Meanwhile, mortars shelled the city itself and the guns landed from Waterford hammered the eastern section of the walls. The old defences quickly began to crumble, and MacElligott, preparing the ground for renewed negotiations, released the Protestant Bishop of Cork and a number of his co-religionists, who lost no time in telling Marlborough of the garrison's precarious situation. Thus, when MacElligott, offered to yield on condition that the garrison were allowed to march away with their arms and colours, Marlborough responded with a demand for unconditional surrender. A potentially fraught situation arose when Württemberg, to whom MacElligott had written separately, offered to let the Jacobites march away if they surrendered their weapons, but a dispute between the allied commanders was avoided when MacElligott chose not to accept Württemberg's offer.

On 28 September the artillery bombardment resumed. A breach was quickly made in the city walls, about 60yd from the south-eastern angle, and at 1 p.m., aided by the low tide, a simultaneous assault was launched through the marshy ground by two bodies of troops, an English detachment led by Marlborough's brother, Brigadier General Charles Churchill, from the south, and a mixed force of Brandenburgers, Danes and Dutch under Württemberg attacking further north. The marshy ground slowed the attackers, and it was discovered that the marsh was separated from the walls and breach by a wet ditch at least 20ft wide. The English attack was led by grenadiers, who crossed the marsh under heavy fire and got to within 20yd of the defences before they were halted. Among their casualties was the Duke of Grafton, an illegitimate son of Charles II, who was mortally wounded.

On the Danish sector, Prince Frederick's Regiment drove the Jacobite outposts back across the marsh to 'a little gate and bridge that joined the island to the town'. About twenty or thirty of the defenders had to jump into the moat.

The remainder of Cork's garrison were manning the walls, from which they saw a further unwelcome sight of two bomb-ketches coming up the river to support the infantry assault. It was enough for MacElligott. His drummers beat for a parlay, and a message was sent out asking for terms. Marlborough insisted that the garrison must become prisoners of war, on the promise that he would intercede with King William for clemency towards them. MacElligott had no option but to agree. Elizabeth Castle was handed over to the besiegers that night, and the next morning the Williamites entered Cork amid considerable looting by some of the sailors.

While the loss of Cork was a serious blow to the Jacobites, that of its 5,000-man garrison was a still greater setback, especially because it had occurred as a result of MacElligott's failure to obey Berwick's order to evacuate the town. MacElligott himself, together with the Earls of Clancarty and Tyrone, was taken to England and imprisoned. Some of the other officers were put aboard the transport *Breda* in the harbour, and were killed when that ship accidently blew up. Most of the rank and file were kept in such crowded conditions that many sickened and died, although this seems to have been caused by negligence rather than by deliberate policy.

With Cork in his hands, Marlborough could move against Kinsale. The 1,700 strong garrison under Sir Charles Scott made no attempt to hold the town itself, but withdrew into Charles and James Forts. Well supplied with provisions and munitions, and confident of relief, Scott brusquely rejected a summons to surrender. While Scott and the bulk of his force garrisoned Charles Fort, about 400 men held James Fort. Marlborough assigned General Tettau, with about 800 men, to deal with the lesser strongpoint. In a carefully planned amphibious night assault, Tettau stormed the fort. Fierce fighting followed, in which, and in an accidental explosion of the magazine, about half of the defenders were killed, after which the remainder surrendered.

Fort Charles, with about 100 guns, was held by around 1,200 men, and Scott was determined to hold out as long as possible. Marlborough spent about a week digging trenches and bringing up his heavy guns from Cork and, on 12 October, opened fire. After three days of bombardment a significant breach had been made in Fort Charles's walls. As Marlborough prepared to mount an assault, Scott asked for terms. Marlborough, concerned about bad weather and the approach of winter, proved generous, allowing the garrison to depart for Limerick with arms and baggage.

Marlborough returned to England in triumph, but to a lukewarm reception from William, who may well have resented his achievements. When Marlborough lobbied for overall command in Ireland for the coming season's campaign he was firmly rebuffed and sent back to Flanders.

Although the remarkable Jacobite successes at Athlone and Limerick ensured that the war in Ireland would continue, Marlborough's capture of the south-western ports not only made assistance for the Jacobites from France more problematic, but confined them to a relatively small area west of the Shannon. The odds would be increasingly in the Williamites' favour when the new campaigning season opened.

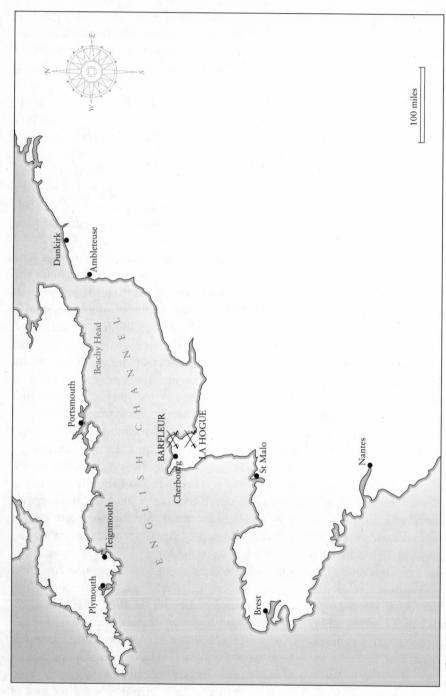

Barfleur and La Hogue, 1692

TEN

• • • • • • • •

The War at Sea

THE RIVAL NAVIES

In 1689 the navy and its associated activities, such as timber production, shipbuilding, logistical support and the personnel of the fleet itself, were collectively England's largest industry. The navy had its own shipyards, bought foodstuffs and clothing in huge quantities from a wide range of producers, and also imported naval stores, masts, yards and rigging from the Baltic States and North America.

The employment of the fleet was in the hands of the Navy Board and the Commissioners, permanent officials. At their head was the Secretary of the Navy. In 1689 William had replaced Samuel Pepys with Daniel Finch (soon to be Earl of Nottingham). Nottingham lacked Pepys's ability, and William was not particularly interested in naval matters. This resulted at times in confusion and lack of direction, although a naval agreement was reached with the Netherlands that allowed for cooperation between the English and Dutch fleets. This would result in a combined fleet of eighty ships of the line for use in home waters and the Mediterranean. It was also agreed that the English, who, with fifty ships, would be providing the largest part of the fleet, should exercise overall command. There were, however, the usual difficulties in manning the English fleet, and William, with his regime as yet not firmly rooted, was reluctant to authorise the customary expedient of pressing men to fill out its crews.

The result was that the French had the initiative in the opening months of the war at sea. The attitude of William III, James II and Louis XIV towards naval matters was influenced by their wider strategic and political aspirations. William saw the war in Ireland and Scotland, and the potential Franco-Jacobite threat to England, as annoying diversions from what he regarded as the main theatre of war in Flanders. To Louis, the British dynastic upheaval was a means of diverting allied resources from the war on the Continent at minimal outlay to himself. For James, the conflicts in Ireland and Scotland were primarily stepping stones to regaining the thrones of all three of his British kingdoms, with England his main objective.

The Comte de Seignelay, son of France's great War Minister, Jean Baptiste Colbert, became Naval Minister in 1689. The current War Minister, Louvois, had been in power since 1672. Although a newcomer, Seignelay had the support of the influential Colbert family and, equally importantly, had the ear of both Louis's mistress, Madame de Maintenon, and James II's queen, Mary of Modena. During his period of office, Colbert had worked energetically to build up the strength of the French navy. By 1683 it had 112 ships of the line including twelve 1st rates and the same number of 2nd rates, and a powerful force of frigates and corvettes, making it the largest navy in the world.

The rapid expansion of the navy necessitated the transfer to the fleet of many former army officers. This had been practised previously by other countries, notably by England during the Commonwealth and Protectorate. Unfortunately, many of the appointees came from Court circles. Some, such as Châteaurenault, had no previous maritime experience.

An increasingly influential bureaucracy was set up to administer the navy, reducing the influence of admirals and other senior naval commanders. Dutch shipwrights were brought in to work in the shipyards that were set up in the burgeoning naval bases at Brest, Rochefort and Toulon. In 1688 France had a fighting fleet of 189 vessels, including 130 ships of the line, compared with 174 English fighting ships, and 25 Dutch warships in commission, with about the same number being fitted out.

The largest ships ideally had crews of 1,700 men, the smallest ship of the line having a complement of around 500 in wartime. The French Toulon Squadron alone needed an establishment of 52,710 men. With their relatively small merchant fleet, the French were never able to obtain sufficient experienced seamen in wartime, unlike the Dutch, who had twice as many seasoned sailors as the British, and ten times as many as the French.

The opening of the war in Ireland presented challenges to all the navies involved. The Irish Jacobites were almost entirely dependent upon supplies brought in from overseas, as indeed were the French and Williamite forces. Both the navies principally involved had to be ready for sea earlier and for longer periods than in the past and, after the Jacobite loss of the south-western Irish ports in the autumn of 1690, the French fleet and supply convoys had to face long and hazardous voyages.

Both Holland and France had land frontiers to defend. This responsibility was particularly demanding in the case of France, who had to defend long frontiers with an average of 150,000 troops against an allied force that at times totalled about 220,000 men. At sea, France had two naval theatres, the Channel and the Mediterranean, which were vital to her security, and which she had to defend with a fleet smaller than the combined allied naval forces.

Financially also, the balance of advantage lay with the allies. After 1688 William had relatively copious funds available from the mercantile centres of London and Amsterdam. Louvois had more limited resources, and had to concentrate the bulk of them on the needs of the army and the defences of the French frontiers. His natural interests also lay with land warfare, where, like many other Frenchmen before and since, he felt the real opportunities for glory lay. Indeed, Louvois only twice in his life set foot aboard a warship. Virtually all senior French naval officers were members of the nobility and, obsessed with matters of precedence, were not willing to take orders from those of lower social standing. The result was bad for discipline at all levels. The main French advantage was generally held to lie in the fields of shipbuilding and design. Indeed, it was said that the best combination was a French warship manned by an English crew.

BANTRY BAY

Louis XIV had not attempted to intervene with his own fleet during William's landing in England in 1688. He was not particularly concerned about saving James, and indeed he expected William to become entangled in a long period of civil conflict in Britain that would remove any prospects of either that country or Holland interfering with his plans in Europe.

By early 1689, however, the situation had changed. James was in exile in France and William, in rather uncertain control of England and Wales, faced significant opposition in Scotland and Ireland. The latter in particular was now seen in France as a useful diversionary theatre of war, especially after Tyrconnel had assured de Pointis, Louis's envoy, of the willingness of the Irish people to fight for James provided they received French support. The French Ministry of Marine played the major role in providing this. The naval base and port of Brest, at the western tip of Brittany, was the main departure point for supplies for Ireland, while Kinsale in south-west Ireland, by virtue of its well-protected harbour, was the main port of entry.

On 17 March the first French convoy, including seventeen warships, thirteen transports, six frigates and three fireships, carrying James II and his entourage, sailed from Brest. At James's request, they flew English flags. The expedition arrived at Kinsale without incident on 22 March, and some ships went on to Cork and Waterford. When the convoy returned to Brest, three frigates remained behind to assist James. March was quite early in the year for a naval expedition to sail, and it may have taken the English by surprise.

The next convoy, which sailed in May, was not so fortunate, and was engaged by Admiral Herbert at Bantry Bay. The convoy that had carried James and his entourage to Ireland had been sent back to Brest to collect the Jacobite troops, now being mustered there, and a large quantity of money and munitions.

Despite Ireland's growing significance as a theatre of war, William had been reluctant to send any of the English navy to operate there because of continuing doubts as to its reliability, not least because some 87 per cent of its officers had held commissions under James. On 11 March Arthur Herbert was appointed Commander-in-Chief in the English Channel and Irish waters. Herbert was a hard-drinking Welshman, noted for his violent temper, who had joined the navy in 1663 at the age of 15, and had seen action in the Mediterranean and in the Third Dutch War. In 1687 Herbert was dismissed by James because of his opposition to the repeal of the Penal Laws. He promptly threw in his lot with William of Orange and, going to Holland with an invitation for William to come to England, in 1688 commanded his invasion fleet. Herbert was one of the few senior naval officers whom William trusted and, hoisting his flag aboard the *Elizabeth*, he was ordered to attempt to intercept James's convoy, instructed by William that the former king was to be well treated if captured.

Herbert was delayed by bad weather and did not put to sea until 4 April. A passing merchant ship informed the English commander that James was already safely ashore in Ireland, but Herbert, unwilling to rely on hearsay, continued towards the Irish coast, 'where I trust to obtain more intelligence than at sea'.[1] Arriving off Cork on 12 April, Herbert received confirmation of James's arrival and headed for Kinsale in the hope of finding some French ships still there.

Although disappointed in this, Herbert continued to cruise off the south-west coast of Ireland, taking a number of small prizes. However, by the middle of April, in continuing heavy weather, several of his squadron were becoming leaky and unseaworthy, and two were ordered back to Portsmouth. On 8 April, with the seas showing no sign of abating, Herbert took shelter with most of the remainder of the squadron in the great natural harbour of Milford Haven in south-west Wales, leaving George Rooke with three ships to continue the watch on Kinsale. Herbert complained bitterly to the Secretary of State, the Earl of Nottingham, about the state of his ships and crew. In one way, however, Herbert's task was clarified when he learnt that England was now formally at war with France, and he was instructed to attack French ships wherever he found them.

Fog delayed Herbert's departure from Milford Haven until 23 April. Two days later a French convoy of twenty-five ships of the line and transports, now under the command of Admiral Châteaurenault, a courtier sailor with no previous experience of senior command at sea, left Brest bound once again for Kinsale. Herbert also headed for Kinsale, correctly deducing it to be the most likely French landfall. On the 28th, off Cork, he received a welcome reinforcement of eight ships of the line and a number of smaller vessels. Next day, while questioning the captain of a Spanish ship off Kinsale, the frigate *Advice* sighted a large fleet to leeward, sailing south. *Advice*'s captain at first took these to be the remainder of the English fleet, but by 5.30 a.m. had discovered them to be French. The *Advice*'s warning guns were ignored by Herbert and the remainder of the English squadron, and it was not until about 6 p.m. that the Admiral became aware of the approaching French and formed his ships into line of battle. With the wind blowing east-north-east, it would be difficult for Châteaurenault to reach Kinsale and Herbert was between him and the port, so the French decided to head into Bantry Bay in order to land their cargo of troops and supplies.

Next morning, Châteaurenault anchored in Bantry Bay, a long narrow inlet, which John Stevens, an English Jacobite among the men being landed, described with distaste as 'a miserable poor place, not worthy the name of a town, having not above seven or eight little houses, the rest very mean cottages'.[2] That afternoon (30 April), when Châteaurenault sighted the English fleet approaching, he hastily crammed the 1,500 English, Scottish and Irish troops and the money and munitions into small vessels, or landed them on the rocks, a task not completed until midnight.

Herbert had been uncertain all day regarding the enemy's location and intentions, but anchored that night off Mizzen Head 'drawn up in line of battle and readiness to engage'. The next day, 1 May, dawned fine and clear, and at around 5.30 a.m. the *Fribbs Yacht* came around the point of Mizzen Head with the news that the French were in Bantry Bay. As the English fleet rounded Sheep's Head they saw the French ships at anchor in the mouth of the bay. They estimated the enemy as twenty-eight to thirty-three 'very stout ships', compared with their own force of between eighteen and twenty-two ships of the line. Despite the disparity in numbers Herbert was eager for action, and the English fleet 'sprung their luffs and plied for them', while the French slipped or cut their cables and formed line of battle, 'keeping their wind'.

The French line made its way further up the bay, closely followed by Herbert's ships, which were, however, hampered by the wind blowing out of the bay against them, and were forced to make a number of tacks as they tried to get close enough to engage. At 10 a.m. both admirals hoisted the red flag as a signal for battle.

Captain John Ashley in *Defiance* (72 guns) led the English line into action, followed by *Portsmouth*, *Woolwich*, *Plymouth* and *Advice*. Châteaurenault signalled for his own van to engage, and three French ships bore down on *Defiance*, 'coming harsh with us, within a pistol shot firing upon us'. *Defiance* responded and 'saluted them with a broadside'. *Portsmouth* quickly joined in, together with *Advice*, and after about three-quarters of an hour of fighting, the French ship of the line *Le François*, while tacking, collided with the ship following her, 'the one lying with his head towards us, the other his stern'. However, neither could be taken, and after another three-quarters of an hour *Defiance* herself was forced to bear off to repair damage to her masts and rigging, which were 'very much damnified'.

There was only a momentary interval, however, before both fleets closed and a 'desperate fight' began. Herbert in *Elizabeth* engaged Châteaurenault's flagship and brought down her main mast. But the French still had the advantage of the wind, and Herbert drew his fleet further out to sea to help keep their line and in the hope that he might gain the advantage of the wind in more open waters. But the French thwarted this hope by 'bearing down that we could never get chance to do it'.

Firing continued for another four hours, during which the English ship of the line *Woolwich* suffered significant damage, the French keeping so far to windward that the majority of English shots fell short of them, while, as an English participant admitted, the French shot 'went over us and through us'. The captain of the *Portland*, George Aylmer, was mortally wounded, although the fireship *Firedrake* managed to set ablaze the French battleship *Diamente* with a hit from her mortar.

At 5 p.m., with his fleet almost clear of the bay, Châteaurenault hauled down his red flag of defiance and tacked away, ignoring a challenging gun fired by Herbert, and pulled back into Bantry Bay. Herbert headed out to sea, the action at an end.[3]

Herbert made the best of a difficult situation, reporting to Secretary of State Nottingham that he had succeeded in 'bringing off the fleet without loss of a ship; after an attempt upon all the disadvantage that ever man lay under'.[4] Damage had been suffered by twenty-one of his twenty-two ships, some cases, such as the *Edgar*, being relatively serious. One captain and 96 men had been killed, and 269 wounded.

Herbert and his battered squadron headed for Portsmouth and Plymouth for repairs, the Admiral himself entering Portsmouth on 12 May. For political purposes it was necessary to proclaim a victory, and official English accounts made no mention of the fact that Châteaurenault had successfully landed his cargo and passengers. Herbert and his officers were given official testimony of William's approval when the King dined aboard the *Elizabeth*, and created Herbert Earl of Torrington, knighting two of his captains, Cloudesley Shovell and John Derby. Every seaman was to be awarded 10s, and the widows of those killed £10 each, with £3 for each child. In a speech to the House of Commons, Herbert called for additional provision for the care of the wounded, which eventually led to the foundation of the Greenwich Hospital for Seamen.

Despite official English attempts to claim otherwise, the action at Bantry Bay had been a tactical victory for the French. Even so, joy on the Jacobite side was far from being unconstrained. James, remarking that if the English fleet had been defeated, 'it is the first time then', and suggesting that it had been the result of the English sailors being reluctant to fight against him, rather reluctantly ordered a celebratory Te Deum to be held in Dublin. Châteaurenault and his captains were, meanwhile, blaming each other for the failure to achieve a complete victory.

There was a widespread feeling that the French had failed to take the opportunity to capitalise on their success. James wanted Châteaurenault to support the planned attack on Derry by blockading the port and transporting heavy siege guns for the Jacobites. He could then clear the Irish Sea of remaining Williamite warships and transport the promised 10,000 Irish troops over to Scotland. D'Avaux, reluctant as ever to support such an increased French involvement, retorted that Châteaurenault's orders forbade him from doing this, and the French naval minister ruled that a much larger fleet would be required to carry out James's demands, and that in turn would depend upon the wider strategic situation. In reality, it would have been very difficult for a fleet of the size required to maintain itself off the coast of Northern Ireland, although a squadron of frigates based at Dublin could have caused serious problems for any supply vessels sent to Derry. All that eventually happened was that three frigates were sent to operate in Irish waters, whose major contribution was to transport Purcell's Regiment of Irish Dragoons over to reinforce Dundee in Scotland.

Nevertheless the troops and supplies aboard the convoy were landed successfully, and Châteaurenault set out on his return voyage on 14 May, reaching Brest safely. He met a lukewarm reception. The general feeling in French government and court circles was that Bantry Bay was 'more a brilliant action than a great loss for the English'.[5]

BEACHY HEAD

Further small convoys reached Ireland during the course of the summer. In August some staff officers and 4,600 muskets arrived safely, and in November another small convoy brought more munitions. In June the three French frigates left behind by the convoy that had carried King James carried Purcell's Dragoons to Scotland, and captured two smaller ships that comprised the 'Scottish Navy'.

By May 1689, the French naval ministry had realised that despite the importance of sending supplies to Ireland, the decisive theatre in the naval war would be the English Channel. Orders were given to the Toulon fleet, under Anne Hilarion de Constantin, Chevalier de Tourville, to sail for the Channel. Tourville, born 47 years earlier in Normandy, had served with the Knights of St John against the Muslims in the Mediterranean before joining the French navy. On 20 July, following a difficult voyage in adverse weather conditions, Tourville reached Brest. His orders from Louis were for the combined French fleet to take on the role of a 'fleet in being', designed to tie down allied naval forces while avoiding a major action. This was not to the liking of Seignelay, who pressed for a more aggressive strategy.

The remainder of the campaigning season passed without the main fleets making contact. The English fleet was under the command of Herbert, ennobled after Bantry Bay as the Earl of Torrington, but known derisively to his men as 'Lord Tarry-town' from his alleged preference for the pleasures of life in London rather than for service at sea.

Although he fought no battle other than Bantry Bay, in the course of the summer Torrington lost as many men to the ravages of scurvy as he would have done in a major action. The main naval events of note in 1689, other than the action at Bantry Bay, had been the successful relief of Derry by an English fleet, the transportation of Schomberg's expedition to Ireland and, on the French side, significant inroads into allied merchant shipping made by privateers such as Jean Bart in the North Sea and the Channel.

In January 1690 the English authorities decided that the main fleet for the coming summer would comprise sixty-four English and Dutch warships. The bulk would be English, and the naval force would also include twenty-seven frigates and corvettes and twenty fireships. The English contingent would require the huge total of 35,000 sailors if it were to be manned adequately.

The English commanders were desperate that the fleet be fitted out as quickly as possible. Late in 1689 Torrington admitted to the Earl of Nottingham that 'I am afraid now in winter, whilst the danger may be remedied, and you will be afraid in summer when it is past remedy'. England's other senior commander, Edward Russell, a nephew of the Earl of Bedford, and happier as an administrator ashore than as a commander at sea, warned Nottingham: 'For god's sake, my Lord, cast your eye sometime towards the next summer's fleet, I dread the French being out before us.'[6]

The French were ready for action by early spring. Their first priority was to provide further aid for the Jacobites in Ireland. On 17 March Lieutenant-General d'Anfreville sailed from Brest with thirty-six ships of the line, fifteen smaller warships and twenty-five transports, carrying over 6,000 French troops. Their commander, de Lauzan, rather ill-advisedly hoped that the expedition might encounter the English fleet. But the latter was occupied during the critical few days, escorting Spain's new queen home from the Netherlands. In any case, d'Anfreville was reluctant to fight a battle when he had so many troops crammed aboard his ships. He reached Cork just before the English fleet left its anchorage at Torbay bound for Spain.

On 18 April d'Anfreville began his return voyage with d'Avaux and von Rosen as his most distinguished passengers. The French fleet also carried Mountcashel's Irish troops, who, according to d'Anfreville, spread disease among his own sailors. By 1 May he was back in Brest, for the moment immobilised as a result of shortage of provisions and the sickness among his crews.

Meanwhile, on 10 May Torrington somewhat reluctantly accepted a commission as Commander-in-Chief and Commander of the 'Red' Squadron. By 22 June he had gathered in St Helen's Roads, off the Isle of Wight, thirty-four English and twenty-one Dutch warships. The same day he heard that seventy-seven French warships had been sighted off Falmouth.

King James had continually been pleading for a French squadron to be sent to operate in the Irish Sea, but the only action of note to take place there had been on 20 May, when Sir Cloudesley Shovell made his audacious raid on Dublin harbour. Chief among the vessels anchored there was the *Pelican*, a twenty-two-gun frigate that was one of the two captured by the French off the Scottish coast in the previous year. Laden with goods for France, she was evidently preparing for sea when Shovell arrived and sent across his boarding parties: 'The captain and all the men fled after firing a very few shots, and losing about five or six more killed in the ship, in the sight of the king and all the army that was in town.'[7] Shovell could probably have taken all of the ships in the harbour had he been so inclined, but after sailing up and down with his ship's fifes and drums derisively playing 'Lillibullero', he headed back out to sea with his prize.

Constant badgering from James and Tyrconnel for more French support resulted in Seignelay dispatching Chef d'escadre Forant to escort some grain ships to Kinsale, and he brought King James back to France after the Boyne. After landing him at Brest on 20 July, Forant returned to Limerick with a large convoy, carrying 400 bags of flour, 500 barrels of grain, 200,000lb of biscuit, and wine and brandy. By then the war at sea seemed to have turned decidedly in France's favour.

Following the news of the large French fleet being sighted off Falmouth, Torrington, protesting that the odds against him were too great, was ordered by a complacent Earl of Nottingham to sail to intercept the enemy.

Tourville had been promoted to Vice-Admiral and given command of the combined French fleet for the coming season. Like the English, Tourville had divided his fleet into three squadrons, and, also like the Anglo-Dutch, subdivided each squadron into three. On 11 June, Châteaurenault, sailing northwards from the Straits of Gibraltar, linked up with Tourville, giving the French fleet a total of seventy-six ships of the line, with eighteen fireships and smaller vessels. By 20 June Tourville was in sight of the English coast, and four days later was approaching the Isle of Wight, with the enemy in sight.

Torrington had been unable to link up with Killigrew and Shovell's squadrons to the west, and slowly retreated up-Channel, with the aim of keeping between the enemy and the Thames estuary. He had a slight numerical advantage, with eighty-two ships divided into three squadrons. He commanded the Red Squadron, the Dutchman Evertsen the White and Sir Ralph Delaval the Blue. Torrington saw his main task as being to preserve a 'fleet in being' in order to provide protection against a French invasion attempt. Consequently he and his council of war were agreed upon the need to avoid battle unless they were able to slip past the enemy fleet and join up with Killigrew and Shovell.

This was probably the soundest option in the circumstances, but Torrington was not permitted to follow his chosen strategy. Admiral Edward Russell, acting as Queen Mary's principal naval adviser in London, sent a curt instruction to fight, and Queen Mary advised Torrington that 'the consequence of his withdrawing to the Gunfleet [at the mouth of the Thames] would be so fatal, that she rather chooses he should, upon any advantage of wind, give battle to the enemy'.[8] Given these uncompromising instructions, Torrington and his captains had no option but to fight. Meanwhile the French forces in Flanders, under Marshal Luxembourg, had gained a major victory at Fleurus. Seignelay, anxious to win similar laurels for himself and the navy, sent Tourville equally firm orders to bring on a battle.

At dawn on 30 June the French sighted the Anglo-Dutch fleet off Beachy Head. The allies were bearing down on their opponent on an ebb tide with the wind from the north-north-east. Tourville formed line of battle on the starboard tack, steering west of north, with twenty-six ships in each of his van and centre squadrons and twenty-five in the rear.

The allied van was formed by Evertsen's twenty-one Dutch ships. Smaller and lighter than their opponents, they were quickly in trouble as Villette, leading the French van, tacked ahead of them and placed them between two fires. Ashby, as Vice-Admiral of the Red Squadron, attempted to go to the assistance of the Dutch, but the remainder of the Red Squadron was forced out of range. Delaval and his outnumbered Blue Squadron engaged the French rear led by D'Estrées, but the wind dropped, forcing the allies to tow their ships clear with their boats.

At about 5 p.m. the eight-hour engagement died down. Having lost one ship captured, the Dutch *Friesland*, the allies drifted out of range. Later in the evening Torrington resumed his retreat towards the Thames estuary. A number of damaged ships, mainly Dutch, were subsequently beached and burnt to avoid their capture. No English ships were lost, but casualties among their crews were heavy, in the region of 400 dead and 800 wounded. With fifteen Dutch ships lost, Torrington withdrew into the mouth of the Thames, where he received emergency reinforcements of additional Dutch vessels and ten of the big armed merchant ships of the East India Company. Torrington declined to accept any blame for his reverse, saying that he had acted 'under command' against his own judgement. Later writers tend to support Torrington's view.

The reverse off Beachy Head caused widespread panic in London, although news some days later of William's victory at the Boyne provided some consolation. As he had expected, Torrington was made principal scapegoat for the defeat, despite there being no obvious replacement for him. On 10 September he was arrested on a charge of 'high treason and misdemeanours', and placed in the Tower of London. On 10 December, he was acquitted of all charges by a court martial, but not re-employed.

The French were, according to Tourville, crippled by sickness and supply shortages, and made little attempt to exploit their victory, other than sending a party ashore in Devon on 22 July to burn the town of Teignmouth, meeting with little resistance. By 7 August Tourville was back in Brest, where he was dismissed by an angry King Louis and Seignelay for failing to follow up his victory at Beachy Head.

In England, the alarm caused by Torrington's reverse resulted in October in Parliament voting for an establishment of 28,000 men for the navy, together with £500,000 to pay for the construction of twenty-seven new warships. Confidence rose, as the summer and autumn passed with homeward-bound convoys reaching port safely without enemy attack. It was becoming clear that the French navy had lost what would prove to have been its best opportunity of the war.

Throughout the summer French attention remained focused on sending supplies to Ireland and on withdrawing the French troops, which Louis was unwilling to leave there to be lost in what he regarded as the doomed Jacobite cause. On 20 August d'Anfraville reached Limerick with fifteen ships of the line, nine frigates and seven fireships to join the ships already there under Forant in evacuating the French troops, which he collected from Galway.

By this time William and his forces were besieging Limerick, but d'Anrafville was unwilling to provide assistance to the defenders. The French were impatient to be home before winter, and on 23 September set sail from Galway, with the French troops and Tyrconnel on board. They reached Brest safely on 10 October. Tyrconnel had provided some of the provisions needed by the French crews despite the fact, as d'Anfraville admitted regarding the supplies earlier taken to Ireland, that 'One would not give to Algerians returning to Barbary biscuit such as that which has been sent to the troops in Ireland'.[9]

The ailing Seignelay died on 3 November and was replaced by Louis Phelypeaux de Pontchatrain. The new minister inherited a situation of growing financial shortages, and made limited use of the fleet. Indeed, at first Pontchatrain wanted to disband the bulk of the navy, but then came round to the more sensible strategy of maintaining a 'guerre de course' by privateers against allied commerce.

In England, Edward Russell had been named to lead the fleet in the campaign of the following year. Unpopular, outspoken and brutal, Russell was disliked by his men, but at least had a clear view on how best to employ the fleet in the national interest in what might well be the decisive months of the war at sea.

ELEVEN

•••••••••••••••

The Bloody Field

Many Jacobites doubted whether they would be able to hold out much longer unless they received substantial assistance from France. Just before his departure on 12 September to lobby King James at Saint-Germain, Tyrconnel estimated that resistance could be maintained until the following spring only if no more Irish troops were sent to France. Although Tyrconnel hoped to persuade James and King Louis to send further troops and supplies to Ireland, his overriding motive was to put his version of events to James before his critics among the Irish leadership could put theirs.

Left behind in control of civil affairs in Jacobite Ireland were twelve commissioners, with the Duke of Berwick in command of the army. The duke was only 20 and, although he had shown considerable potential in two years of fighting against the Turks in Hungary and in the war in Ireland, he was inexperienced in high command, and was unable to curb continuing dissension between the supporters of Tyrconnel, who favoured a speedy end to the war on the best terms possible, and the 'Irish' faction led by Sarsfield, who wished to fight on at least until their estates and religious freedom were assured. Berwick was on particularly poor terms with Sarsfield, commenting that the success of his raid on the Williamite artillery train had 'puffed him so that he thought himself the greatest general in the world'.[1] The dissension hindered any coherent Jacobite strategy in the closing months of 1690. Another cause of inactivity was the state of the army, which still lacked almost every necessity. Even John Stevens, no great admirer of the Irish, paid tribute to their soldiers' endurance and spirit. Their basic rations were salt beef, and grain with which to bake their own bread, and their pay, when received, was in the now almost worthless brass money, a crown coin of which would buy no more than a quart of poor ale and a very small loaf. Yet:

It is really wonderful, and will perhaps to after ages seem incredible, that an army should be kept together above a year without any pay . . . And what is yet more to be admired the men never mutinied nor were they guilty of any disorders more than what do often happen in these armies that are best paid. Nor was this all they might have complained of. In Limerick . . . all the garrison lay in empty houses, where they had neither beds nor so much as straw to lie on, or anything to cover them during the whole winter, and even their clothes were worn to rags, insomuch that many could scarce hide their nakedness in the daytime, and abundance of them were barefoot or at least so near it that their wretched shoes and stockings could scarce be made to hang on their feet and legs. I have been astonished to think they lived and much more that they should voluntarily choose to live so, when if they had forsaken the service they might have been received by the enemy into good pay and want for nothing. But to add to their sufferings the allowance of meat and corn was so small that men rather starved than lived upon it. These extremities endured as they were with courage and resolution are sufficient with any reasonable person to clear the reputation of the Irish from the malicious imputations of their enemies; and yet this is not all that can be said for them. We have already seen them defend an almost defenceless town against a victorious disciplined army, and we shall see them the following summer under all these hardships fight a battle with the utmost bravery, though overcome by numbers rather than valour. Let not any mistake and think I either speak out of affection or deliver what I know not; for the first I am no Irishman to be anyway biased, and for the other part I received not what I write by hearsay but was an eyewitness.[2]

With the Jacobites now effectively confined to Connaught and part of Munster, and their numbers swollen by a large amount of refugees, starvation was a very real threat. Sergeant Robert Parker of the Williamite forces wrote in the spring of 1691 that some particularly unfortunate refugees, attempting to survive in the disputed zone between the two armies, were 'wretches . . . devouring all the filth they could meet with. Our dead horses crawling with vermin, as the sun had parched them, were delicious food to them; while their infants sucked those carcasses, with as much eagerness, as if they were at their mothers' breasts.'[3]

The Williamites, preparing to go into winter quarters, had established a line of outposts running south from Mullingar to the east of the Shannon. On 16 September Berwick, with a few hundred infantry, attempted to retake one of these outposts at Birr but, after a half-hearted siege, withdrew on the approach of relief forces under Kirke and Lanier. With the approach of winter, the Williamites temporarily reduced their own forces. The three battalions of Dutch Guards returned to England, as did Count Solms, after establishing the Williamite headquarters at Tipperary. Solms was replaced by Ginkel, another experienced veteran.

Throughout the winter small-scale, but occasionally intense, fighting continued along and to the east of the River Shannon. The river basically formed the boundary of Jacobite Ireland, with Limerick, Sligo and Athlone as their key defensive posts. The Williamites lay well back from the river, their front line running from Cork up the middle of Ireland through Cashel, Birr, Mullingar, Longford and Cavan to Enniskillen, and westwards along the River Erne to Ballyshannon, giving them Ulster and most of Leinster and Munster. Ginkel's own headquarters was at Kilkenny.

Sarsfield ordered the major crossing points of the Shannon, at Portumna, Lanesborough and Jamestown, to be fortified, and Douglas and Kirke tried to seize Lanesborough and Jamestown. Both attempts were thwarted by Sarsfield's cavalry, leaving an area of disputed territory east of the Shannon. Here raiding parties from each side operated, seizing cattle and burning houses and farms to deny them to the enemy.

The winter also saw an increase in the activities of the Irish irregulars known as rapparees. King James had been squeamish about unleashing such a scourge on the countryside, but in the increasingly nationalistic conflict that followed his departure there was no such hesitancy. Some of the rapparees were dispossessed or vengeful civilians, others were soldiers from the main field army sent to operate in their home territory during the winter, with orders to report back in the spring. They attacked Williamite supply columns even in the outskirts of Dublin, burnt farms, ambushed patrols and killed collaborators. By the end of the winter they were several thousand strong, operating throughout much of 'occupied' Ireland. They were hated and feared by their opponents: 'all of them were armed, of all sorts, sexes and ages, the old women and young children providing their skeans and half-pikes, which they cut before our faces'.[4] The guerrillas also displayed an impressive ability to melt into the surrounding countryside. Storey related:

When the rapparees have no mind to show themselves upon the bogs they commonly sink between two or three hills grown over with very long grass that you might as soon find a hare as one of them. They conceal their arms thus, they take off their lock and put it in their pocket or in a dry place. They stop the muzzle with a cork and the touch-hole with a small quill and throw the piece into a pond or running water. You may see one hundred of them and they look like the poorest slaves in the world and you can search until you are weary and you will not find one gun.[5]

The rapparees were a major obstacle to Williamite efforts to set up local administration in the areas under their control, and the Williamites responded by forming local militias to combat the guerrillas. As the majority of militiamen were Protestant, the result was an ongoing and increasingly vicious small-scale conflict, in which neither side gave quarter. Storey noted a far from isolated incident in which 'The militia kill some rapparees and bring in their heads, a custom in that country, and encouraged by a law which allows so much for every head, according to the quality of the offender.'[6] The rapparees, in their turn, frequently mutilated the bodies of Williamite soldiers who fell into their hands, reserving a particular animus for the Enniskilleners.

The ongoing guerrilla war hardened attitudes, with reprisal and counter-reprisal, in which the innocent suffered along with the guilty. The Danish troops were said to be the worst offenders on the Williamite side, and there were protests that 'Tartars could hardly do worse'. Ginkel found the rapparees a serious hindrance, commenting that they 'are in so great number that we can neither find forage nor corn, which hinders much our march . . . we must do what we can against the rapparees, who will ravage us if they be not timely prevented . . . one must begin early and think what we are to do against the rapparees who will do us much damage'.[7]

If the Williamites passed an uneasy winter due to the activities of the rapparees and Sarsfield's cavalry, the slackening of military operations did nothing to ease animosities in the Jacobite camp. As King James observed in a rare moment of insight, 'when the enemy gave them some respite their whole attention was to make war upon one another'.[8] The Irish army officers were opposed to King James's men, Tyrconnel and Berwick, but, although they were following an agenda of their own designed primarily to serve 'Old English' interests, continued to pay at least lip service to the Stuart King. They sent a deputation to put their case to the King, but this was delayed by bad weather, allowing Tyrconnel time to entrench his position with James, before returning to Ireland. Tyrconnel assured James that he would bring Sarsfield, whom he described as a 'mutineer', back into order.

During the winter there were further abortive peace moves. The failure at Limerick had made some Williamites feel that the Irish should be offered better terms, and Ginkel, the new Commander-in-Chief, also wished to bring the war to a quick end. William was reluctant, partly because he intended to reward some of his supporters with land confiscated from Jacobites. However, Ginkel's agents reported that most of the Irish Catholic gentry were eager for peace if their property was guaranteed. By late winter King William, anxious to release troops for the war in Flanders, agreed to offer a general pardon, with certain exceptions. As intended, this caused a sharp division on the Jacobite side between those who had lost their lands during Cromwell's time or earlier, to whom the amnesty offered little, and others, who still theoretically owned their property, who were more receptive. Sarsfield remained implacably opposed to acceptance, and persuaded Berwick to arrest the leading members of the 'peace party'. By spring, peace feelers had died away.

In January 1691 Tyrconnel returned to Ireland and the Duke of Berwick left for France. Tyrconnel's position had been strengthened by James's support, and he saw himself not only as running the civil government of Jacobite Ireland, but also as Commander-in-Chief of the army. Sarsfield had been created Earl of Lucan by the King, which did little to mollify him. The majority of the army officers sided with Sarsfield, while Balldearg O'Donnell, still lurking with 7,000 or 8,000 men near Sligo, refused to accept anyone's authority.

All, however, were in agreement that, if the war were to be continued with any prospect of success, massive French aid, a French general to act as de facto commander in the field, and a reorganisation of the army were essential. Tyrconnel had brought with him in January 8,000 muskets and 4,000 pikes, and French War Minister Louvois had been sufficiently impressed by a disingenuous assessment of Irish military prospects by James and Tyrconnel to agree to send French officers and supplies, although no more units of troops. Sarsfield was tasked with reorganising the army, raising ten new infantry battalions, bringing the total to forty-six, although, with only 30,000 men, many remained understrength. To these were added 3,000 dragoons and 3,500 cavalry, the latter being justifiably regarded as among the best troops on either side in Ireland. Artillery, however, remained inadequate.

Efforts were made to strengthen the defences of the key towns still in Jacobite hands. Work went on at Limerick from February until late April, and further efforts were made at Athlone, where Richard Grace seems to have been replaced as Governor, perhaps on the grounds of age, although possibly because his approach was causing increasing discontent among the local Protestant population. During the winter Sarsfield established a forward outpost at Ballymore, halfway between Athlone and the Williamite garrison at Mullingar, as well as a number of smaller outposts.

On 9 May the promised French general arrived at Limerick. Lieutenant-General Charles Chamont, Marquis de St Ruhe (commonly rendered as 'St Ruth'), was appointed Marshal General of the Irish forces. A native of Alsace, St Ruhe had served as a professional soldier in eastern Europe before entering French service, where he had been noted for his vigorous operations against the Huguenots. During this period he had Mountcashel's Irish Brigade under his command, and was accounted particularly skilful in leading Irish troops. Others, however, saw him as vainglorious and obstinate. St Ruhe brought with him '146 officers, 150 cadets, 300 English and Scots, 24 surgeons, 180 masons, 2 bombardiers, 18 cannoniers, 800 horses, 19 pieces of cannon, 12,000 horse shoes, 6,000 bridles and saddles, 16,000 muskets; uniforms, stockings and shoes for 16,000 men, some lead and balls, and a large supply of biscuit'.[9] With St Ruhe also came two lieutenant-generals, d'Usson and du Tesse.

The Williamites scorned these reinforcements, likening them to pouring brandy down the throat of a dying man. St Ruhe for his part was dismayed by the indiscipline and shortages of all kinds in the Irish forces. Nor was

Tyrconnel entirely willing to cede control of military matters to the Frenchman. Although St Ruhe set to work energetically, it remained to be seen whether the enemy would grant him time to prepare.

King William began the campaigning season in discontented mood. He blamed the Royal Navy for its failure to prevent three major French convoys from reaching Ireland, and he was also dissatisfied with Godert de Ginkel, whose winter offensives had all come to nothing. Ginkel was not seen as ideal for the Irish command. He had had difficulty in controlling his subordinates, and was felt by some to be lacking in resolution. William considered replacing him with the younger Schomberg, but eventually decided to leave Ginkel in command. Telling him to make Athlone the first objective of the new campaign, William warned: 'you know what sort of people you have to deal with, such as cannot always be controlled by mildness'. To ease Ginkel's task, William transferred two of his most difficult subordinates, Percy Kirke and James Douglas, to Flanders, replacing them with Hugh Mackay and Thomas Tollemache.

Throughout the winter there had been a continuing build-up by the Williamite forces. At the beginning of the campaigning season they were deployed broadly as follows. In Ulster there was a mixed Scottish–English force, whose eventual objective was Jacobite-held Sligo. Dutch and Huguenot troops under Württemberg were at Waterford, there was a Danish contingent in south-east Ireland, while Ginkel had his own headquarters at Kilkenny.

Both sides recognised the importance of Athlone. While the Jacobites had no reasonable alternative to staying on the defensive, the Williamite plan was to force a crossing of the Shannon and thrust into Connaught, capturing Limerick and Galway and striking a death blow to continued Irish resistance.

BALLYMORE AND ATHLONE

Ginkel was ready for action by the end of May. At his forward headquarters at Mullingar he had eight regiments of foot, six of horse and one of dragoons, with thirty siege guns, six mortars and twelve field pieces. Wintering in Ulster were eight infantry regiments, one of horse and two of dragoons, which were ordered to muster at Bellinbet and then march south to join Ginkel.

The Duke of Württemberg's polyglot forces, which included Danish, Dutch and French Huguenot infantry, with three English foot battalions and 2,000 horse and dragoons, mustered at Cathel on 28 May, reached Birr on the 30th and marched on towards Athlone to rendezvous with Ginkel. The latter expected his army, when fully assembled, to total over thirty battalions of foot, with forty squadrons of horse and dragoons, a total of some 25,000 men.

Meanwhile St Ruhe was mustering all available forces to meet the attack. After bringing in as many as possible of the rapparees, and stripping his garrisons, he may have mustered some 20,000 men, including 3,000 horse and 2,000 dragoons, who were assembled at Ballinasloe, some 20 miles south-west of Athlone.

On 7 June Ginkel's army appeared before the Jacobite outpost at Ballymore. The defences incorporated an old castle at the end of a narrow peninsula that jutted at its southern end into a lake. The garrison totalled 1,130 men, including many rapparees, and they had two old Turkish guns. The governor, Colonel Bourke, was forced to surrender after a ferocious two-day bombardment. Ginkel spent the next ten days repairing the castle, and waiting for a pontoon train that was on its way from Dublin. In the event, the pontoons would prove useless in bridging the Shannon, and the delay enabled St Ruhe to reach Athlone before Ginkel did.

The Williamite forces arrived before the 'English' town of Athlone on 19 June. This had been abandoned by Grace in the previous year, but Sarsfield had decided during the winter that its defences should be repaired and strengthened. Work had not gone well, allegedly as a result of a quarrel between Major-General John Wauchope, whose troops were responsible for carrying out the work, and the French engineer in charge of the design, over whether French or English measurements should be used. It was still incomplete when Ginkel arrived.

On 20 June Ginkel began a bombardment with fourteen siege pieces. Within two days the defences of the 'English' town had been shattered, and Wauchope had to be dug out of the ruins by his men before they withdrew across the Shannon into the 'Irish' town, having inflicted some 400 casualties on their attackers. As they withdrew, the Irish broke down two arches of the medieval bridge. St Ruhe and the main army had reached the western outskirts of Athlone on the previous day, and were confident of stalling Ginkel's offensive. St Ruhe ill-advisedly boasted: 'Ginkel deserved to be hanged for attempting to take Athlone while he [St Ruhe] was at the head of so great an army to defend it, and he himself deserved to be hanged if he should lose it.'[10]

St Ruhe established his camp 2 miles west of Athlone. He had with him around 16,000 foot, 3,000 horse and 2,000 dragoons. He placed Lieutenant-General d'Usson in command in the town, and decided to adopt the seemingly reasonable strategy of rotating his infantry regiments in defence of Athlone in order to give them experience of combat conditions.

The Williamites, meanwhile, faced major difficulties in crossing the Shannon. The pontoon bridge could not be set up in the face of heavy enemy fire. Mackay wanted to detour around Athlone and make a crossing either downstream at Banaghr or Meelick, or upstream at Lanesborough, using a picked force of Ulster troops. Ginkel, however, decided on a prepared assault, either over the bridge or across immediately adjacent fords. In the meantime a bombardment of the 'Irish' town was maintained, which, as well as doing a great deal of damage, steadily lowered the morale of the often raw Irish troops enduring it.

On 24 June a Williamite party was sent upstream to reconnoitre a ford. They had been told not to cross, but disobeyed orders and went cattle rustling. They were spotted, and the Jacobites promptly fortified the Connaught end of the ford, frustrating any planned crossing at that point. The battle now became increasingly focused on the bridge. On 26 June the Williamites, under heavy fire, attempted to advance towards the bridge: 'we labour hard to gain the bridge, but what we got there is inch by inch as it were, the enemy sticking very close to it, though great numbers of them were slain by our guns'.[11]

During the struggle the Williamites managed to bridge one of the broken-down arches, but the gap where the other had been remained. The Williamite artillery was meanwhile systematically smashing the Jacobite defences in continuous fire, day and night. However, the Jacobites worked furiously under fire to repair their barricades and, during daylight hours on 27 June, continued to frustrate all enemy attempts to span the last breach in the bridge. Early on 28 June, probably while it was still dark, planks were placed across the gap, but a Sergeant Custane and sixteen men of Maxwell's Ulster Dragoon Regiment volunteered to try to throw them down. All were killed, but a lieutenant and twenty men followed and succeeded, though all but two of them were casualties. This incident was typical of the fighting at Athlone, whose fierce defence seems to have owed more to junior officers and rank and file than to the generals. Furious firing continued all day, with the Williamites setting alight some houses near the Jacobite end of the bridge. John Stevens was caught up in the action:

The great and small shot never ceased firing, and sometime before noon the enemies with their grenades fired our faggots on the bridge, which, being dry and not covered with earth, burnt most furiously. I was commanded with a detachment of forty men of our regiment, and other officers of other regiments in the town with proportionable numbers of their men to put a stop to the fire, which notwithstanding all our endeavours raged so violently that it took hold of the houses adjoining to the bridge. The enemy in the meantime bent thirty pieces of cannon and all their mortars this way, so that what with the fire and what with the balls and bombs flying so thick that spot was a mere hell on earth, for the place was very narrow which made the fire scorch, and so many cannon and mortars incessantly playing on it there seemed to be no likelihood of any man coming off alive. However we threw down one house, and the men, being hasty to run off with the timber for their own security, that gave a stop to the progress of the fire, which then began to decline until it ceased. We had very many men killed here of the detachment that came to work, and the rest being gone off, a French major we had in our regiment, besides the Irish, commanded me back to my post. And this I think was the hottest place that ever I saw in my time of service . . . Many who had served long in France said they had never seen such furious firing for so long a time . . . The whole action continued about four hours, most of the men who got away returning no more, which made our work the longer for those who were forced to continue it . . . By this means only seven of my detachment were killed and nineteen wounded out of forty, and I received no hurt myself. Yet returning to my post in the trenches I was knocked down with a stone that flew from the castle wall, which only stunned me, a good beaver I had on saving my head. Another stone from the wall gave me a small hurt on the shin, which was not considerable.[12]

By the end of the day, with all attempts at crossing repulsed, Ginkel was growing desperate. The season was already well advanced, and unless Athlone were taken soon, it seemed that the campaign would end in frustration. St Ruhe, for his part, seems to have believed that the repulse of the attacks of the 28th had effectively ended the danger, and that the Williamites would soon withdraw.

However, at this point Major-General Thomas Tollemache presented Ginkel with his own plan. Three Danish soldiers awaiting execution following courts martial were offered their lives if they agreed to test a ford across the river. Crossing at three points, with their own men firing over their heads as if at deserters, all three reached the west bank of the Shannon and returned unscathed. A crossing was clearly feasible, and at around 6 p.m. on 30 June, Major-General Hugh Mackay led a picked force onto the bridge, while Major-General Tettau headed another party, including sixty grenadiers wearing body armour, wading waist-deep across the river, which dry weather had rendered abnormally low.

Fortuitously, the attack had been made at a time when a changeover of units in the garrison was taking place. The defenders currently were the three raw infantry regiments of O'Gara, Cormac O'Neill and MacMahon. Although they opened a hot if inaccurate fire on the attackers, they urgently required reinforcements. But St Ruhe had chosen the same afternoon to hold a party for his senior officers, which slowed down any reaction. As Mackay swept across the bridge with 1,500 men, O'Gara's soldiers were the first of the defenders to break. D'Usson attempted to lead MacMahon's men in a counter-attack, but they panicked and fled, trampling and knocking unconscious the Frenchman. English and Danish troops poured into the town, though:

the rubbish and stuff thrown down by our cannon was much more difficult to climb over than a great part of the enemy's works, which occasioned our soldiers to swear and curse even among the bullets themselves, upon which Major General Mackay told them that they had more reason to fall on their knees and thank God for the victory and that they were brave men, and the first of men if they would swear less.[13]

Jacobite attempts to send reinforcements into Athlone were frustrated by the defences on the westward side of the town, St Ruhe having ignored suggestions that gaps should be made to allow swift entry in just such a contingency.

Within half an hour Athlone had fallen, apart from the castle, which surrendered next day. The Williamites admitted to thirteen dead and thirty-four wounded, and claimed to have killed 500 of the enemy. More were massacred by Danish troops in the course of mopping-up operations amid the ruins, in which 'one could not set down his foot at the end of the bridge, or castle, but on dead bodies; many lay half-buried under the rubbish, and more under faggots, and many not to be seen under the ruins, whereby the stench is insufferable'.[14] Among the dead was Richard Grace.

The sudden loss of Athlone caused widespread recriminations among the Jacobites: 'never was a town which was so well defended before so basely lost'.[15] There were dark rumours of treachery, the principal scapegoat being the Scot, Major-General Thomas Maxwell, who had directed the initial defence that day and who was conveniently now a prisoner in enemy hands. More appropriately, St Ruhe could be censured for failing to ensure that reinforcements could enter the town quickly if needed.

The Williamite bombardment of Athlone had expended about 50 tons of gunpowder, 12,000 cannon balls and 600 mortar-bombs, together with uncounted tons of stone which the mortars also fired, making Athlone the most bombarded town in the British Isles.

AUGHRIM: THE APPROACH

The next day St Ruhe pulled his army back 20 miles to Ballinasloe. Morale had slumped even lower than after the Boyne. Stevens recorded that there was 'great confusion and disorder, such a panic fear having seized our men that the very noise of ten horsemen would have dispersed as many of our battalions, above half the soldiers scattering without any other thing but their own apprehension to fright them'.[16]

By the time the army reached Ballinasloe, half of the infantry had deserted. St Ruhe was angry and humiliated, and determined to repair his injured *amour-propre* by meeting Ginkel in a pitched battle. This was not a prospect that appealed to most of the Irish commanders, who had a realistic view of their soldiers' limitations. They were strengthened in their view by the knowledge that Tyrconnel had ordered St Ruhe to bring the army back to

Limerick, hoping to wear out Ginkel's men in an abortive siege similar to that of the previous year, and prolong the war into another spring, when French troops might arrive.

Sarsfield, for once, was in agreement with Tyrconnel: the infantry could hold Limerick and Galway while the cavalry raided deep into Williamite territory, perhaps as far as Dublin, threatening Ginkel's lines of communication and forcing him to withdraw. Eventually, St Ruhe reluctantly accepted the majority viewpoint and issued orders for the foot to pull back into Limerick and Galway. Lieutenant-General d'Usson, who had supported the Irish, was sent to command at Galway, John Wauchope was dispatched to Limerick, while Sarsfield was sent to Loughrea. St Ruhe, having thus disposed of his three principal critics, remained at Ballinasloe, where, partly as a result of his own strenuous efforts, the Irish army recovered much of its lost morale. St Ruhe proved particularly successful in gaining the confidence of Irish junior officers and the rank and file, setting out to be 'very kind and familiar with the Irish officers, whom formerly he had treated with disrespect and contempt; and to caress the soldiers, though a little before he would hang a dozen of them in a morning'.[17]

With morale restored, and many stragglers and deserters returning to the colours, St Ruhe reversed his original decision. He would stand and fight, and found what appeared to him to be the perfect position about 5 miles from Ballinasloe, on a hill called Kilcommodon, above the village of Aughrim. The eastern slopes of the hill were protected to their front by a bog, crossed only by two narrow passes at its northern and southern ends. The northernmost pass or causeway was partly protected by Aughrim Castle, and the hillside itself was covered with hedges and ditches which, when the Irish army took up position along a 2-mile front, the troops began to improve into more substantial earthworks.

There are various estimates of Jacobite strength; the army included thirty-five infantry battalions, many of them considerably understrength, and probably totalled about 15,000 effectives. The eleven cavalry and eight dragoon regiments present totalled around 5,000 men. The Jacobites fielded nine, mainly light, guns.

Following his capture of Athlone, Ginkel had halted until 7 July, awaiting the arrival of fresh supplies of ammunition. That day the Williamite army began moving slowly westwards, on the 11th reaching the River Suck, where, approaching Ballinasloe, Ginkel learnt for the first time of St Ruhe's whereabouts. The Williamites halted for the night on the east bank of the Suck, sending scouts to occupy the high ground on the opposite bank.

At dawn the Williamites could see the slopes of Kilcommodon Hill, covered with grass, bracken and brambles, and with the tents and rough shelters of the enemy spread along its crest. George Storey observed that:

The enemy's camp lay along the ridge of a hill . . . from thence to the bog below was nigh half a mile, and this cut into a great many small enclosures which the enemy had ordered so as to make a communication from one of them to another, and lined all these very thick with small shot [musketeers]; this showed a great deal of dexterity in M. St Ruth in making choice of such a piece of ground as nature itself could not better, considering all circumstances; for he knew that the Irish naturally loved a breastwork between them and bullets, and here they were fittest to the purpose with hedges and ditches to the very edge of the bog.[18]

St Ruhe planned to fight, initially, a defensive battle. His left wing rested on the castle and the right on the Tristaun stream, a distance of about 1½ miles. The front of the Irish position was protected by the bog that ran from in front of the castle to Tristaun Bridge, and another area of bog lay to the left, making any outflanking attempt in that direction very difficult. Approach from the east was made still more tortuous by a number of streams that ran down from the ridge, eventually to join the River Suck. There appeared to be only two approaches to the ridge from the east: a narrow causeway led towards the castle, and on the Irish right a low, irregular ridge or 'drumlin', only wide enough for two horsemen to ride abreast, ran across the bog.

On the Jacobite left were two regiments of horse and three of dragoons, commanded by Major-General Dominic Sheldon; on the right, probably led by Sarsfield accompanied by General du Tesse, were the Lifeguard troop, three regiments of horse and some dragoons. In reserve, to the left rear, was the Earl of Galmoy's excellent Regiment of Horse. The main body of Irish foot was deployed in two lines. The first was commanded by Major-General William Dorrington, the second was under Major-General John Hamilton.

The slope of the ridge was fairly gentle, and was traversed along its length by a road, below which, running down to the bog, were a number of small fields divided up by hedges and ditches. The left centre of the Irish foot occupied these, which were especially suitable for the many raw troops in the Irish ranks. Another area of rough ground, divided up by hedges and ditches, lay on the Irish right, near Tristaun Bridge, and was also occupied by musketeers.

The second line of Irish foot was deployed in orthodox fashion, with its pikes, probably reinforced by those of the front line, stationed behind its musketeers, and following approximately the line of the road. On the far left, Aughrim Castle and associated ditches and trenches were occupied by 200 musketeers of Walter Burke's Regiment. Commanding the causeway to the south of the castle, two more battalions were drawn up in a field or enclosure. At least three of the Jacobite guns formed a battery near to the site of the present-day church.

St Ruhe's deployments were designed to make the best possible use of the terrain. Sheldon's Horse on the left were positioned slightly to the rear in a

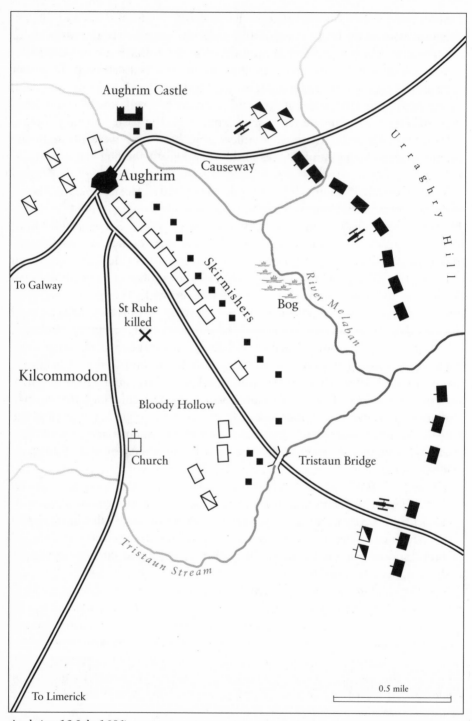

Aughrim Castle

Causeway

Urraghry Hill

To Galway

Aughrim

Skirmishers

Bog

River Melaban

St Ruhe killed

Kilcommodon

Bloody Hollow

Church

Tristaun Bridge

Tristaun Stream

To Limerick

0.5 mile

Aughrim, 12 July 1691

hollow, with firm ground, suitable for cavalry, to their front, and covered further forward by some dismounted dragoons. On the Jacobite right, the horse were deployed behind the foot lining the hedges of the enclosures between Tristaun Bridge and Kilcommodon church, with rough ground to their front occupied by dragoons.

On paper the Jacobites occupied an extremely strong position. Its main weakness was that the terrain would make it virtually impossible for them to manoeuvre or make a major attack. It may well be that the poor overall state of the Irish army would have made such an option impossible anyway, but St Ruhe's position has been described with some aptness as one for a 'last stand taken up before the end'.[19] Another weakness, which was to become increasingly apparent once fighting began, was the failure to protect the line of retreat to Limerick, which actually lay beyond the Jacobite right wing. Furthermore, while probably unavoidable, the lack of a substantial reserve was a major weakness.

St Ruhe's plan was probably the best available in the circumstances. He would allow Ginkel to make a frontal attack on his right across the ford of the river and on his centre across the bog. He seems to have assumed that the narrowness of the causeway leading to the castle would preclude any assault on his left. Once the Irish had repulsed the Williamite attack, which with all their advantages of terrain St Ruhe was confident they would do, his cavalry would attack across the causeway into Ginkel's flank, and his foot would advance to roll up his front. Irish morale was high; according to Storey, St Ruhe delivered an inspirational speech to his troops, although, as his English was evidently limited, even if his men understood anything but Gaelic, and most of them would be out of earshot, its effectiveness was perhaps questionable:

stand to it, therefore, my dears, and fear no more the reproaches of the heretics who brand you with cowardice, and you may be assured that King James will love and reward you, Louis the Great will protect you, and all good Catholics applaud you, I myself will command you, the church will pray for you, your posterity will bless you, God will make you all saints and his holy mother will lay you in her bosom.[20]

THE BATTLE BEGINS

Ginkel's army, approximately equal in numbers to its opponents, broke camp at dawn on 12 July and, hindered by early morning mist, began cautiously moving forward, the foot crossing the Suck by means of a bridge, the horse using fords above and below the bridge.

The Williamite army had twenty-eight battalions of foot, most averaging around 500 men compared with their nominal establishment of 806 privates, and so totalling around 14,000. They included twelve or thirteen English battalions, three from Ulster, six Danish, three Dutch and three Huguenot. The horse and dragoons, around 4,000 to 6,000 men, formed thirty-four or thirty-five squadrons of cavalry and thirteen or fourteen troops of dragoons. Four each of the horse and dragoon units were Enniskilleners, and there were also some Danish horse. Once in sight of the enemy position, Ginkel halted and, apart from some skirmishing between outposts, no serious action occurred during the morning. It may have been as late as three in the afternoon before the Williamites were fully deployed.

Ginkel also formed his foot up in two lines, with horse and dragoons on the wings. General Hugh Mackay, loser at Killiecrankie, commanded the right wing of the first line of foot, which consisted of seven battalions of English infantry. On the left were seven battalions of Danes and Huguenots commanded by Brigadier General La Melloniere, a veteran of the Boyne. The second line was weaker, with seven battalions of English and Ulster foot under Major-General Tollemache on its right, and a similar number under the Count of Nassau forming its left. The horse on the right consisted of twenty-six or twenty-eight squadrons of horse and dragoons, some of the latter being dismounted to protect the right flank. The first line was led by Major-General Schravemoer, while the second was under the Marquis de Ruvigny. On the left were twenty-one squadrons, including three Danish, under La Forest Suzannet. Again, there were dismounted dragoons on the left flank.

Ginkel was never an adventurous commander, and he may have hesitated to attack the strong enemy position. Although he had numerical superiority in cavalry, the nature of the terrain would make it difficult to utilise this effectively, and he had had ample testament to the ability of the Irish horse. Ginkel called a council of war to consider his next move. It was left to Hugh Mackay to come up with a proposal. He had noted that although more troops might be hidden behind the ridge, the bulk of the Irish horse appeared to be stationed on St Ruhe's right, suggesting, as might be expected from its proximity to the road to Limerick, that the Jacobite commander was most concerned about that flank. A major attack here might cause St Ruhe to divert more troops from his left and any reserve. At the same time, a frontal attack across the bog might pin down the Irish centre and perhaps draw in more troops from the Jacobite left. This would make easier an assault aimed at breaking through along the causeway and then swinging in to attack the left flank of the Jacobite centre. This was a very high-risk strategy, and was probably not greeted by Ginkel with great enthusiasm. But events were about to force his hand.

Fighting flared up early in the afternoon when Donop's Danish horse encountered Jacobite outposts south of Urraghry Hill. The Danes were reinforced by Cunningham's Enniskillen Dragoons, switched from the inactive Williamite left flank, and by the Earl of Portland's Regiment of Horse. The

Jacobite outposts were pushed back along the ridge towards Tristaun Bridge. Ginkel, on the high ground half a mile east of Tristaun Bridge, could see the main Jacobite forces before him. The Tristaun Pass would clearly be difficult to force, but there did seem to be a slim possibility of turning the Irish flank beyond the stream at the south end of the ridge. Meanwhile the main part of the Williamite army was completing its deployment on the high ground around Urraghry.

By about 2 p.m. the fog was clearing and a long-range artillery duel began. Firing could be heard near Tristaun Bridge, where Cunningham's Dragoons were trying to force their way forward through the ditches and enclosures. Ginkel had still not decided whether or not to bring on a full-scale engagement that day, but the scale of the fighting increased anyway, as more troops were fed into the action. Ginkel's initial intention seemed not to follow Mackay's suggestion, but to seize Tristaun Bridge and Ford, and so threaten the Jacobite right flank and the road to Limerick, forcing St Ruhe to evacuate his strong position. More troops were brought over from the Williamite right, including Sir John Lanier's and part of Ruvigny's Regiments of Horse. The Irish reacted by sending in reinforcements of their own, and throughout the afternoon fighting around the ford intensified.

After about an hour's dispute, the Jacobites on the right were forced back a short distance across a stream. By 4 p.m., Ginkel's left was so heavily engaged that a major engagement seemed inevitable.

St Ruhe, meanwhile, was riding constantly from one part of his army to another, 'to give the necessary orders, when he saw occasion'. Despite what Mackay evidently believed, the Jacobite left had not yet been seriously weakened in order to reinforce the troops of the right wing engaged around Tristaun Ford. But, as the fighting continued to intensify, St Ruhe made the serious error of ordering the second line of the left wing to march to the right. He may also have transferred some of the first line of cavalry stationed near the castle, believing his position there to be sufficiently safeguarded by the bog to its front. The Irish commanders were justifiably concerned about the threat to their right and to their line of retreat to Limerick but, as a result, they neglected other points of their defences.

The extensive boggy ground initially discouraged action in the centre of the field but, as evening approached, the rest of the Williamite forces began a general advance.

THE CRISIS

Because of the difficult going, the Williamite formations became disordered, in some cases to such an extent that elements of the second line of foot overtook parts of the first and were in action before them. On the Jacobite right, Sarsfield was faced by Ginkel's Dutch Huguenot and Danish cavalry, some 1,500 of whom, representing five regiments, charged across the ford at about 6 p.m. to engage Sarsfield's men in a major engagement. Although the Williamites established a foothold on the far bank, they quickly found themselves pinned down.

More allied cavalry were committed, and managed to push Sarsfield's first line back on to his second, where they were held. Some Danish infantry were sent forward in an attempt to clear the boggy ground of enemy dragoons, but found themselves entangled in the difficult ground 'all cut up by the marsh and by hedges [while] the enemy resisted much more vigorously than we had expected'.[21] After a fierce struggle the Williamite horse fell back to the western edge of the ford.

So far, the battle seemed to be going as St Ruhe had intended, and he soon had further cause for satisfaction.

In the centre the advance of the allied infantry received covering fire from their artillery, which was double the number of their Jacobite opponents. Slightly to the north of the main Williamite battery, the Huguenot foot battalions under La Melbonière advanced against the enemy in what was later to be known as the 'Bloody Hollow'. They were quickly checked, and were soon desperately defending themselves behind hastily erected barricades of stakes and pikes against fierce enemy counter-attacks.

As the allied foot struggled, waist-deep in places, through the bog, they could see no sign of the enemy, who were in the cover of hedges and ditches and holding their fire until the Williamites were at close range. According to Storey, some believed that the Jacobites had no 'men in that place . . . but they were convinced of it at last, for no sooner were the French [Huguenots] and the rest got within twenty yards or less of the ditches than the Irish fired most furiously upon them'.[22]

On the Jacobite left a Williamite battery was manhandled onto the causeway leading to the castle, and exchanged fire with some Jacobite guns. Once again the advancing Williamite foot were thrown into disorder by the terrain. The bog to the right of the causeway was felt to be too wide to make a crossing feasible, and so the Williamites were forced to make their assault on the south side of the causeway, although here they faced both the bog and a stream. The advance was spearheaded by four English battalions (those of Earle, Herbert, Creighton and Brewer), about half a mile south of the Galway road at Melehan Bridge. The advancing English troops were struggling in the bog, up to their middles in mud and water.

Thomas Earle's battalion was first through the bog, and was ordered to re-form its ranks, occupy the nearest ditches and stand on the defensive until supporting troops of horse came up to back them. The foot battalions of Foulkes, from the first line, and Stuart from the second, were also moving up in support. But the English troops at once found themselves under heavy fire from the hitherto unseen Irish foot lining the ditches and hedges, and they were also suffering from the significant disadvantage (in the days of dense smoke produced by black powder firing) of having the wind and the sun in their faces. Rather than stand still, taking casualties from the enemy fire, Earle's men pressed on and cleared the first line of hedges, but discovered that the fight had only just begun:

> When we, on the right, attacked them, they gave us their fire and away they ran to the next ditches and we, scrambling over the first ditch, made after them to the next from where they gave us another scattering fire and away they ran to other ditches behind them, we still pursuing them from one ditch to another until we had them out of four or five rows of these ditches into an open plain where was some of their horse drawn up. Here in climbing these ditches and still following them from one to another, no one can imagine we could possibly keep our order, and here in this hurry there was no less than six battalions so intermingled together that were at a loss what to do.[23]

The Jacobite skirmishers had now fallen back on their second line, positioned where gaps had been cut in the banks and hedges to allow for cavalry counter-attacks, and Dominic Sheldon's Horse bore down on the English foot before they could re-form their ranks. The English broke and fled back towards the bog, Earle being taken prisoner. Brewer, Creighton, Earle and Herbert's Regiments, consisting of half the foot that Mackay had ordered to attack, all broke.

Meanwhile, to their right, Mackay's remaining foot and some horse were also fiercely engaged. Mackay sent forward the foot regiments of Kirke and Gustavus Hamilton to cover the horse, and also to engage Walter Burke's Regiment of Foot around Aughrim Castle. The English forces were halted by the Irish musketeers firing from behind cover, but managed to stand their ground. At about the same time, the battalions of Bellasis and George Hamilton also crossed the bog 'by the defile or dirty lane which leads to Aughrim'. Reaching a gap in the hedges that had been made for the Irish horse, the Williamites crossed a cornfield and, despite heavy fire from the castle, established themselves in some entrenchments that had apparently been evacuated by Irish troops who had been shifted to the right.

Thus, by 8 p.m. there were four Williamite battalions established on the enemy side of the bog. But Ginkel's overall position was far from secure. Mackay had launched a second assault to the south of the ill-fated attack by Earle's men, using the Ulster battalions of Tiffin and St John from his second line, together with Foulkes and Stuart and a Huguenot regiment from his left. Once again, the Irish, in their hedges and ditches, allowed the enemy to come within 20yd before they opened fire. Amid heavy fire and dense clouds of smoke, the allied troops pushed on, but were first halted and then forced back.

Possibly acting on his own initiative, the Prince of Hesse brought his German battalion and some Dutch troops forward in support from the second line, and a fierce combat followed in which the Irish gradually gained the upper hand and, in furious close combat, using their clubbed muskets, drove the Williamite forces back into the bog.

Most of the centre of the allied line was now in total confusion, and St Ruhe's men exploited their success. The Irish counter-attack was spearheaded by Dorrington's Foot Guards and John Hamilton's Regiment, who pursued the enemy until 'the blood flowed into their shoes'. In places both sides were intermingled in total confusion as they struggled in the bog. Men of Gordon O'Neill's Regiment, following their banner of white bearing the Red Hand of Ulster, reached the far side of the bog and briefly captured a Williamite battery.

St Ruhe was delighted with the success, calling out excitedly and unintelligibly to his men: 'Le jour est nous, mes enfants!', and talked of advancing to the gates of Dublin. But reason quickly reasserted itself. His horse on the left were occupied by those of Mackay's men who had held their ground, and were in no position to begin exploiting the enemy's disorder. St Ruhe recalled his men to their original positions.

On the Jacobite right, the cavalry fight around Tristaun Ford was still stalemated. The Huguenot cavalry commander, La Forest, had ordered up further troops so that he could support the infantry attack by breaking through Sarsfield and attacking the flank of the Irish foot. A new division under Major-General van Holzapfel came up, but the Williamites found themselves still unable to overcome the determined resistance of Sarsfield's men, who had probably been reinforced from Sheldon's wing.

On the Williamite side, Major-General Thomas Tollemache, the ablest of Ginkel's subordinates, rallied the second line of foot on the right, brought up the remaining reserves, and recrossed the bog. By now virtually all of the Williamite foot were in action and the only remaining uncommitted troops were the English cavalry on the right flank. If Ginkel were to salvage a victory, they were his only realistic hope. But thanks to the failure of Mackay's foot, they still had to negotiate the causeway before they could make their presence felt.

THE BREAKTHROUGH

Although the two Irish foot battalions that had begun the battle stationed at the northern end of the causeway had been drawn off by Dorrington to take part in the infantry action in the centre, Burke's Regiment was still in position, with an unknown number of Sheldon's cavalry beyond. The Williamite cavalry commanders, unaware of the extent of the bog, hesitated, until an angry Mackay rode out himself to investigate the ground. His temper was not improved when he was thrown from his horse into the mud. Ginkel now sent Ruvigny direct orders to advance. Ruvigny gave the task to Villier's brigade, which had only six squadrons available, joining it himself.

The only feasible route of advance for the horse (who were covered by the fire of some dragoons) was along the 'old broken causeway only large enough for two horses to pass it a time and sixty yards long'. It was not an inviting prospect, but represented Ginkel's only remaining chance of victory. The horse, headed by Ruvigny's Regiment and Oxford's Royal Regiment of Horse, set off in a desperate, straggling charge along the causeway, passing about 30yd in front of the trenches and castle held by Burke's men. Now was the time for the Irish musketeers to deliver a devastating volley. But Burke's men discovered to their horror that the reserve ammunition with which they had been issued was for English muskets, and unusable in their French weapons. As their fire faltered, some of Burke's desperate soldiers tried to load their muskets with stones or with buttons from their coats. With light losses, the English horse had passed their first obstacle.

They were now faced by Henry Lutterell's Dragoons, who opened fire but then began to pull back towards Sheldon's Horse, reduced to two regiments by the reinforcements sent to Sarsfield. Even so, if Sheldon had followed customary cavalry tactics and counter-charged Ruvigny before he was deployed or reinforced, there was every chance that the Williamites would have been routed. Instead, he hesitated, and Ruvigny was quickly joined by several more squadrons, Wolseley's Enniskillen horse, and some dragoons, who steadily widened and deepened their bridgehead at the northern end of the causeway.

Even now, it was not necessarily too late for the Jacobites to at least stabilise their position. St Ruhe did not seem particularly concerned. He ordered Sheldon, reinforced by the sole Jacobite reserve, consisting of Galmoy's Horse, to prepare to counter-charge, and ordered the Lifeguard of Horse from Sarsfield's wing to reinforce them. Then St Ruhe himself set off to command their attack, exclaiming: 'They are beaten, let us beat them to the purpose.' Hardly had the words left St Ruhe's mouth than he was killed instantly, decapitated by a cannon ball.

The result was a paralysis of command. Although his aides hastily covered St Ruhe's body with a cloak to avoid panic among the troops, valuable time was lost. A year previously Dominic Sheldon had fought with bravery and determination at the Boyne, but now he seemed stricken by indecision. He hesitated, awaiting St Ruhe's arrival, like the other Irish commanders, further confused by not having been informed of the General's full intentions for conducting the battle.

By now back in the saddle, Hugh Mackay was quick to follow up the
advantage gained by Ruvigny's advance. He sent four foot battalions and
some horse against the Irish left wing, positioned in the dozen or so cabins
that made up the village of Aughrim. At the same time the rest of the horse
under Ruvigny swung south-eastwards, linking up with Tollemache's
advancing foot. Fierce fighting continued, with 'nothing but a constant fire
and a very hot dispute all along the line'[24] as the Irish foot struggled to hold
their ground and prevent their line from being enfiladed. They looked in vain
for support from the horse and dragoons of their left wing. Henry Lutterell,
having decided that the battle and, indeed, the war were lost, mounted up his
dragoons and left the field. Sheldon was left heavily outnumbered, and
Ruvigny was able to detach a portion of his force to contain him while the
remainder moved against the left flank of the Irish foot.

The latter were utterly unprepared. Their defences were mostly to their
front, and they lacked the discipline and cohesion to face the cavalry. The
Williamite cavalry tore into them and panic began to spread, as Irish foot fled
desperately towards the crest of the ridge, in many cases throwing down their
colours and muskets.

Lieutenant-General du Tesse had at length learnt of St Ruhe's death and
attempted to restore the situation, but it was too late. He led two squadrons of
horse, including the Lifeguards, in a counter-charge, but was hurled back by
superior numbers. Du Tesse was seriously injured and the Lifeguard was
effectively destroyed, with the loss of seventy-two men.

The triumphant Williamite horsemen swept on to the crest of the ridge,
trampling down, shooting or sabring the droves of panic-stricken Irish who
fled before them. By the time the tidings of disaster reached Sarsfield on the
right wing, it was too late for him to take any effective action other than
make successive charges to slow down La Forest's Horse. Sarsfield and
Galmoy did what they could to cover the flight of the foot, to whom the
Williamites were offering no quarter. Those who escaped mainly did so by
hiding in the bogs or taking advantage of gathering rain and darkness.

A Williamite eyewitness, the Dane Andreas Claudianus, saw the horror of
the closing stages of the battle:

At the very top of the hill the cavalry were mixed with the infantry. The
firing was so intense that the ridges seemed to be ablaze. As dusk fell the
cavalry began to move away and take flight, abandoning the infantry who
in turn threw down their arms, left their colours and ran. Terrible scenes
followed as the English fell on the rear of the fugitives. Stricken with terror
we saw them fleeing in all directions across the countryside into the
mountains, woods, bogs and wilderness. Like mad people, the women,
children and waggoners filled every road, weeping and wailing. Worse still
was the sight after the battle of many men and horses too badly wounded

to get away, who when attempting to rise fell back unable to bear their own weight. Some, mutilated and in great pain, begged to be put out of their misery, and others coughed out blood and threats, their bloodied weapons frozen in their hands as if in readiness for some future battle. The blood from the dead so covered the ground that one could hardly take a step without slipping. This grisly scene of slaughter remained untouched and unchanged for several days . . .[25]

Storey also saw the aftermath of the battle:

We killed seven thousand of the Irish upon the spot, as was generally believed, and there could not be many fewer for looking amongst the dead 3 days after when all our men and some of theirs had been buried, I reckoned in some small enclosures a hundred and fifty, in others a hundred and twenty etc, lying most of them by the ditches where they were shot, and the rest from the top of the hill where their camp had been looked like a great flock of sheep scattered up and down the country for about four miles around.[26]

Estimates of total losses varied. Storey's figure for the Irish seems too high. Robert Parker probably came closest with an estimate of 'near' 4,000 Irish and 3,000 Williamites. The Jacobites had also lost thousands of muskets, all their artillery and huge quantities of powder, ammunition and provisions. Two brigadiers and nine colonels were dead, Dorrington and Major-General John Hamilton, a brigadier and nine other colonels captured.

Blame for the defeat was placed on the treachery of Lutterell and the suspected disloyalty of the Englishman Sheldon. 'And so let them keep their pridding cavalry to stop bottles with', wrote one Jacobite bitterly.[27] The former charge is possibly true, but more doubtful in the case of Sheldon. St Ruhe erred in deciding to meet the enemy in the open field, certainly in not making his intentions clearer to his subordinates. As it was, the fighting qualities of his Irish troops had come within measurable distance of pulling off a surprise victory.

But even defeating Ginkel would have been very unlikely to turn the tide of the war. Dublin was for ever out of the Jacobites' reach, and at most they might have prolonged their resistance into another year. As it was, as the remnants of the Jacobite army reeled back on Limerick, the end of Jacobite Ireland seemed near.

TWELVE

· · · · · · · · · · · · · ·

The Flight of the Wild Geese: Ireland 1691

SECOND SIEGE OF LIMERICK

It is probable that if, after Aughrim, Ginkel had moved rapidly on Limerick, the Irish war would have been over within days. But Ginkel was a cautious man; he decided first to deal with Galway, but before doing so he halted on Kilcommodon Hill for a week to wait for his siege guns to come up from Athlone. The delay gave the Jacobite army, with its customary resilience, time to recover. Many of the fleeing infantry, almost by instinct, headed back for the sanctuary of Limerick. Here they were gradually re-formed, as Tyrconnel, now in effectively undisputed control and regarding himself as vindicated by the result of Aughrim, was making what preparations he could for the inevitable siege.

Meanwhile d'Usson was preparing to defend Galway. He was not optimistic, having a garrison of only about 2,000 'poor sorry fellows with hardly a rag on their backs'.[1] There was no prospect of reinforcements, and most of the Irish leaders realised that there was little hope of holding Galway. The townspeople, or at any rate the prosperous merchants, although Catholics, had never been very enthusiastic in the Jacobite cause, mainly because they had more to lose in the event of defeat. The main concern of the citizens of Galway was to make peace with the victors. Messages were sent to Ginkel by some of the leading citizens, urging him to march on Galway as soon as possible.

The Williamite army arrived before Galway on 19 July. D'Usson hoped to resist, despite the lack of enthusiasm of the citizens and some of his own officers. But early on 20 July, when Williamite troops attacked some of the outworks, the defenders, from the Earl of Clanricarde's Regiment, fled without a fight. It was the end, as d'Usson's officers, headed by Lord Dillon, told the Frenchman of their intention to ask for terms. Ginkel, anxious to move on

Limerick as quickly as possible, proved generous. The citizens were confirmed in their properties, and were even promised religious freedom, while d'Usson and the garrison, with their weapons, were allowed to march away to Limerick.

The only towns of importance now left in Jacobite hands were Sligo and Limerick. The former, under the command of the redoubtable Sir Teague O'Regan, was well fortified, but effectively contained by Ulster troops. Before moving on Limerick, Ginkel sent a detachment of troops to strengthen the blockade of Sligo. En route, they encountered Balldearg O'Donnell and his force of 10,000 irregulars. After only token resistance, O'Donnell proved as ready as the defenders of Galway to accept lenient terms and make his peace with King William. Some of his men chose to fight on, but another major threat to Ginkel's progress had effectively been neutralised. At Sligo neither side was strong enough to take the offensive, but O'Regan knew resistance to be futile, and used the arrival of more Williamite troops as an excuse to make terms.

Only Limerick remained. For a time there seemed a possibility that the story of the previous year's siege might be repeated. Ginkel did not arrive before the town until 25 August, after advancing with some difficulty through countryside again devastated by the Jacobites. The Irish army had regained much of its numerical strength, totalling some 17,000 men, although there were only sufficient arms for about 10,000 of them. Tyrconnel wisely rejected proposals that the Irish should once more engage Ginkel in a pitched battle. Instead his plan was to stand siege behind the strengthened defences of Limerick until the end of the campaigning season, in anticipation of more aid from France. The infantry would hold the city, while the horse, based in County Clare, operated against enemy outposts and lines of communication. But Jacobite morale suffered a devastating blow on 14 August when Tyrconnel, who had had a stroke four days earlier, died. No one else had the authority or prestige to unite the Irish and influence the French.

Even so, the Williamite commanders regarded victory as far from certain. To add to their concerns over provisions and fodder and the still potent threat of Sarsfield's Horse and the remaining rapparees, the weather had turned foul in a manner uncomfortably reminiscent of the previous summer. Although Ginkel seems to have favoured establishing a blockade of Limerick in the hopes of starving the defenders into surrender, the Duke of Württemberg successfully urged the need for a close siege if the town were to fall before French aid arrived.

The Williamites had a far stronger siege train with much more ammunition than had been the case a year earlier, and this time the besiegers were supported by a naval squadron. On 30 August Ginkel's siege guns opened fire. With considerable difficulty batteries were established to fire across the Abbey River at the walls of the 'English' town, which were much weaker than those of the Irish town, 'being thin and without a rampart, and void of outward fortifications'.[2]

After one day's bombardment, on 8 September, a breach had been opened in the defences. However, it became clear to the Williamite commanders that the garrison was still too numerous and determined for an assault to have any prospect of success, and Ginkel decided to force a crossing of the Shannon in order to threaten Limerick from both sides.

Ginkel feared that the Irish might bring superior numbers to bear against part of his army. The crossing was planned for the night of 16 September, at Partine, where the defenders, a brigade under Robert Clifford, were spread thinly. Helped by darkness and a thick mist, Williamite troops occupied three islands in the river without detection, and by dawn on 17 September their engineers had a pontoon bridge in place for the final crossing. As Williamite infantry closed in on their encampment on the far bank, Clifford's unready men broke and fled for the safety of Limerick, scarcely firing a shot. Clifford was accused of treachery and imprisoned pending court martial. But greater blame could be attached to Dominic Sheldon, who, with over 3,000 cavalry and 1,000 foot, had been stationed nearby at Annaghbeg, and might have destroyed the detached part of Ginkel's force and compelled him to abandon the siege. But, as at Aughrim, Sheldon hesitated and then pulled back deeper into County Clare, leaving Limerick to its fate.

On the same day Ginkel offered the defenders of the town generous terms, similar to those granted to Galway. The Jacobites were given eight days to decide; in the meantime Ginkel tightened his ring around Limerick. On 22 September, after sending a strong detachment into Clare to counter the Irish horse, he launched an assault on a fort covering the road from Limerick to Clare across Thomond Bridge. After two hours of bombardment, the Williamites prepared to assault the breached fort, and the 800 Irish defenders prepared to retreat across Thomond Bridge, back into Limerick. However, a French officer panicked and ordered a drawbridge halfway across the bridge to be raised while most of the Irish soldiers were still trying to reach safety. Trapped, over 600 of them were mercilessly slaughtered.

The repercussions of Thomond Bridge were far greater than the immediate casualties. The infuriated Irish turned against the French, and d'Usson and du Tesse had no option but to hand over command to the Irish officers, headed by Patrick Sarsfield.

THE END IN IRELAND

Sarsfield and his supporters were ready to talk to Ginkel. They realised that the war in Ireland was lost, with the fall of Limerick sooner or later being inevitable. However, the wider war would still continue, and might well provide opportunities for an intact Irish army in exile, fighting at least nominally for King James, to regain on English or European battlefields that which had been lost in Ireland. Sarsfield was therefore ready to make a quick settlement, while the defences of Limerick were still strong enough to make Ginkel inclined to grant lenient terms. On 24 September Sarsfield and John Wauchope came out of the city, asking for a ceasefire while terms were agreed.

The aim of both the Irish and the French commanders (provided that the responsibility could be placed on Sarsfield) was the same – to reach an agreement by which the Irish army could be transported to France, there to take up arms once more. They found a receptive ear in Ginkel, who, William was demanding, should bring the Irish war to a speedy conclusion in order to release troops for the war in Europe. If this meant providing King James with an army in exile, Ginkel believed that it would appear to William an acceptable price.

Some Irish diehards were reluctant to end the fight, and scattered rapparee bands remained active for some time, with the Williamites using surrendered guerrillas in a 'poacher-turned-gamekeeper' role to hunt them down. Sarsfield may have exaggerated the lack of future French support in order to gain majority support in the army, although most of the ordinary soldiers and the civilians in what remained of Jacobite Ireland were ready enough to end the struggle.

Terms were agreed on 28 September. Those governing the rights of the Irish population as a whole were fairly worthless without the agreement of the English and Irish parliaments being obtained for them, and they would never in fact be fully observed. But Sarsfield obtained the military concessions that were his principal objective. The Irish army could go to France.

The Treaty of Limerick was signed on 3 October and next day the town was occupied by the Williamite forces. Ginkel soon felt that he had been too lenient in the terms he had granted. Although he was not prepared to break the agreement, he authorised energetic efforts to persuade the Irish soldiers either to enlist with the Williamite forces or to return to civilian life after selling their arms and horses to the English. Those planning to go to France were warned that they would not be allowed to return to Ireland. In response, Sarsfield and Wauchope harangued their men, urging them to go to France so that they might then restore King James and their own fortunes by invading England. The officers would be retained on their English rates of pay, which were higher than their French equivalents, while priests threatened damnation to any men who succumbed to the blandishments of the 'heretics'.

The troops were plied with large quantities of brandy, then marched over into County Clare to await transport to France. Here they were addressed by Williamite officers, who recounted Ginkel's offer – although the fact that they spoke in English meant that few of the Irish soldiers could understand them. Then Ginkel's officers instructed that each regiment should march past Thomond Bridge. Those who were willing to accept the Williamite offer should turn aside while the remainder marched over the bridge to await French shipping.

The response varied; all but seven men of the 1,400-strong Foot Guards, the most fervently Jacobite of the Irish units, opted for France. It was not so with all; for example Lord Dillon's and Lord Iveagh's Regiments chose to stay behind. In all about 70 per cent of the Irish foot opted for France. In general, it was those with landed estates in Ireland who tended to feel that it was in their own and their families' interests to make their peace with the victors. Professional soldiers and younger sons and landless men preferred to seek their fortunes in France. Of the cavalry, two colonels, one of them the already deeply suspected Henry Lutterell, persuaded their regiments to enlist with William. The remainder opted for France.

There were considerable difficulties in actually carrying out the terms of the Treaty. Some of the Williamite soldiers bitterly resented what they saw as the overly lenient concessions that Ginkel had made: 'We fight like heroes, but like fools we treat.'[3] Many of the Irish soldiers were reluctant to take ship for France if that meant separation from their families. The Treaty had allowed for families to accompany their menfolk, but Sarsfield intended this to apply only to officers. However, it was evident that such a restriction would result in mutiny, so on 14 October Wauchope agreed that families, or at any rate those who were in the Limerick area, should be included.

Most of the Irish were to be transported in English ships, although others would be carried by the large French supply convoy that had been en route to Limerick when the town fell. In the interim, the Irish were quartered on King's Island, outside Limerick, from where a number deserted despite the efforts of their officers, with the English doing nothing to prevent such defections.

The French fleet arrived in the Shannon on 20 October, and the Irish were ferried the 40 miles downriver to the anchorage in smaller ships. The French were not, however, expecting to carry the soldiers' families as well, and Wauchope, anxious to take as many troops as possible, insisted that priority should be given to loading soldiers. The result, in some cases, was tragedy:

Accordingly, a vast rabble of all sorts were brought to the waterside then the major general, pretending to ship the soldiers in order according to their lists they first carried the men on board; and many of the women at the second return of the boat for the officers, catching hold to be carried on board were dragged off and through fearfulness, losing their hold, were drowned; but others who held faster had their fingers cut off and so perished in the sight of their husbands or relations.[4]

This Williamite account certainly exaggerates the number of fatalities. Many of the soldiers were from distant parts of the country and their families were not with them. On 2 November Wauchope sailed for France with 6,000 men and 800 women and children.

Meanwhile Sarsfield was organising a similar evacuation from Cork. More shipping was available there, and the troops to be embarked included the cavalry. However, reports of the cold reception given to the first arrivals in Brittany were filtering back and, as a result, at least three regiments refused to embark and disbanded themselves. To some extent they were compensated for by a steady stream of stragglers from elsewhere who were arriving at Cork, and for whom Sarsfield delayed sailing as long as possible. Finally, on 22 December Sarsfield sailed for France with around 10,000 men.

Although the war in Ireland was at an end, the 'Wild Geese' were confident that they would soon gain their revenge.

THIRTEEN

• • • • • • • • • • • • • • • • •

La Hogue

PLANS FOR INVASION

Back in France, King James recovered his equanimity with remarkable speed. The defeat at the Boyne he dismissed as an unfortunate setback for which the pusillanimity of his Irish troops was to blame, and he seemed oblivious to the fact that his uninspired performance there had destroyed any remaining respect for his abilities as a military commander. He was happily unaware of the comment that Marshal Luxembourg, France's leading general, had made on James's return to France: 'Those who love the King of England should be glad to see him in safety, but those who love glory will deplore the figure he has made of himself.'[1]

However, James's complacency received a shattering blow from the cool reception that he received from King Louis at their first meeting after his return. The exiled monarch was informed brusquely that an invasion of England was impossible until more troops arrived from Ireland. James was bitterly hurt that Louis patently had such little faith in him and his ability.

With the French victory off Beachy Head, James redoubled his efforts to persuade Louis to follow up this success. He professed confidence that 'his own Sailors would never fight against one, under whom they so often had conquered'.[2] However, Louis remained adamant, and James's case was not helped by events. From Scotland came news of Cromdale and the disintegration of Cannon's army, while in Ireland the Jacobite leadership appeared paralysed by dissension.

The Williamite regime in England was alarmed by evidence of Jacobite activity. Much of this consisted of little more than loud talk in London coffee houses and drinking dens by cashiered officers from James's English army. There were some seemingly serious activities. In the summer of 1689 Jacobite officers from Ireland had been landed in strongly Catholic Lancashire with commissions for the local gentry to raise men for King James, and there were scare stories of military equipment being smuggled ashore at night.

The reality was much less threatening. The English Jacobites, with no military potential, professed loyalty to James – but coupled with the stipulation that they were prepared to take up arms only after a landing by James himself with powerful French support. In the meantime, in Lancashire, the suspected hotbed of Jacobitism, loyalist militia rounded up many of the most dangerous malcontents and threw them into prison in Manchester, although the autumn brought renewed rumours of secret gatherings in Northumberland and Yorkshire. Around the same time, Jacobite officers from Ireland, again carrying commissions for supporters in England and Wales, were captured in Chester and Flintshire.

But these activities were small scale and poorly organised. Two of the leading Jacobites in England, Lord Clarendon and the Bishop of Ely, urged that, before an invasion of England were attempted, King Louis should reassure English Protestants by extending toleration to the Huguenots, and James should promise to grant similar freedom to the Church of England and to rule through Parliament, and to ensure that French troops should maintain as low a profile as possible. The first of their demands was clearly unacceptable to the French. The messages were intercepted by government agents; the Bishop fled to France, while Clarendon and James's former fleet commander, the Earl of Dartmouth, along with various other suspects, were imprisoned. Clarendon and Dartmouth were eventually placed under more lenient house arrest, but a number of lesser players were executed.

Following the defeat at Cromdale, James had ordered his commanders in Scotland, Alexander Cannon and Thomas Buchan, to join him in France, and the Edinburgh Convention was very willing to facilitate their departure. James meanwhile hesitated between attempting to keep armed resistance in Scotland alive and seeking a political accommodation with the Episcopalians – both, in the current circumstances, highly unrealistic hopes. As a result, James temporised over the requests of the Jacobite clan chiefs to be permitted to accept the government's offer of amnesty.

The stage was set for a tragic outcome. Throughout the winter of 1691–2 James continued to hope that the French might be persuaded to land men and supplies in Scotland in order to reinvigorate the clans, while the chiefs themselves hoped that their threats of continued rebellion might intimidate the Edinburgh government into making concessions. In fact, these threats merely served to stiffen Presbyterian opposition to any compromise, although the Scottish Convention lacked a solution to the Highland problem.

King William had even less interest in Scotland than he had in Ireland, and largely delegated responsibility for Scotland to its Secretary of State, Sir John Dalrymple of Stair, merely emphasising that he wanted the situation north of the Border resolved quickly. Many clans submitted to the government before the stated deadline of 1 January 1692. Among them were MacIain of Glencoe and his MacDonalds. Dalrymple, however, determined to make a punitive example to deter other would-be rebels, suppressed all evidence of the MacDonalds' submission, and on 13 February the infamous Massacre of Glencoe took place, in which forty-five MacDonalds, including MacIain himself, were butchered by government troops. There were ample precedents for the action taken at Glencoe, although it was particularly brutal. In any event, it served its immediate objective of ensuring that Jacobite resistance, with the exception of the tiny garrison of Bass Rock in the Firth of Forth, came to an end.

If only for lack of other viable options, King James continued to pin his hopes on increased French support. In July 1691 prospects seemed more favourable, following the death of War Minister Louvois. King Louis now became directly involved in formulating the war effort and took a more positive view of aid for James, providing it served French interests.

By the winter of 1691 there was apparently growing evidence of English support for James. Intelligence reports from England spoke of growing strains between Queen Mary and her sister, Princess Anne. There was English resentment towards William and his Dutch officials and generals. A number of leading figures, including the Earl of Marlborough, while professing loyalty to William, were maintaining a secret correspondence with the Jacobite court in exile. Marlborough, in particular, seemed close to changing his allegiance. William appeared to be isolated, and James was confident that a coalition of leading figures was about to turn to him, a possibility that seemed to be heightened after Marlborough was dismissed, following allegations of corruption.

French agents were reporting rising popular discontent with the Williamite regime, coupled with apparent increased sympathy for James. Of more practical importance, the arrival of the 'Wild Geese' from Ireland would at last give James an invasion force (even if, realistically, its composition would make it hardly more acceptable in English eyes than the French army would have been). The new French Naval Minister, Pontchartrain, was eager to follow up the success at Beachy Head with operations designed to catch the English and Dutch fleets divided, and then launch an invasion of England.

There were, however, various problems to be overcome before the Irish army could be ready for action. In all about 15,000 men, with 4,000 dependants, arrived in France, to a very cold reception. The French authorities had never displayed any particular regard for the Irish army and, following the Boyne, this grew into positive contempt. In particular, Louvois and Barbezieux – his son and less influential successor as War Minister – despaired at what they saw as the incompetence of the Jacobite leadership.

Jacobite aims and strategy often seemed enigmatic, and by early 1692 French loss of confidence extended to James himself. Although James must shoulder a major share of the blame for Jacobite ineffectiveness, there were other factors. Endemic internal dissensions in the ever-swelling ranks of the Jacobites in exile were worsened by nationalistic feuding in a group of which around 60 per cent were Irish, 35 per cent English and 5 per cent Scottish.[3] Many of the minority groups preferred to enlist with the French army rather than to join the Irish forces. James himself did not inspire confidence as a leader. Viscount Clare, whose sons had fought in Ireland, said of the King: 'Leaving aside the respect I owe him, he would do best to go and pass the remainder of his days praying to God in a cloister than think of commanding armies or governing a state.'[4]

There were several French motives in allowing the Irish army to come to France. Least important was a desire to maintain James's status by providing him with an 'army'. More relevant was France's own need for additional military manpower. Furthermore, in an age when most leading European powers were ready to employ foreign mercenaries, there was a clear need to secure the use of the Irish army before anyone else did.

Even so, the reception given to the Irish troops demonstrated the underlying lack of French regard for them. From James himself they received a message of welcome:

We are extremely satisfied with your conduct and of the valour of the soldiers during the siege [of Limerick], and most particularly of your and their declaration and resolution to come and serve where we are. And we assure you, and order you to assure both officers and soldiers that are come along with you, that we shall never forget this act of loyalty, nor fail when in a capacity to give them above others a particular mark of our favour.[5]

Unfortunately, James's fair words were not matched by present realities. Troops arrived in French ports piecemeal, their original units hopelessly fragmented, and some 1,500 were sick. The Irish soldiers struggled to survive in appalling conditions. Still wearing the often ragged clothing in which they had fought in Ireland, they found themselves shivering in the depths of a bitter Breton winter. Supplies of all kinds were scanty, and the welcome of the Breton villagers on whom they were billeted was often as frosty as the weather. An eyewitness lamented:

Alas it is a miserable sight to see the condition the poor gentlemen are in, and the women and children invited to go along with their husbands are now begging their bread from door to door, and cannot get it. The soldiers wish they had died in Ireland before they came here, and many of the officers express themselves to the same purpose, and are extremely dejected and melancholy.[6]

To make matters worse, James lacked the means to support his troops and would have to rely on French aid. Not surprisingly, the French government was unwilling to pay the Irish on a higher rate than its own troops, which meant that the promise the Irish soldiers had been given of payment at English army rates was immediately broken. The lower French rate was barely adequate for a single man, and certainly would not support the soldiers' families: 'For when they were reduced in France to four pence a day they were obliged to leave their children to the wide world and only lament with the prophet Jeremiah that their children lay naked in a starving condition at the top of every street.'[7] The French also felt that the Irish army had far too many officers, the result of hundreds of new commissions hastily issued after Aughrim for units whose ranks were never refilled.

The upshot was that the Irish army was reorganised under French direction. It was to include all troops in France who were subjects of King James, with the exception of Mountcashel's Brigade, which was to remain part of the French army. The reorganisation was rushed through while Sarsfield was still in Cork, so that most senior posts went to supporters of James rather than to the 'gaels' of Sarsfield's faction.

Eventually the new Irish army was organised on the French pattern. Its two regiments of horse were under the command of Dominic Sheldon (whose loyalty was not seen to be in doubt) and Lord Galmoy. The two troops of Lifeguards were commanded by the Duke of Berwick and Patrick Sarsfield and two regiments of dismounted dragoons were under the command of Thomas Maxwell and Francis Carroll. The foot were eventually formed into six regiments, each of fourteen to sixteen companies, forming two battalions and totalling around 1,000 men. Their colonels were the Lord Grand Prior, William Dorrington, John Wauchope, Simon Luttrell, Gordon O'Neill and Richard Talbot. This establishment required 50 per cent fewer officers than James had hoped to employ. Some of the surplus went, with 600 men, to fill out Mountcashel's Brigade; the Scots formed two independent companies, while the remainder were offered the dubious option of service in the French navy.

James had optimistically hoped that the Irish army would retain its autonomy under his command, but it quickly became apparent that this would not be the case. Louis XIV retained the right to decide on its deployment and, regarding the reduction in pay, James could do no more than issue a proclamation that 'when it shall please God to restore him to his kingdoms, [the troops] shall receive so much in money or lands as shall complete their full pay'.[8]

However, James did gain some small satisfaction from an incident that occurred when the French tried to issue the men of the Regiment of Clare with French army grey coats. The troops mutinied until they were at length given red coats like those they had worn throughout their careers in Ireland. This at least helped James to preserve the fiction that he had an independent army, and he set up headquarters at Nantes, where he busied himself in signing batches of commissions for officers in the reorganised regiments, gave others employment in command of Jacobite privateers operating out of Brest and Saint-Malo, and convinced himself that the time was ripe for his invasion of England. He relished reports that English Jacobites had bought arms in preparation for his landing and had even begun raising troops – including no less than eight regiments of horse and dragoons in the north of England. That none of these actually existed outside the minds of overenthusiastic Jacobite agents never seems to have occurred to James.

Throughout the winter of 1691/2 the officers of the Irish army, assisted by instructors from the Garde Française, drilled their men in preparation for the invasion of England. Louis had been sufficiently convinced by reports from England to agree to give James naval and artillery support, together with 7,000 troops. The devoutly Catholic, and therefore to James eminently suitable, Marshal Bellefonds was to command the army. Lieutenant-General du Tesse, experienced with Irish troops, would be second in command, and Patrick Sarsfield and Richard Hamilton would be major-generals. There were, however, continuing uncertainties about the details of the invasion plan. In January the intention was for the main French fleet to move northwards through the Irish Sea to the Firth of Clyde, where it would land its troops and supplies at Glasgow. The invasion force would then march southwards into England via Carlisle and Cumbria, and on into Lancashire, hopefully picking up recruits on the way. James planned to land with 25,000 to 30,000 men, including 3,000 horse and dragoons, for, 'If I come with smaller, I shall run a great risk of not being joined by the English, who, in that case, will wait for the issue before they hazard themselves. Whereas, on the contrary, if they see me at the head of such a good army, they will not hesitate to join me immediately upon my landing.'[9]

The French, however, remained unwilling to supply more than 7,000 to 8,000 troops, and the projected large-scale Scottish landing was abandoned. Only Major-General Thomas Buchan, with the three Scottish companies of the Jacobite army in a handful of transports escorted by two frigates, would make landfall on the east coast of Scotland in Aberdeenshire or the Merse.

With England now the target for the main invasion force, James wanted to embark his troops on the northern coast of France, at the port of Ambleteuse, and land in Kent, preferably at Dover. From there he would march on Rochester, scene of his humiliation in 1688, and seize the naval stores and ships in the Medway. James believed that after this London would surrender, and the rest of the country soon follow. However, the French decided that the invasion force's cavalry should embark at Le Havre, and the infantry at the harbour of La Hogue in the Cotentin peninsula, for a general rendezvous off Ushant.

From the end of March 1692 some 14,000 Irish soldiers, newly equipped and clothed, and with their morale higher than it had been at any time since the first siege of Limerick, began moving towards their embarkation ports in Brittany. All now depended upon the outcome of events at sea.

THE NAVAL CAMPAIGN

The year 1691 had seen increased activity by privateers, mainly operating out of Dunkirk, but no fleet action. Admiral Edward Russell did not, however, spend all his time in fruitless searches for the enemy. A set of 'Fighting Instructions', usually credited to the disgraced Torrington, was issued, that would be the basis of British naval tactics throughout the age of sail. They depended on the use of a simple signalling system employing one or two flags hoisted in a series of different positions on different masts. The line of battle was now clearly established as the fighting formation, although some degree of flexibility was allowed for in case some captains found themselves to windward or leeward of the admiral.

By the end of 1691 the English authorities were concerned by signs of Jacobite sympathy among naval officers. King James's former fleet commander, the Earl of Dartmouth, had offered to man ships for James if the French could send them to the English coast with skeleton crews. Wisely – for Dartmouth certainly exaggerated the amount of support he had – the French declined.

As 1692 dawned, Russell knew that James was planning his invasion for the early summer, and he spent the opening months of the year trying to fill out the depleted crews of his fleet, initially by paying bounties to merchant seamen who voluntarily enlisted and, from 17 March, by pressing men with official sanction, although he had been doing so without authorisation since early January. The two marine regiments were sent to reinforce the fleet which, by virtue of all of these efforts, was, by the end of March, only 1,200 men below its authorised full complement.

With the onset of spring, the initiative passed to the French. Their plan was to launch the invasion before the English fleet could be reinforced by the Dutch, and shipping began to gather in the Breton ports in order to carry the troops and supplies. The Toulon Squadron, under Admiral d'Estrées, was to provide close escort for the massive convoy, while Tourville and the Brest fleet were to prevent any interference by the English fleet, which, if unsupported by the Dutch, would find itself outnumbered.

But French hopes for a swift resolution received a serious setback when d'Estrées, making a very slow voyage from the Mediterranean, encountered adverse weather in passing through the Straits of Gibraltar and lost two ships. In the meantime Tourville, Louis and the King's Council had decided that the invasion should follow in the footsteps of King William in 1688 and make its landfall at Torbay. Once the troops were ashore, Tourville, supported by the Toulon and Brest squadrons, would prevent the English fleet from interfering with their supply lines. The Navy Minister warned Tourville in uncompromising terms of the need for haste: 'You would anger the King if on pretext of waiting explanations of the orders received, you were to postpone your departure by a single tide.'[10]

After his failure to follow up the success at Beachy Head two years previously, King Louis had grave doubts concerning Tourville's commitment, and on 25 April sent him further orders to sail 'even though he receives word that the enemy are outside with a superior number of ships. In case he meets them on passage to La Hogue [where King James and the bulk of the Irish troops were to embark], His Majesty wishes him to engage, whatever their strength.' In his own hand, Louis added that that 'is my will and I wish it to be exactly followed'. Explaining the King's orders to his officers, Tourville told them that they must not lay themselves open to accusations of cowardice by slowness in carrying out their instructions.[11]

By the end of April the volume of reports and rumours had convinced William that the invasion threat was real. He realised that the support of the Dutch fleet, for the moment delayed by contrary winds, was vital. William was currently in Holland, but kept his yacht and escorts on standby off the Dutch coast to carry him back to England if an invasion began.

In England itself plans had been under way for an amphibious attack on Normandy, but these were laid aside as all efforts focused on preparing to meet an invasion. On 9 April Russell instructed his flag officers to ensure that all of their ships were fully provisioned, manned and ready for sea. Three days later the frigate *Dolphin* set sail from Plymouth to gain intelligence of French preparations. From neutral ships her commander learnt that the French totalled 'near 40 sail' but that they were so short of men that they were pressing boys aged 12. 'If true', Russell commented, 'the French are not much to be feared.'[12]

The English fleet began to leave its winter anchorage at the Nore on 29 April, and by 7 May had taken up station in the Downs, where Russell was joined by the Dutch. Now he needed only Delaval, who, with the bulk of the 3rd rates, had returned from duty off the French coast to the anchorage of St Helens off the Isle of Wight. Here Russell joined him on 12 May, and sent out scouting forces in search of the French.

Tourville, stung by the King's evident displeasure, had begun leaving the Brest Roads on 29 April, but contrary easterly winds meant that he did not clear the coast until 2 May. He had left Vice-Admiral Châteaurenault to complete the manning of twenty ships, whose crews were still 2,000 men below strength. Initially Tourville had only thirty-seven warships and seven fireships, but on 15 May he was joined off Plymouth by Villette and the Rochefort Squadron, with seven warships and four fireships.

On 12 May Russell learnt that the enemy had been sighted off Start Point on the Cornish coast. Some of his own ships were still poorly manned, with many raw recruits. Of the 612 men aboard the 2nd rate, *Vanguard*, 150 had not previously been to sea. However, the Dutch had sent more ships and now had twenty-six sail of the line. Lieutenant Admiral Almonde, aboard the 92-gun *Prins*, was in command and had eight vessels comparable to the English 1st and 2nd rates, and was assisted by three Dutch vice-admirals and three rear admirals – known to the Dutch as 'schout-by-nacht'.

The English Red and Blue Squadrons each had eight 1st and 2nd rate ships. The Red Squadron was commanded by Vice-Admiral Sir Ralph Delaval, aboard the 100-gun *Royal Sovereign*, with Rear Admiral Shovell in the 100-gun *Royal William* (formerly *Prince*) as his second-in-command. Admiral Sir John Ashby, aboard *Victory*, led the Blue Squadron, with Vice-Admiral George Rooke in *Neptune* as his deputy. As well as their larger ships, each admiral also had a mixture of 3rd and 4th rates and three or four fireships. Ironically, six of the ships in the English fleet still carried the names of royal bastards of Charles II and James.

Russell was doubtful whether the French would seek an engagement with the combined English and Dutch fleets. He was not concerned about defections by his own men, particularly as, with typical ineptness, James had actually stiffened resistance by compiling a list of those who would be exempted from pardon on his return to England which, as well as leading political figures, even included the fishermen who had foiled his first attempt to escape to France in 1688. The list had fallen into English hands, and Queen Mary had ordered its publication and also sent personal messages to the captains of the fleet, assuring them of her confidence in their loyalty. Privately, however, the Queen commented that she had not 'much opinion of what could be done at sea by Mr Russell'.

But 'Mr Russell' outnumbered his French opponents by a margin of two to one, for d'Estrées and the Toulon Squadron had not arrived to join Tourville. With belated realisation of the odds stacked against the admiral, on 9 May the French Navy Minister countermanded his instructions to fight whatever the odds and circumstances, but he was too late.

The French had forty-four sail of the line, eight of them carrying more than eighty guns. Tourville flew his flag in the 104-gun *Soleil Royal*, commanding the White Squadron. The Marquis d'Amfraville led the White and Blue Squadron in the 94-gun *Merveilleux*. The Blue Squadron was under Gabaret in the *Orgueilleux* (94 guns). In all the French fleet numbered between seventy and eighty ships.

Tourville appeared off the English coast on 17 May. The invasion threat was being taken very seriously, with a round-up of leading Jacobite suspects, and all Catholics were ordered to remove themselves at least 10 miles outside of London. If a landing took place, cattle and livestock were to be driven away from it for at least 15 miles inland, while troops and local militia throughout southern England were placed on standby.

THE BATTLE OF BARFLEUR

Throughout 16 and 17 May Russell had been held up by light winds, but next day, receiving definite intelligence of the French, he weighed anchor at

5 a.m. and, with a fresh south-westerly wind, put to sea on the starboard tack. An hour later, 15 miles from the Isle of Wight, he formed his fleet into line of battle, with the smaller craft scouting ahead. Russell had received news as he sailed that the French were off Portland Bill, to the west of the Isle of Wight.

At 4 a.m. the next day, with a light breeze still blowing from the south-west, the French fleet lay about 21 miles north of Cap Barfleur on the Normandy coast, steering north-east in six columns under easy sail. At dawn the Anglo-Dutch fleet was sighted 9 miles to the leeward. Tourville conformed by coming round on to the starboard tack and lay to, to call a council of war. He knew that he could not load and successfully transport the invasion force without first defeating the enemy fleet, but he also knew that the invasion plan had depended on the troops being landed before the English and Dutch fleets had united. However, he was still burning with indignation at the aspersions cast on him earlier by the Naval Minister and King Louis. Holding the advantage of the weather gauge, the French could decide whether or not to accept battle. At the council of war all of the French flag officers were opposed to seeking action, but they could hardly disobey a written order from the King himself. They had no option but to fight, and the French formed line and bore down on the Anglo-Dutch fleet with their crews saying last-minute prayers and gulping down fortifying swigs of brandy.

At between 3 a.m. and 4 a.m., while about 20 miles north-east of Cap Barfleur, Russell had heard the distant sound of signal guns. As the mist cleared, he saw the French fleet steering south and ordered his own ships to clear for action. The flagship lay to, while the rest of the fleet took up its stations. By 8 a.m. a reasonable line of battle had been formed, running from the Dutch in the rear through to the English Red Squadron. The Blue Squadron still lay to leeward, its crews struggling in the light wind to use their boats to tow their ships into the line.

By now Tourville was bearing down on the allied line, aiming for Russell's flagship, *Britannia*, with the leading French division, under Nesmond, pressing on under all sail and towed by their boats in an effort to prevent the Dutch from doubling around or breaking their line.

As the French closed with *Britannia* the time was ripe for any disloyal captains to defect. Indeed, to the allied commanders, watching in astonishment as the French drove in to attack almost twice their number, such an expectation seemed the only rational explanation. It is difficult to see why Tourville, even bearing in mind the orders he had received, should have acted in such a near-suicidal fashion. The most likely reason, perhaps, is that poor visibility had caused him to underestimate the strength of his opponents.

The rival fleets closed to within musket range without firing a shot. Then, at about 11.15 a.m. a Dutch ship opened up on the French *Saint-Louis* in the van, and within seconds both sides commenced a furious fire.

For the next couple of hours, too shrouded in the smoke to have a clear idea of how the battle was going, the fleets hammered each other at close range. Neither side gained a clear advantage until, at around 1 p.m., the wind shifted to the north-west and freshened slightly. Sir Cloudesley Shovell saw his opportunity, and luffing up to the new breeze, forced his way through the French line ten ships from the rear, isolating Coetlogon's Blue Squadron. Shovell was followed by six more of his squadron. The Blue Squadron, headed by the *Suffolk* and piling on all sail, began to close with the French rear. The Dutch broke through the French van, and, Shovell wrote later, 'from that moment they began to run'.[13]

Both fleets had already suffered severe batterings. The French *Soleil Royal* and Villette's flagship, *Ambiteux*, had been badly hit, but so had several English ships. The *Eagle* had lost her top and mizzen masts and over 200 casualties, and had to haul out of line, while the *Grafton*, at the rear of Russell's division, was also severely damaged. At least three other French ships were badly hurt, the *Perle* having a third of her crew out of action.

As the opposing fleets turned in a westerly direction, Russell's *Britannia* continued to hammer Tourville's *Soleil Royal*, other ships coming to the aid of their respective flagships. By now the French fleet had lost its line formation and was bunched around its flagship. After five hours of fighting, a number of ships on both sides were in dire straits, but at around 4 p.m. fog and a flat calm descended, giving both admirals a respite to recover their formations and carry out emergency repairs. On the English side both the *Royal Catherine* and *Centurion* had suffered serious damage, the former with twenty-two guns out of action, the latter with her hold flooded to a depth of 7ft. But both were back in the line of battle after an hour of feverish repairs.

At around five in the evening a light breeze sprang up from the east, clearing the fog sufficiently for Russell to sight the French flagship being towed in a northerly direction by her boats. He went in pursuit, and at around 5.30 p.m., as the breeze freshened, ordered the entire fleet to take up the chase. The French in turn hoisted all available sail in an attempt to extricate themselves from the trap. Their line of retreat westwards was blocked by the bulk of Carter's Blue Squadron and some of Shovell's ships but, as the French prepared to try to fight their way through, at about 6 p.m. the wind died away and the fog descended once more.

In order to avoid being carried up-Channel by the flood tide, Tourville dropped anchor with all sails still set. Most of Shovell's vessels conformed, but Captain Hastings's *Sandwich* was too slow in reacting, and was carried through the French fleet, Hastings being killed and his ship badly damaged by heavy enemy fire. Carter's squadron was also carried through the enemy fleet, Carter, aboard his flagship *Duke*, being mortally wounded. At about 7 p.m. the breeze freshened sufficiently for George Rooke to bring the remainder of the Blue Squadron back into action, inflicting further damage on the *Soleil Royal* and *Ambiteux*.

Shovell joined in the attack, launching fireships in an unsuccessful attempt to drive the French from their anchorage. However, he now saw that the hitherto unengaged French rear squadron was bearing down on him and, fearing being caught between the newcomers and Tourville, cut his cables and drifted through the main fleet in the same manner as Carter, suffering a similar hammering in the process. As a result, the English no longer lay between Tourville and the safety of Saint-Malo and Brest.

By 10 p.m. the battle of Barfleur was over.[14] Despite a tremendous expenditure of ammunition, and the severe damage suffered by ships on both sides, not a single vessel was actually sunk. But although Tourville had survived against all the odds, largely due to the intervention of the weather, he was by no means safe, especially if the largely undamaged Dutch squadron closed with him.

If Barfleur had been a disappointment for the allies, it was clear that the French fleet, even reinforced by d'Estreé's squadron, was no match for superior allied numbers. The chances of James's invasion flotilla ever reaching England were fast disappearing. Throughout the night the French fleet headed westwards, with Russell signalling to his own ships to pursue. In an urgent dispatch to England on the day's events, he expressed himself confident, given clear weather, of destroying the French.

THE END OF AN ARMADA

At dawn on 20 May the French were sighted 8 miles to the leeward of Russell's fleet and all morning, with the aid of an easterly wind, continued to head westwards along the coast of Normandy, with the allies slowly closing the gap. But by nightfall action had not been resumed, and at 4 a.m. on 21 May, with the new flood tide, both fleets had to anchor again. By 7 a.m. the flood was so strong that the French began to drag their anchors and eventually some of them had to cut their cables and run eastwards with the tide. Tourville, who had shifted his flag to the *Ambiteux*, one of the group of ships being carried helplessly eastward, realising that he had lost control of his fleet, signalled *sauve qui peut*! However, the prompt action of Rear Admiral Pannetier, the most senior officer still with the twenty-one ships forming the major portion of the French fleet, succeeded in rallying them, while Tourville, with eleven others, was carried eastwards along the coast.

Concerned about risking their ships in the dangerous waters of the Alderney 'race', the allies failed to close with Pannetier's force, which, soon after midnight, stood to the south and reached the safety of Saint-Malo. Russell was keenly aware of the opportunity that had been lost, and a fortnight later was admitting that he could not sleep 'for thinking of the stupidity which lost the French fleet'.[15]

But as dawn broke on 21 May, Russell and Shovell were still in pursuit of Tourville's portion of the French fleet. At around 11 a.m. the three most heavily damaged French battleships, *Soleil Royal*, *Triomphant* and *Admirable*, ran ashore under the inadequate shore defences of Cherbourg (whose great harbour did not yet exist). Russell, continuing the chase of the remainder, ordered Sir Ralph Delaval to detach some ships to deal with the beached enemy. That afternoon Delaval led several 4th rates close inshore, but was held off by heavy enemy fire. 'They galled me so extremely' Delaval admitted, that he anchored out of range for the night. Next morning, however, with a combined force of fireships and small boats, Delaval completed the destruction of the three French ships, including the once-splendid *Soleil Royal*.

Meanwhile the other ten French ships, shadowed by Shovell, had anchored in the roadstead of La Hogue, joining two of Nesmond's squadron which were already there. At dawn the next morning, 22 May, Russell, who had now arrived, could see the French warped close to the shore with their topmasts and yards struck, aground at low water, but shored upright by spars and yards so that their guns could still be fired, and given some additional protection by Fort de l'Ilet and the fort at St Vaast.

Watching events from the nearby cliffs was King James, who, with the Duke of Berwick, had reached Caen on 24 April. The foot of the Irish army were bivouacked around the village of Morsalines, south-west of La Hogue. Here, for the best part of four weeks, they had been held by contrary winds and rough weather, which had damaged some of the transports.

Nemond's approaching ships were at first thought to be the vanguard of a victorious French fleet, but the true situation became apparent a day and a half later, when Tourville's battered remnant hove into view, with the allied fleet gathering out at sea.

Tourville was not entirely pessimistic. He could claim to have held the enemy to a draw and to have extricated his fleet from a very difficult situation without losing a single ship. But the reality was that the battered French fleet was split into three parts, with no prospect of reuniting in the face of the enemy, or of defeating them. Tourville came ashore to consult with James, Marshal Bellefonds and other senior officers on what to do next. Both James and Tourville were opposed to simply beaching the ships and leaving them to be burnt by the enemy. Instead, supplies of powder were to be brought to them from the Normandy magazines.

But Tourville changed his mind. The ships were to be run ashore and stripped of their guns and stores, to try to prevent the enemy from burning them by means of boats filled with armed sailors patrolling the shoreline, while additional platforms were to be constructed for shore batteries. James made the suggestion, which was rejected, that the ships should be packed with Irish soldiers to repel any boarding attempts. Tourville felt that this would reflect adversely on the honour of his own men – and he probably saved many Irish soldiers from being victims of Russell's guns.

On the evening of 22 May Edward Russell called a council of war aboard *Britannia*. Shovell was to lead the 3rd and 4th rates, frigates and fireships to destroy Tourville's squadron. A small warship, the *Greyhound*, was sent to take soundings close to the enemy, and found that with 7½ fathoms there was ample water for the inshore squadron. After a night of preparation, during which the larger ships of Russell's fleet armed and manned their pinnaces and barges, at 6 a.m. Shovell prepared the inshore squadron to attack, only to find that there was too little wind. By midday, Shovell, suffering from the effects of a wound received at Barfleur, handed over command of the operation to George Rooke, who, at 3 p.m., ordered all longboats, barges and pinnaces to muster near his flagship, *Eagle*.

Command of the small-boat attack was given to Captain the Earl of Danby and, with the breeze now freshening, Rooke, with fourteen 3rd and 4th rates, and several smaller vessels and fireships, closed the range and opened fire.

After an hour's bombardment the English small craft moved in on the northern group of French ships, which consisted of four large 82- to 96-gun vessels, the *Ambiteux*, *Merveilleux*, *Saint-Phillippe* and *Foudroyant*, and two slightly smaller, the *Magnifique* and *Terrible*, both of 76 guns. At 8.30 in the evening a fireship got alongside *Terrible* and set her ablaze, and at about 9 p.m. the small boats attempted to close with the rest of the group of French ships, but were held off by heavy musket and cannon fire. Danby ordered his boats to tow a fireship towards the enemy, which attracted most of their fire, allowing the smaller craft to close. The French gunners had already abandoned the incomplete shore batteries, and the men aboard the stranded warships also began to quit their posts and scramble ashore. An attempted counter-attack by a dozen French boats was fairly easily repulsed. One English boat, under Lieutenant Stephen Martin of the *Eagle*, ran aground and was attacked by Irish troops. An attacking cavalry trooper was pulled from his horse by a boathook before the boat was refloated.

The seamen of the flotilla boarded the by now almost deserted French ships and set them ablaze, in one case training loaded guns round at the enemy fort so that they would discharge in that direction when triggered by the heat of the flames. French resistance had been surprisingly feeble, and they had begun firing several of their own ships before the English boarded.

With the turn of the tide, the English boats pulled back to the main squadron for the night. Six enemy ships had been destroyed, but there were still a further six at the opposite side of the bay, protected by the 68-gun St Vaast fort.

The attack was resumed at dawn on 24 May. Once again the English boats pressed home their attack, despite a heavy if ill-directed fire from French batteries and infantry. King James, watching from the cliffs, was delighted

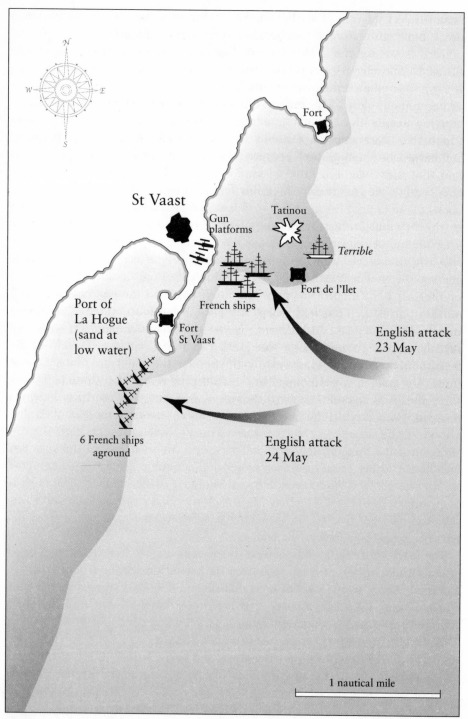

Fort

St Vaast

Gun platforms

Tatinou

Terrible

French ships

Fort de l'Ilet

English attack 23 May

Port of La Hogue (sand at low water)

Fort St Vaast

6 French ships aground

English attack 24 May

1 nautical mile

La Hogue, 23–24 May 1692

with the performance of the attackers: 'Ah! None but my brave English could do so brave an action!'[16] Surrounded as he was by French army and naval officers, it was not the most appropriate of observations, but James was never noted for his tact. He may have been less favourably impressed when an English cannon ball narrowly missed him.

The remaining six French warships were set ablaze; an exultant Danby, replying to a enquiry from Rooke as to whether his men could also destroy the mass of transports lying within the narrow harbour of La Hogue, replied: 'Ay! It can be safely done, for now I believe our men will do anything!'[17] Rooke himself led the column of small boats, accompanied by two fireships, into the attack. Enemy fire this time was heavier, one boat being sunk and about ten men killed in total, but a number of the twenty or thirty transports in the harbour were set ablaze. There were too few to have carried the intended invasion force, in any case.

It is questionable whether James's invasion ever had any real prospect of success, for, even if they had made landfall on English soil, the spectacle of the deeply mistrusted Stuart monarch returning at the head of thousands of Irish and French Catholic troops would probably have united in resistance many who otherwise had little enthusiasm for 'Dutch William'. At worst the British Isles might have been plunged into another bitter civil war, which, from Louis's point of view, would have been the ideal outcome. One of James's tragedies was his apparent inability to realise how much he was merely seen as a useful tool to advance French interests. Perhaps it was a final humiliation which he never dared recognise, even to himself.

FOURTEEN

• • • • • • • • • • • • • • • • •

Epilogue

La Hogue spelt the end of James's hopes of invading England and, as it proved, of regaining his lost kingdoms. The French no longer saw any point in maintaining a separate Irish army and, although for administrative convenience the Irish troops remained in separate brigades, they transferred to French service with the same status as Mountcashel's Brigade. During the coming years they fought in Flanders, eastern France, the Pyrennes and northern Italy.[1]

The focus of the war was in Flanders, where King William's generalship proved as uninspired as usual. On 3 August the bloody battle of Steinkirk inflicted heavy losses on both sides. Among the dead was General Hugh Mackay, who was killed at the head of his brigade, in the midst of the enemy. Two more stalwarts of the War of the Three Kingdoms, Major-General James Douglas and one-eyed Sir John Lanier, also died. The Duke of Berwick and Patrick Sarsfield, fighting in the French army, were both distinguished for their bravery.

In July the next year, Sarsfield's potentially brilliant career was snuffed out when he was mortally wounded at the battle of Landen. The Irish were in the thick of the action, another veteran of the Irish war, Colonel Barrett, dying at the head of James's Foot Guards. In October the Irish Brigades played a key role in the French victory at Marsaglia near Turin, when, led by Thomas Maxwell and John Wauchope, they routed the Savoyards in a furious charge with swords and clubbed muskets, during which both their commanders were killed, two of the more than 40,000 casualties suffered by the Irish Brigades in the next quarter of a century.

King James, meanwhile, clinging to ever-decreasing hopes of restoration, in 1693 issued a Declaration promising a free pardon to all his subjects, and a confirmation of all legislation passed by Parliament since the Restoration. It was far too late; although Queen Mary died in 1694, his British kingdoms accepted William as sole ruler – if not with enthusiasm, at least with determined resignation. Jacobite plotting continued, with abortive schemes to kill William, but it would be some years in the future before discontent in Britain would reach a scale to make Jacobitism a serious force again.

The sole remaining Jacobite foothold in the British Isles was tiny Bass Rock in the Firth of Forth, seized on 16 June 1691 by Jacobite prisoners housed there. For the next three years the garrison maintained itself by raids on the Scottish mainland and occasional supplies run in by French ships, until, faced by starvation, King James's men surrendered in June 1694. James by now had few hopes of a change in his fortunes. He had been devastated by the defeat of La Hogue, seeing it as the judgement of God. It shattered his always fragile self-confidence, and he increasingly turned to religion as a spiritual consolation for his worldly misfortunes.

By 1697 all sides in the war were exhausted, and in September hostilities were ended by the Treaty of Ryswick, in which Europe effectively returned to the status quo that had existed before the war. Louis withdrew his recognition of James's rights to the British throne, although he would maintain the former king at Saint-Germain for the rest of his life. The Irish army was fully incorporated in the French forces, and would face its English foe on many occasions in the next half century.

The leading participants of the war met various fates. King James died from a stroke on 16 September 1701, seven months before his greatest enemy, King William, who succumbed to the effects of a fall from his horse on 9 March 1702. Louis would live until 1715, to see his country worsted once again in the War of the Spanish Succession. The latter war brought glory, wealth and fame to John Churchill, Duke of Marlborough, whose principal English rival, Thomas Tollemache, had died in 1694 in an unsuccessful attack on Brest – some said betrayed to the enemy by Marlborough. Ginkel, created Earl of Athlone in 1693, died peacefully, at the age of 73, at his home in Utrecht.

Of the Jacobites, the Duke of Berwick gained mounting military fame in a career that extended until his death in 1735. Richard Hamilton died in poverty in 1717; William Dorrington and Dominic Sheldon continued their military careers, reaching the rather empty ranks of lieutenant-general in James's army. Lord Galmoy achieved the same rank, and died in his bed in 1740, aged 90.

In hindsight, the war of 1689–92, although easily the most wide ranging, was one of the Jacobites' lesser challenges for the thrones of Great Britain. It never came as close to success as the 1715 rebellion, or, arguably, the '45. From the start, Jacobite strategy had been bedevilled by confusion of aims. Tyrconnel and many of the Irish were primarily fighting for Ireland, James never saw Ireland and Scotland as more than stepping stones back to England, while the French aimed only to prolong the contest in the British Isles for as long as possible, with a minimum outlay of their own resources, in order to divert part of the Williamite war effort from the Continent. As a result the French navy was never utilised effectively, nor were French troops fully committed.

The hugely expanded Irish army never had either the training or the equipment to match William's European forces. Although the Irish troops frequently equalled their opponents in bravery, their lack of equipment and training proved decisive in three of the four major actions of the Irish war. The Scottish Jacobites were never more than a marginal force, and only a major injection of Irish, or preferably French, support could have offered them the chance of victory.

The Williamites, however, had a clearer strategy of achieving speedy and decisive victory in Scotland and Ireland in order to concentrate on the war in Europe. William was no great general, but was at least an inspirational leader. James was neither and, arguably, was never whole-heartedly committed to the risks and exertions necessary for victory. In the end, a capable team of commanders, and vastly greater resources, rather than brilliance of generalship, sufficed to bring William victory.

Notes

CHAPTER 1 INTRODUCTION

1. T. Harris, *Revolution*, London, 2006, p. 11.
2. *Ibid.*, p. 21.
3. J. Callow, *King in Exile*, Stroud, 2004, p. 61.
4. *Ibid.*, p. 62.

CHAPTER 2 WARFARE IN THE LATE SEVENTEENTH CENTURY

1. D. Chandler, *The Art of Warfare in the Age of Marlborough*, London, 1976, p. 15.
2. A quintal is an ancient unit of measurement equivalent to 100kg (or one hundredweight imperial measure).
3. Chandler, *Art of Warfare*, p. 17.
4. G. Perjes, *Army Provisioning, Logistics and Strategy in the Second Half of the Seventeenth Century*, Amsterdam, 1972, pp. 35–51.
5. *Military Dictionary*, London, 1702.
6. G. Storey, *An Impartial History of the Affairs of Ireland during the Last Two Years*, London, 1691, p. 21.
7. *Ibid.*, p. 34.
8. *Ibid.*, p. 97.
9. Chandler, *The Art of Warfare*, p. 113.
10. *Ibid.*, p. 146.

CHAPTER 3 THE RIVAL ARMIES

1. J. Childs, *The British Army of William III 1689–1702*, Manchester, 1987, p. 14.
2. *Ibid.*, p. 24.
3. National Army Museum, *1688: Glorious Revolution?*, London, 1988, p. 19.

4. R. Parker, *Memoirs of the Most Remarkable Military Transactions in Ireland from 1683 to 1715*, Dublin, 1746, p. 27.

5. P. Lenihan, *The Battle of the Boyne, 1690*, Stroud, 2003, p. 29.

6. K. Danaher and J.G. Simms, *The Danish Force in Ireland, 1690–1*, Dublin, 1962, p. 101.

7. *Négociations de M. le Comte D'Avaux en Irelande 1689–90*, Irish Manuscripts Commission, Dublin, 1934, pp. 296–311.

8. *Ibid.*, p. 388.

9. *Ibid.*, pp. 112–16.

10. *Ibid.*, pp. 334, 389, 471.

11. S. Mulloy (ed.), *Franco-Irish Correspondence, December 1688–February 1692*, Dublin, 1983, vol. 2, p. 377.

12. S. Reid, *Killiecrankie*, Southend-on-Sea, 1989, p. 23.

CHAPTER 4 JACOBITE HIGH TIDE

1. *Négociations de M. le Comte D'Avaux*, pp. 274–5; 517–21.

2. P. Macrory, *The Siege of Derry*, Oxford, 1988, p. 152.

3. R. Simpson, *The Annals of Derry*, Londonderry, 1847, pp. 105–6.

4. *Négociations de M. le Comte D'Avaux*, pp. 53–4.

5. Simpson, *Annals of Derry*, p. 98.

6. *Ibid.*

7. *Ibid.*, pp. 98–9.

8. Macrory, *The Siege of Derry*, pp. 176–7.

9. Revd G. Walker, *A True Account of the Siege of Londonderry*, London, 1689, p. 24.

10. Simpson, *Annals of Derry*, p. 122.

11. *Négociations de M. le Comte D'Avaux*, p. 23.

12. Macrory, *The Siege of Derry*, p. 235.

13. T. Ash, 'Extracts from a Circumstantial Journal of the Siege of Londonderry', in J. Hempton (ed.), *The Siege and History of Londonderry, etc.*, 1861, p. 74.

14. Macrory, *The Siege of Derry*, p. 258.

15. Walker, *True Account*, pp. 32–4.

16. *Ibid.*, p. 36.

17. *Ibid.*, p. 41.

18. *Ibid.*, p. 45.

19. Irish Manuscripts Commission, *Analecta Hiberniae*, Dublin, 1932, xxi, p. 141.

20. *Négociations de M. le Comte D'Avaux*, supplement, p. 37.

21. Historical Manuscripts Commission, *8th Report, Part 1, MSS of Lord Talbot de Malahide*, London, 1881, p. 497.

CHAPTER 5 THE BRAES OF KILLIECRANKIE

1. G. Burnet, *Bishop Burnet's History of His Own Time*, 6 vols, Oxford, 1833, vol. 4, p. 47.
2. H. Mackay, *Memoirs of the War Carried on in Scotland and Ireland, 1680–1691*, ed. J.M. Hogg *et al.*, Edinburgh, 1833, p. 230.
3. P. Hopkins, *Glencoe and the End of the Highland War*, Edinburgh, 1986 p. 122.

CHAPTER 6 STALEMATE IN IRELAND

1. W. McCarmick, *A Further Impartial Account of the Actions of the Inniskilling Men*, London, 1690, p. 57.
2. R. Doherty, *The Williamite War in Ireland, 1688–1691*, Dublin, 1998, p. 73.
3. A. Hamilton, *The Actions of the Enniskillen Men*, Belfast, 1813, p. 20.
4. P. Wauchope, *Patrick Sarsfield and the Williamite War*, Dublin, 1992, p. 62.
5. Storey, *Impartial History*, pp. 85–6.
6. *Ibid.*, p. 88.
7. J. Stevens, *Journal, 1689–91*, ed. R.H. Murray, Oxford, 1912, ff. 51–52a.
8. *Ibid.*, f. 52a–b.
9. *Ibid.*, f. 53a.
10. *Négociations de M. le Comte D'Avaux*, pp. 251–4.
11. *Ibid.*, supplement, p. 31.
12. *Ibid.*, p. 443.
13. J.-F. Morsier, 'Journal de Jean-François de Morsier', in A. Jullien (ed.), *Soldats Suisses au Service Etranger*, Geneva, 1913, iii, p. 90.
14. Storey, *Impartial History*, p. 15.
15. *Calendar of State Papers Domestic*, 1689–90, ed. W.J. Hardy, London, 1885, p. 256.
16. Storey, *Impartial History*, pp. 11–14.
17. *Ibid.*, p. 30.
18. Stevens, *Journal*, f. 60b.
19. *Ibid.*, f. 62b.
20. Storey, *Impartial History*, p. 13.
21. *Ibid.*, p. 18.
22. Ibid., p. 39.
23. *State Papers*, 1689–90, p. 382.
24. Quoted in J.G. Simms, *Jacobite Ireland, 1685–91*, London, 1969, p. 131.

CHAPTER 7 THE END OF THE HIGHLAND ARMY

1. Mackay, *Memoirs*, p. 259.
2. *Ibid.*, p. 261.

3.   J. Howie, *Faithful Contendings Displayed*, Glasgow, 1780, pp. 390–405.

4.   *Ibid.*

5.   *Register of the Privy Council of Scotland*, 3rd ser., Edinburgh, 1891, xiv, p. 28.

6.   *The Exact Narrative of the Conflict at Dunkeld*, London, 1689.

7.   *Ibid.*

8.   *Ibid.*

9.   *Ibid.*

10. *Ibid.*

11. J. Blackadder, 'Letter', *Blackwood's Magazine*, 1, 1817, p. 609.

12. See p. 35.

13. Blackadder, 'Letter'.

14. Hopkins, *Glencoe*, p. 188.

15. *Ibid.*, p. 186.

16. Blackadder, 'Letter'.

17. *Ibid.*

18. *Ibid.*

19. *Exact Narrative*.

20. Mackay, *Memoirs*, p. 290; Howie, *Faithful Contendings*, p. 436.

21. Hopkins, *Glencoe*, p. 190.

22. See pp. 74–8.

23. Mackay, *Memoirs*, p. 93.

24. Hopkins, *Glencoe*, pp. 215–19.

CHAPTER 8 THE ROAD TO THE BOYNE

1.   *Négociations de M. le Comte D'Avaux*, pp. 648–9.

2.   *Ibid.*, p. 701.

3.   Lenihan, *Battle of the Boyne*, p. 72.

4.   Storey, *Impartial History*, p. 62.

5.   *Ibid.*, p. 71.

6.   Irish Manuscripts Commission, *Analecta Annales Hiberniae*, iv, p. 133.

7.   *Ibid.*, p. 27.

8.   Storey, *Impartial History*, p. 79.

9.   Lenihan, *Battle of the Boyne*, p. 120.

10. *Ibid.*, p. 27.

11. *Ibid.*, p. 139.

12. Storey, *Impartial History*, pp. 89–90.

13. Lenihan, *Battle of the Boyne*, p. 141.

14. P. Berresford-Ellis, *The Boyne Water*, London, 1976, p. 109.

15. Storey, *Impartial History*, p. 92.

16. Morsier, 'Journal', p. 97–8.

17. Lenihan, *Battle of the Boyne*, p. 156.

18. *Ibid.*
19. Sir George Clarke, quoted Berresford-Ellis, *The Boyne Water*, p. 115.
20. Morsier, 'Journal', p. 101.
21. R. Davies, *Journal of the Very Rev. Rowland Davies, Dean of Ross, from March 8, 1688–9 to September 29, 1690*, ed. R. Caulfield. London, 1857, pp. 123–4.
22. Lenihan, *Battle of the Boyne*, pp. 181–2.
23. *The Royal Inniskilling Fusiliers from December 1688 to July 1914*, Regimental Historical Records Committee, London, 1934, p. 20.
24. Berresford-Ellis, *The Boyne Water*, p. 98.
25. Lenihan, *Battle of the Boyne*, pp. 195–6.
26. *An Account of King William's Royal Heading of the Men of Inniskillin*, London, 1690.
27. Lenihan, *Battle of the Boyne*, p. 204.
28. Stevens, *Journal*, ff. 79b–80b.

CHAPTER 9 THE IRISH RECOVERY

1. A.G. Finch, *Report on the Manuscripts of Allan George Finch*, Historical Manuscripts Commission, 1913, vol. 2, p. 324.
2. Storey, *Impartial History*, p. 88.
3. Harris, *Revolution*, p. 474.
4. Stevens, *Journal*, f. 84b.
5. *Ibid.*, ff. 84b–85a.
6. *Ibid.*, f. 85b.
7. J. Barratt, 'The Last Cavalier', *Military Illustrated* 138, 1999, pp. 34–41.
8. T. Wright, *The History of Ireland*, 3 vols, London, 1854, vol. 2, p. 483.
9. Stevens, *Journal*, f. 89a.
10. *Ibid.*, f. 97b.
11. Storey, *Impartial History*, p. 114.
12. *Ibid*, p. 184.
13. Stevens, *Journal*, f. 104a.
14. Storey, *Impartial History*, p. 129.
15. Stevens, *Journal*, f. 104b.
16. *Ibid.*, ff. 104b–106a.
17. Storey, *Impartial History*, p. 130.

CHAPTER 10 THE WAR AT SEA

1. Finch, *Manuscripts*, vol. 2, p. 198.
2. Stevens, *Journal*, f. 10a.
3. The fullest account of Bantry Bay may be found in P. le Fevre, 'The Battle of Bantry Bay, 1 May 1689', *IS* 18, no. 70, 1990, pp. 1–16.
4. *Ibid.*, p. 156.

5. *Ibid.*, p. 16.

6. Finch, *Manuscripts*, vol. 2, pp. 206–7.

7. E.B. Powley, *The Naval Side of King William's War*, London, 1972, p. 350.

8. *Ibid.*, p. 353.

9. S. Mulloy, 'The French Navy and the Jacobite War in Ireland, 1689–91', *IS* 18, no. 70, p. 28.

CHAPTER 11 THE BLOODY FIELD

1. Duke of Berwick, *Memoirs*, 2 vols, London, 1779, vol. 1, p. 72–3.

2. Stevens, *Journal*, f. 114a–b.

3. Parker, *Memoirs*, pp. 25–6.

4. *Relation of the Inniskillen Men*, London, 1693, p. vii.

5. Storey, *Impartial History*, p. 153.

6. *Ibid.*

7. Historical Manuscripts Commission, *4th Report*, app. (Ginkel Corr., de Roos MSS), London, 1874, p. 318.

8. *Life*, vol. 2, p. 421. J.S. Clarke, *Life of James II*, London, 1816, vol. 2, p. 421.

9. J.T. Gilbert (ed), *A Jacobite Narrative of the War in Ireland*, repr. Shannon, 1971, p. 131.

10. Wauchope, *Sarsfield*, p. 227.

11. G. Storey, *A Continuation of the Impartial History of the Wars in Ireland*, London, 1693, pp. 100–1.

12. Stevens, *Journal*, ff. 124a–124b.

13. Storey, *Continuation*, p. 108.

14. *Dublin Intelligencer*, 7 July 1691.

15. *The Inchiquin Manuscripts*, ed. J. Ainsworth, Dublin, 1961, p. 30.

16. Stevens, *Journal*, f. 118a.

17. Storey, *Continuation*, p. 114.

18. *Ibid.*, p. 122.

19. G.A. Hayes-McCoy, 'The Battle of Aughrim 1691', *Galway Archaeological Society Journal*, 20, 1941, p. 4.

20. Storey, *Continuation*, pp. 123–4.

21. *Ibid.*, p. 125.

22. *Ibid.*, p. 122.

23. Richard Kane, *Campaigns of King William and Queen Anne*, London, 1723, p. 12.

24. Storey, *Continuation*, p. 125.

25. Wauchope, *Sarsfield*, p. 232.

26. Storey, *Continuation*, p. 131.

27. Gilbert, *Jacobite Narrative*, p. 143.

CHAPTER 12 THE FLIGHT OF THE WILD GEESE

1. *A Diary of the Siege and Surrender of Lymerick*, London, 1692, p. 8.
2. J.G. Simms, *Jacobite Ireland 1685–91*, London, 1969, p. 125.
3. Doherty, *The Williamite War*, p. 131.
4. *An Account of the Capitulation and Surrender of Limerick*, [London], 1691, p. 6.

CHAPTER 13 LA HOGUE

1. J. Callow, *King in Exile*, Stroud, 2004, p. 156.
2. P. Aubrey, *The Defeat of James Stuart's Armada, 1692*, Leicester, 1979, p. 83.
3. *Ibid.*, p. 91.
4. G. Rowlands, *An Army in Exile: Louis XIV and the Irish Forces of James II in France, 1691–1698*, Royal Stuart Society, Occasional Paper No. 60, London, 2001, p. 4.
5. Gilbert, *Jacobite Narrative*, p. 311.
6. J.G. Barry, 'The Groans of Ireland', *IS*, 2, p. 132.
7. *Ibid.*, p. 133.
8. Callow, *King in Exile*, p. 184.
9. *Ibid.*, p. 185.
10. C. de la Roncière, *Histoire de la Marine Française*, Paris, 1932, p. 99.
11. *Ibid.*, p. 102.
12. Finch, *Manuscripts*, vol. 2, p. 114.
13. R. Allyn, *A Narrative of the Victory . . . near La Hogue*, London, 1744, p. 34.
14. The fullest English account of this rather neglected battle is in Aubrey, *Defeat*, pp. 96–111.
15. Finch, *Manuscripts*, vol. 4, p. 205.
16. Callow, *King in Exile*, p. 200.
17. Aubrey, *The Defeat*, p. 111.

CHAPTER 14 EPILOGUE

1. The classic account remains J.C. O'Callaghan, *History of the Irish Brigades in the Service of France*, Glasgow, 1870.

Bibliography

(IS – *Irish Sword*, Journal of the Military History Society of Ireland)

A Diary of the Siege and Surrender of Lymerick, London, 1692

Allyn, R. *A Narrative of the Victory . . . near La Hogue*, London, 1744

An Account of the Capitulation and Surrender of Limerick, [London], 1691

Ash, T. 'Extracts from a Circumstantial Journal of the Siege of Londonderry', in J. Hempton (ed.), *The Siege and History of Londonderry, etc.*, 1861

Aubrey, P. *The Defeat of James Stuart's Armada, 1692*, Leicester, 1979

Barratt, J. 'Drunk on Brandy: Catholic Cavalry at the Boyne', in *Military Illustrated*, no. 106 (1997)

——. 'The Last Cavalier', *Military Illustrated* 138 (1999)

——. 'Rorke's Drift in Tartan [Dunkeld]', *Military Illustrated* 153 (2001)

Barry, J.G. 'The Groans of Ireland', *IS* 2, p. 132.

Bartlett, T. and Jeffrey, K. (eds). *A Military History of Ireland*, Cambridge, 1996

Baxter, S.B. *William III*, London, 1966

Berresford-Ellis, P. *The Boyne Water*, London, 1976

Berwick, James Fitzjames, Duke of. *Memoirs*, 2 vols, London, 1779

Blackadder, J. 'Letter', *Blackwood's Magazine* 1 (1817), p. 609

Burnet, G. *Bishop Burnet's History of His Own Time*, 6 vols, Oxford, 1833

Calendar of State Papers Domestic,1689–90, ed. W.J. Hardy, London, 1885

Callow, J. *The Making of James II*, Stroud, 2000

——. *King in Exile*, Stroud, 2004

Carter, T. *Historical Record of the Twenty-Sixth, or Cameronian Regiment*, London, 1867

Chandler, D. *The Art of Warfare in the Age of Marlborough*, London, 1976

Chatrand, R. *Louis XIV's Army*, London, 1988

Childs, J. *The Army, James II and the Glorious Revolution*, Manchester, 1980

——. *Armies and Warfare in Europe, 1648–1789*, Manchester, 1982

——. *The British Army of William III 1689–1702*, Manchester, 1987

Clarke, J.S., *Life of James II*, 2 vols, London, 1816.

Cox, L. 'A Diary of the Siege of Athlone, 1691', *IS* 4, no. 15, p. 88

——. 'The Williamite War in West Meath and Ginkel's March to Athlone', *IS* 9, no. 37, pp. 308–17

Danaher, K. and Simms, J.G. *The Danish Force in Ireland, 1690–1*, Dublin, 1962

Davies, R. *Journal of the Very Rev. Rowland Davies, Dean of Ross, from March 8, 1688–9 to September 29, 1690*, ed. R. Caulfield. London, 1857

Doherty, R. *The Williamite War in Ireland, 1688–1691*, Dublin, 1998

Douglas, H. *Jacobite Spy Wars*, Stroud, 1999

Dublin Intelligencer, 7 July 1691

The Exact Narrative of the Conflict at Dunkeld, London, 1689

Ferguson, K. 'The Organisation of King William's Army in Ireland 1689–92', *IS* 18, no. 70, pp. 62–79

Finch, A.G. *Report on the Manuscripts of Allan George Finch*, Historical Manuscripts Commission, vol. 2, 1913, vol. 4, 1919

Garland, J.L. 'Galmoy's Horse', *IS* 1, no. 3, p. 228

——. 'MacElligott, The Regiment of, 1688–89', *IS* 1, no. 2, pp. 121–7

Gebler, C. *The Siege of Derry*, London, 2005

Gilbert, J.T. (ed). *A Jacobite Narrative of the War in Ireland*, repr. Shannon, 1971

Hamilton, A. *The Actions of the Enniskillen Men*, Belfast, 1813

Harrington, P. 'Images of the Boyne', *IS* 18, no. 70, pp. 57–61

Harris, T. *Revolution*, London, 2006

Hayes-McCoy, G.A. *Irish Battles*, London, 1969

—— 'The Battle of Aughrim 1691', *Galway Archaeological Society Journal* 20, 1941, 1–20

Hennessy, M. *The Wild Geese*, London, 1973

Historical Manuscripts Commission, *4th Report*, app. (Ginkel Corr., de Roos MSS), London, 1874

——. *8th Report, Part 1, MSS of Lord Talbot de Malahide*, London, 1881

Hopkins, P. *Glencoe and the End of the Highland War*, Edinburgh, 1986

Howie, J. *Faithful Contendings Displayed*, Glasgow, 1780

The Inchiquin Manuscripts, ed. J. Ainsworth, Dublin, 1961

Irish Manuscripts Commission, *Analecta Hiberniae*, Dublin, 1932

Kane, R. *Campaigns of King William and Queen Anne*, London, 1973

Kinross, J. *The Boyne and Aughrim: The War of the Two Kings*, London, 1990

Le Fevre, P. 'The Battle of Bantry Bay, 1 May 1689', *IS* 18, no. 70, 1990, pp. 1–16

Lenihan, P. *The Battle of the Boyne, 1690*, Stroud, 2003

Lenman, B. *The Jacobite Risings in Britain, 1689–1746*, London, 1991

McCarmick, W. *A Further Impartial Account of the Actions of the Inniskilling Men*, London, 1690

Mackay, H. *Memoirs of the War Carried on in Scotland and Ireland, 1680–1691*, ed. J.M. Hogg *et al.*, Edinburgh, 1833

McNally, M. *Battle of the Boyne, 1690*, Oxford, 2005

Macrory, P. *The Siege of Derry*, Oxford, 1988

Maguire, W.A. (ed.). *Kings in Conflict*, Belfast, 1990

Mangan, H. 'Sarsfield's Defence of the Shannon', *IS* 1, no. 1, pp. 24–32

Melvin, P. 'Jacobite Infantry, 1691', *IS* 2, no. 6, p. 121

——. 'The Irish Army and the Revolution of 1688', *IS* 9, no. 37, pp. 288–307

——. 'Irish Troop Movements and James II's Army in 1688', *IS* 10, no. 39, pp. 87–105

——. 'Justin MacCarthy, Lord Mountcashel', *IS* 12, no. 49, pp. 305–6

——. 'Irish Soldiers and Plotters in Williamite England', *IS* 13, no. 52, pp. 256–67; no. 53, pp. 353–68; 14, no. 57, pp. 271–86

Morsier, J.-F. 'Journal de Jean-François de Morsier', in A. Jullien (ed.), *Soldats Suisses au Service Etranger*, Geneva, 1913

Mulloy, S. 'French Eyewitnesses of the Boyne', *IS* 15, no. 59, pp. 105–11

——. 'French Engineers with the Jacobite Army in Ireland, 1689–91', *IS* 15, no. 61, pp. 222–32

——. 'The French Navy and the Jacobite War in Ireland', *IS* 18, no. 70, pp. 17–31

Mulloy, S. (ed.). *Franco-Irish Correspondence, December 1688–February 1692*, Dublin, 1983

Murtagh, D. 'The Regiment of Walter Bourke', *IS* 1, no. 1, pp. 40–9

——. 'Colonel Richard Grace', *IS* 1, no. 3, pp. 173–80

Murtagh, D. and Murtagh, H. 'The Irish Jacobite Army, 1688–9',*IS* 18, no. 70, pp. 32–48

Murtagh, H. 'Galway and the Jacobite War', *IS* 12, no. 46, pp. 1–14

——. 'Unusual Artillery at the Siege of Crom Castle, 1689', *IS* 18, no. 70, pp. 81–2

National Army Museum, *1688: Glorious Revolution?*, London, 1988

Négociations de M. le Comte D'Avaux en Irelande 1689–90, Irish Manuscripts Commission, Dublin, 1934

O'Callaghan, J.C. *History of the Irish Brigades in the Service of France*, Glasgow, 1870

O'Carroll, D. 'An Indifferent Good Post: The Battlefield of the Boyne', *IS* 18, no. 70, pp. 49–56

O'Ciardha, E. *Ireland and the Jacobite Cause, 1685–1766*, Dublin, 2002

O'Danachair, C. 'The Danish Corps in Ireland, 1690–91', *IS* 5, no. 18, pp. 2–9

Parker, R. *Memoirs of the Most Remarkable Military Transactions in Ireland from 1683 to 1715*, Dublin, 1746

Perjes, G. *Army Provisioning, Logistics and Strategy in the Second Half of the Seventeenth Century*, Amsterdam, 1972

Powley, E.B. *The Naval Side of King William's War*, London, 1972

Prebble, J. *Glencoe*, London, 1966

Register of the Privy Council of Scotland, 3rd ser., Edinburgh, 1891

Reid, S. *Killiecrankie*, Southend-on-Sea, 1989

——. *Highland Clansman, 1689–1746*, Oxford, 1997

Relation of the Inniskillen Men, London, 1693

Rodger, N.A.M. *The Command of the Ocean*, London, 2004

de la Roncière, C. *Histoire de la Marine Française*, Paris, 1932

Rowlands, G. *An Army in Exile: Louis XIV and the Irish Forces of James II in France, 1691–1698*, Royal Stuart Society, Occasional Paper No. 60, London, 2001

The Royal Inniskilling Fusiliers from December 1688 to July 1914, Regimental Historical Records Committee, London, 1934

Sapherson, C.A. *William III at War: Scotland and Ireland, 1689–1691*, Leeds, n.d.

Scott, A.M. *Bonnie Dundee: John Graham of Claverhouse*, Edinburgh, 2000

Shepherd, R. *Ireland's Fate*, London, 1990

Simms, J.G. *Jacobite Ireland 1685–91*, London, 1969

——. 'The Surrender of Limerick, 1691', *IS* 2, no. 5, pp. 22–32

——. 'Eyewitnesses of the Boyne', *IS* 4, no. 22, pp. 16–27

——. 'Sligo in the Jacobite War', *IS* 7, no. 27, pp. 124–35

——. 'Marlborough's Siege of Cork, 1690', *IS* 9, no. 35, pp. 113–23

——. 'Schomberg at Dundalk, 1689', *IS* 10, no. 38, pp. 14–25

——. 'An Invasion of Kerry, 1690', *IS* 14, no. 55, p. 171

Simpson, R. *The Annals of Derry*, Londonderry, 1847

Stevens, J. *Journal, 1689–91*, ed. R.H. Murray, Oxford, 1912

Storey, G. *An Impartial History of the Affairs of Ireland during the Last Two Years*, London, 1691

——. *A Continuation of the Impartial History of the Wars in Ireland*, London, 1693

Symcox, G.W. *The Crisis of French Sea Power, 1688–1697*, The Hague, 1974

Terry, C.S. *John Graham of Claverhouse*, London, 1939

Tincey, J. and Embleton, G. *The British Army, 1660–1704*, London, 1994

Walker, Revd G. *A True Account of the Siege of Londonderry*, London, 1689

Wauchope, P. *Patrick Sarsfield and the Williamite War*, Dublin, 1992

Wright, T. *The History of Ireland*, 3 vols, London, 1854

Index